The
Quest
for
the
Dream

JOHN P. ROCHE was born in Brooklyn, New York, and studied at Hofstra College and Cornell University. He has been Professor and Chairman of the Department of Politics at Brandeis University; a Fellow of the Fund for the Advancement of Education and of the Rockefeller Foundation; and national chairman of Americans for Democratic Action. He is the author of *Courts and Rights* and *Shadow and Substance,* and co-author of *The Dynamics of Modern Government.*

The
Quest
JOHN P. ROCHE
for
the
Dream

The Development of
Civil Rights and Human Relations
in Modern America

QUADRANGLE PAPERBACKS
QUADRANGLE BOOKS / CHICAGO

Q

SECOND PRINTING

THE QUEST FOR THE DREAM. © 1963 by
the Anti-Defamation League of B'nai B'rith. This
book was originally published in 1963 by The
Macmillan Company, New York, and is here reprinted by arrangement.

First QUADRANGLE PAPERBACK edition
published 1968 by Quadrangle Books, Inc., 12 East
Delaware Place, Chicago 60611. Manufactured in
the United States of America.

This work was made possible by a grant from the
Jacob Alson Memorial Fund to commemorate the
Fiftieth Anniversary of the founding of the Anti-
Defamation League of B'nai B'rith.

The author wishes to thank the following publishers
for permission to quote from copyrighted material:
Harcourt, Brace & World, Inc., for an excerpt from
Essays in Biography by John Maynard Keynes; J. B.
Lippincott Company for an excerpt from *The Story
of Huey P. Long* by Carleton Beals; and The
Ronald Press for an excerpt from *A Catholic Runs
for President* by Edmund A. Moore, copyright 1956
by The Ronald Press Company.

This book is dedicated to that noble band
of brave, dedicated, and joyous men and women
who fought the winter war for civil liberty
in the United States.
With respect, affection, and some envy . . .

PREFACE

The foundations of this book were laid almost a decade ago when Gilbert A. Harrison, publisher of the *New Republic*, invited me to write a series of articles on the current vitality of civil liberty in the United States.

Like most liberal intellectuals—I suspect—I began with the unarticulated assumption that McCarthyism symbolized a new low in what I took to be a steady process of decline in the vigor of American liberty, a drastic falling away from the standards of some Golden Age of freedom located in the misty past.

However, as I began industriously to disinter the actual data in an area of research that has, except for narrow legal studies, been curiously neglected, it began to dawn upon me that my initial hypothesis was wrong, incredibly wrong. That in fact by all the standards of historical evidence civil liberty has a meaning in contemporary American life which never existed in the past. That never since the foundation of the Republic has there been such a concern for the basic principles of decency and civility in intergroup relations as we know today. It should become abundantly clear to the reader that this historical judgment is neither a justification of the many violations of human dignity that still occur nor a call for relaxation and somnolent self-esteem on the part of militant civil libertarians. We are committed to an ideal which is both our daemon and our justification—we are proudly utopian and perfectionist in our quest for the good society, our *Quest for the Dream*.

Over the intervening years, I have published various articles indicating in fragmentary fashion the results of my labors, but this work is an effort to develop the story in its totality. Because I do not see judicial decisions as the key to social change, the emphasis here is the broader context, on the basic transformations in American life over the past half-century which have made this country civil-liberties-conscious and have driven to the margin of society the religious and ethnic bigotry which flourished well within the memory of living men and often seemed to dominate American life.

A happy confluence of events resulted in my receiving a grant from the Anti-Defamation League of B'nai B'rith to make possible the writing of this book. The ADL, as part of a program marking its 50th anniversary, sought to stimulate the writing, by an independent scholar, of a history of the past half-century which would explore changing intergroup attitudes among Americans and the direction of civil liberties and human rights. Discussion soon established that my own interests and studies, in broad outline, coincided with the project ADL had in mind. During the year I worked on this book, I made use of ADL research facilities and accepted some helpful suggestions. In all of this, however, the ADL remained faithful to its purpose of having this a work of independent scholarship and did not intrude upon my freedom. In short, this is my book.

I want to thank my old friends Murray S. Stedman, Jr., and Leonard W. Levy for the time they gave to the manuscript and to disputing fine points with its stubborn author. I also wish to express my gratitude to the Rockefeller Foundation which subsidized my early research into this problem by a fellowship which gave me time to read and meditate, and to the *New Republic, The Reporter, The New Leader,* and the Cornell University Press for permitting me to draw on earlier versions of some of these observations. My research assistant, Stanley B. Bernstein, besides laboring far beyond the call of duty searching out obscure tracts, provided a number of extremely penetrating insights for which I am thankful.

It is difficult, finally, to convey my deep appreciation to my wife Constance for her encouragement, her willingness to put up with the selfishness that writing brings out in me, and for her successful campaign to limit the freedom of assembly of our daughter Joanna.

J. P. R.

CONTENTS

THE DAWN
OF AN EPOCH

For an American born and reared in the period since the First World War, the years which preceded that holocaust have a curious, misty character. The world was different, the structure and pace of existence were different, and perhaps most importantly, the Americans who came of age before 1914 have always spoken a different language, one which their children and grandchildren have only comprehended with great difficulty if at all.

True, the language was the same in its externals—that vital hybrid which is American-English—but at the essential level of definition, there was, and still is, an abyss between the generations. When Ernest Hemingway announced (on the authority of Gertrude Stein) that the intellectuals of the 1920's were the "lost generation," he was in part indulging the characteristic self-pity of the social critic, but he was also voicing a far more profound insight. At the key points, the young had lost the power to communicate effectively with their elders. There was an existential gap between the outlooks, between the value systems of the fathers and the sons. They just took different things for granted in the equation of life.

We who have grown up through the Depression, Nazism, World War II, and the Cold War cannot help but look back with nostalgic envy to that warm, leisurely world without crises, that American Garden of Eden isolated from and insulated against the alarms and perils of the Old World. For its inhabitants seemed to have one priceless attribute which has been denied to us through all of our lives: that feeling of certainty which emerges from knowing the mind of the Maker. They were at home in their universe and they knew its rules. Above all, they knew that the Future was Progress. Can we, who live with a nuclear sword of Damocles suspended over our heads, be blamed if we look back to this golden age, with all its naïvete and illusions, as a time of happiness and security?

A father or mother who has observed the blissful untroubled sleep of a child has often momentarily regretted the emotional price one pays for adulthood. And in our time a whole school of sociologists have made a career out of glorifying the sleeping child that was pre-urban America. The United States, we are told, has become an impersonal, atomized society of conformists who are far removed from the meaningful, participative life of earlier generations. A "lonely crowd" of "status seekers" have brought an "end of ideology" and an "eclipse of community." Caught up in "mass society," the average American has not only lost the power but the will to be "inner directed." Fundamental to this diagnosis is the assumption, either explicit or submerged, that the United States today is far closer to the atomized collectivism of *1984* than to the vision of a free society which has always been the American Dream.

The thesis of this book, put simply, is that these diagnoses, though often founded on important and useful insight, are fundamentally misconceived. They are misconceived, first of all, because their authors have made no real effort to break through the barrier of myth that shrouds the pre-1914 period. (From a sociological point of view, history seems to begin the day a researcher gets his foundation grant.) They are misconceived, in the second place, because of the intellectual bias which the authors hold toward contemporary American life. Secret Platonists, they deplore the refusal of the affluent masses to pay homage to the intelligentsia—in fact, these critics have pretty well abandoned the populace to its materialistic revels. Denouncing "popular culture" in a fashion strangely reminiscent of aristocratic excoriations of the democratic principle, they heap contempt on suburban "togetherness" while extolling the abstract merits of a (medieval?) "sense of community." Similarly, when they define nonconformity, one realizes with a start that the ideal type they applaud is the rural eccentric, the village atheist. Given this definition, it is hardly surprising that they find little nonconformity in a United States where less than 8 percent of the labor force is engaged in agriculture.

But their greatest sin has been an overpowering emphasis on the insecurities of present life, as if somehow past generations had received survival guarantees from the cosmos. In 1900 the life expectancy of a white male American at birth was forty-seven years—for a Negro it was thirty-two years [1]—and one can only imagine what the chances of life were of that overwhelming mass of humanity which did not live in a society as advanced as the United States. It is possible that modern technology will lead to the destruction of civilization, but it is equally the case that only in our time and in a relatively small segment of advanced society has human life become a precious commodity. Our anxieties, in other words, are a function of our good fortune, not of our deprivations. This does not make them any less meaningful, but it does mean that we should put the contemporary philosophies of gloom and *angst* in intelligent perspective. After all, nobody has ever survived this life, but only a psychotic allows the inevitability of death to deprive existence of its joyous creative fulfillments.

And it is the view of this essay that twentieth-century Americans have much to be proud of beyond their superficial, but nonetheless significant, triumphs in the realm of technology. That in fact the last fifty years have seen the most meaningful development, the greatest breakthroughs, in human freedom in our history. That it is indeed possible that the United States stands on the verge of a new historical form: a great industrial, urban society dedicated to freedom and equal opportunity. We still have a good way to go—and the Orwellian nightmare of *1984* reminds us of the perils—but when the historian looks empirically at the distance we have traveled, and the dangers we have overcome, in the past half-century, he has reason for optimism. We may yet be worthy of our dreams.

With this as an introduction, let us abandon the broad sweep for the narrow. Before we can understand where we are, we must know where we have been. Thus, difficult as it is, the effort must be made to penetrate the epistemological curtain that divides modern urban America from its rural antecedents. In particular we are concerned in this chapter with the state of American liberty in the first decade of the twentieth century, and this necessarily involves us in an analysis of the key institutions and the dominant social realities of that period.

First of all, the United States was a great *empty* country. The Census of 1900 showed a total population of 76 million. (In 1963 we are pressing rapidly toward 190 million.) And an overwhelming proportion of the population lived in small towns or rural areas; only 24 million inhabited communities of more than 10 thousand people. (Today roughly two-thirds live in so-called conurbations, great urban complexes centering around a "core city.") The federal government in 1900 lived quite nicely on its revenues which totaled 567 million dollars. The Internal Revenue Service turned in roughly 300 million—this year it should disgorge into federal coffers nearly 90 *billion* dollars. (There was, of course, no income tax, and in 1895 the Supreme Court had insisted that there could be none until the Constitution was amended.) [2]

The United States in 1900 was, in short, a huge underpopulated nation of small towns and rural villages. It was a white, Protestant country dominated by a rural value system. The legal system, for example, treated the monster trusts which developed in the 1880's and 1890's as if they were simply oversized village merchants and artisans. Consumers and workers who did not like Mr. Rockefeller's way of doing business were told by the judges to try another storekeeper. The worker injured in the steelworks was similarly treated in law as though he were the blacksmith's helper who had been kicked by an eccentric horse. Litigation thus went wandering into the labyrinth of "contributory negligence" and the "master-servant rule." It was not until later that men would realize that the United States had a profound urban-rural schism, one which established new value systems as well as new ways of life.

To the ancient masters of rural America—the white, Protestant, predominantly Anglo-Saxon elite which had managed the destinies of the Republic for more than a century—the City was enemy ground. They echoed Thomas Jefferson's detestation of these sores on the body politic and his fears that urbanization in the New World would lead to the demoralization of the populace and the degeneration of the democratic way of life. The City was a foreign body infecting the whole society. And it was foreign in another sense: the great immigration from Southern and Eastern Europe which swelled in the nineties was reaching the proportions of a tidal wave. Between 1900 and the outbreak of the First World War, over thirteen million immigrants reached the "Golden Shore." Roughly two and a half million emigrated from Italy alone, no less than six million from Central and Eastern European nations. Needless to say, this was a Catholic invasion which made the earlier arrival of the Irish look like a commando raid. From this period also, beginning with the great exodus from the Czarist pogroms of 1890, dates the real history of the Jewish community in the United States. In hardly more than a decade, New York became one of the leading centers of world Jewry.[3]

The America to which this massive immigration flooded was not the small town or the bucolic homestead. It was the factory city, where people congregated in great ethnic blobs to live in what was all too often a state of industrial peonage. Suddenly—almost overnight it must have seemed to those who had grown up in small-town America—the country was full of foreigners jabbering away in unknown tongues, insecure and secretive, and worst of all, perhaps, "Romans," members of that international conspiracy against religious freedom which Protestant children learned in cradle and conventicle to dread. And if the "Roman" conspiracy was not enough, it was "common knowledge" that many of the Jewish immigrants were anarchists and Communists. It seemed as though they were hardly in the country a week before they began to organize trade-unions and engage in other forms of subversive activity. (The truth, as those who labored to create the United Hebrew Trades in the 1890's knew, was far from the myth, but the critics knew no Yiddish and were thus cut off from the vitriolic denunciations of the Jewish *petit bourgeoisie* which enlivened the pages of the socialist *Daily Forward*.) [4]

The nation faced an "Americanization" problem. Agitation to limit immigration grew, and in 1905 and 1906, for the first time in our legal history, the laws of nationality were codified, defined, and extended to make the process of conferring citizenship more than the mere formality it had been for over a century. The problem in part arose from the political entrepreneurial talent of the Irish who demonstrated a superb capacity for "Americanizing" the new immigrants. Both from history and from their situation, the Irish politicians were ideally equipped to act as the bridge between the English-speaking Protestant Establishment and the non-English-speaking Catholic immigration: they were English-speaking Catholics. They also had learned a lot since they streamed off the boats in the 1840's and 1850's. Their own experience with the Protestant ethic led them understandably to set up a toll bridge.

The key to their power lay in the immigrant vote. Under the free and easy rules of the time, United States citizenship (in some states, only a declaration of intention, i.e., "first papers") and residence were virtually the only prerequisites to exercising the franchise. There was no Immigration and Naturalization Service to check on the naturalization process. Indeed, state and municipal courts were authorized to naturalize aliens, and, with a cooperative judge (elected by the machine), an incredible number of immigrants could be admitted to citizenship in a remarkably brief period of time. In fact, as memoirs from that time confirm, the political machines simply marched the immigrants through the courtroom to the registry of voters—and subsequently marched them to the polling booths. The United States Government, until the reforms mentioned above, literally had no control over admission to the political community. [5]

Of course, under these circumstances, those who instructed and mobilized the newcomers—the political machines of the big cities—stood to profit from the enterprise. The immediate effect was to create a large block of votes which they could deliver one way or the other, a package which could on occasion determine presidential elections (the impact of the famous "Rum, Romanism and Rebellion" episode in 1884 on the fortunes of James G. Blaine could not be forgotten) and which in practical terms put the big city machines above the law. But while the representatives of the old order who ran the state legislatures and the states were prepared to make deals with these potent upstarts, they were always on the lookout for ways and means to destroy the authority of the cities. One way, obviously, was to cut down on immigration and to tighten, and make enforceable, the standards for naturalization.

Another was to demand the "Americanization" of the immigrant before he was permitted to participate in the affairs of the Republic—a move which found practical expression in the demand for literacy tests, proof of loyalty, and more elaborate residence requirements as a prerequisite for voting. This effort was frustrated in its essentials until the United States entered World War I. Then the "Americanizers" went wild. Using wartime chauvinism as their justification, they attempted to eliminate foreign language newspapers, parochial schools, the teaching of foreign languages in the public schools, and—momentarily—even changed sauerkraut to liberty cabbage and dachshunds to liberty hounds. And when in November, 1917, Morris Hillquit ran for Mayor of New York on an antimilitarist, if not antiwar, platform, and received a third of the votes, their judgment was confirmed: the cities were the strongholds of disloyalty, radicalism, and un-Americanism.

But to discuss this is to get ahead of the story. In the first decade of the twentieth century, there was an uneasy equilibrium between the growing industrial, urban sector of the nation and the shrinking rural and agrarian section which sustained the Establishment on the national and state levels. The state and national machines of the small-town politicians were not less immoral (despite their fondness for prohibition and antigambling legislation) than those of the big cities. The big city bosses, generally of Irish extraction, were no more altruistic in their approach to the immigrant than were their Brahmin opponents. Indeed, politics generally was conducted on such a level of blatant self-interest, and with such a shameless dedication to pelf, that the American Socialist Party gained strength geometrically from its foundation in 1901 as an expression of public indignation against the "two old parties."

The point of this is that there was no national community in 1900; there were a number of subcultures living side by side within the geographical expanse of the nation. As a consequence, any generalizations have to be qualified by a recognition that one group's meat was another group's poison, that, for example, the broad religious tolerance of the Establishment was reserved for those within the traditional Protestant ambience. Just as John Locke excluded from the benefits of religious tolerance "opinions contrary to human society, or to those moral rules which are necessary to the preservation of civil society," the leaders of the nation could in the last decades of the nineteenth century ruthlessly suppress polygamous Mormonism.[6] (When the question of Mormon religious freedom under Article I of the Bill of Rights came to the Supreme Court in 1879, the Justices disposed of the matter summarily: *Mormonism was not a religion!*) Thus if one were Protestant, the odds were that he would live out his life in an atmosphere of toleration, but if he were Catholic or Jewish (to omit the Mormon, admittedly an extreme case), he would probably feel the whiplash of religious discrimination. (The village atheist, that landmark of rural nonconformity, apparently had a special dispensation: perhaps he denied the existence of a *Protestant* God?)

To put the matter this way is not to suggest that the Catholics or Jews were innocent devotees of civil liberty. On the contrary, in their city ghettos, where their jurisdiction ran unchallenged, they dealt in their own rough fashions with religious and cultural nonconformity. (Jewish freethinkers, who celebrated their "liberation from superstition" by organizing a "Yom Kippur Ball," narrowly escaped lynching at the hands of the Orthodox for thus defiling the Day of Atonement.) By contemporary standards of civil liberty, the rights of an individual were largely defined by the will of *his* majority, i.e., the majority in whatever subcultural unit of sovereignty he inhabited. And, as we shall see, when jurisdictions crossed, life got complicated. The "sturdy, individualist worker" who was beaten up as a "scab" by his neighbors was a classic instance of what might be called conflict of jurisdictions. This was not a new problem in American life. In 1794 Congressman Albert Gallatin, who had told his neighbors in western Pennsylvania to pay their whiskey excise and stop behaving like a "mob," was ominously referred by his audience to a recent resolution which stated that "any one who refers to the People as a 'mob' shall be tarred and feathered." [7]

But, despite what we with hindsight see as the evils of the age, there was little sense of oppression. Indeed, if we examine the epoch in terms of its own values—as we must if we are to come to grips with it—there was a pervasive optimism and sense of freedom. This was understandable in the instance of the white, Protestant, rural majority, but paradoxically it thrived among the exploited immigrants. (The Negroes are a special case to be examined shortly, but it might be noted in passing that the *Zeitgeist* even permeated that oppressed community: the motto of the Class of 1886 at Tuskegee Institute was "There Is Always Room at the Top!") [8] To poor people, accustomed to the oppression of Czarist Russia, the "Black Hundreds," the semiofficial pogroms, or to the unbelievable filth of the slums of Naples or Palermo, accustomed above all to life in a brutalized atmosphere of authority, the United States, even the slums of New York's lower East Side or Chelsea district, was the land of promise. The immigrant in short was exploited, but not alienated. He never lost his most priceless possession—his hope. The greatest justification of twentieth-century American accomplishment is that this hope, this trust in freedom, has been so grandly vindicated.

But if we must deal with states of mind, we must also deal with states of reality. Let us therefore switch from an examination of this paradoxical and turbulent society, which all unknown to itself was carrying the embryo of a new industrial civilization, to a discussion of the legal institutions which, in the last analysis, determined the concrete meaning of American liberty. Here we must begin with the sad story of the rise and fall of the Fourteenth Amendment. The original Bill of Rights, the first ten amendments added in 1791, were designed under states' rights auspices to limit the authority of the new Leviathan, the national government which some feared might become an engine of oppression. In fact, with few exceptions, the Bill of Rights forbade the national government to do things which it had little inclination to undertake. With the eruption of the slavery crisis and the ensuing Civil War, a new spirit briefly invigorated the nation; the result was the "War Amendments" (Thirteen, Fourteen, and Fifteen) designed both to put an end to human slavery and to establish national protection of fundamental human rights. Along with the Fourteenth Amendment went a corpus of civil rights acts based on the principle that agencies of the national government had the jurisdiction and the duty to protect basic civil and property rights from state and local governmental action, and even from local "custom."

The high pitch of idealism which accompanied the Civil War soon degenerated into the shambles of business and governmental corruption which Mark Twain called the "Gilded Age," Vernon L. Parrington "the Great Barbecue." The Republican Party, whose attachment to Negro rights had been partly motivated by political self-interest (the goal of building a strong Republican movement in the South on a foundation of Negro voters was always in the background of any discussion of civil rights), simply lost interest in the freedmen by 1877. Not only was this lack of interest in the Negro characteristic of Southern and Democratic opinion, but it also pervaded liberal and radical Republican circles. On April 5, 1877, for example, the *Nation*, liberal Republican in orientation, observed coldly that "the negro will [now] disappear from the field of national politics. Henceforth the nation, as a nation, will have nothing more to do with him." [9] The radical Republican *National Intelligencer*, which had vigorously supported military reconstruction, similarly noted on February 21, 1877, that all seemed peaceful in Southern race relations: "Satisfied with his personal liberty, [the Negro] appears now, as a rule, willing to vote with his former master." [10] No Negro comments have survived.

On the basis of an arrangement too simple to be called a conspiracy and too complex to style a compromise, jurisdiction over the Negro was returned in 1877 to the states—white supremacy was effectively reinstituted in the very shadow of the Fourteenth Amendment. The political aspects of this arrangement have been told with brilliance and perception by C. Vann Woodward in his *Reunion and Reaction* and *Origins of the New South*. What concern us here are the legal formalities by which the Fourteenth Amendment was converted into a battle monument.

Once the white guardians had deserted their posts, it was predictable that the Fourteenth Amendment could be interpreted to justify this desertion. What was surprising was the speed with which this rationalization was accomplished. By 1883, the Supreme Court (with the approval, it should be noted, of Congress, President, and parties) had turned the Fourteenth Amendment into a vague set of libertarian aphorisms with no effective cutting edge in the enforcement of civil rights. Essentially it was held to limit only formal state action infringing upon narrowly stipulated rights; for example, a state law banning Negroes from jury service. All private actions, even those which relied for their effectiveness on the support of the police power of the state, were beyond the reach of the amendment. Thus a theater owner could bar Negroes—and call the sheriff to arrest those who persisted in seeking admission—without violating in any way the injunctions of the Fourteenth Amendment.[11]

As if this definition of "private action" were not broad enough, the Court in the famous case of *Plessy* v. *Ferguson* (1896) sustained a "Jim Crow" law, a Louisiana statute requiring the segregation of the "races" on railroad trains. (Race has been put in quotes not only from deference to genetic theory, but also to suggest the problem created in this very litigation: *Plessy was one-eighth Negro!* Indeed, no hero in the cause of race relations, he claimed to be a white man unfairly discriminated against by the state.) By analogy this Court decision was used to justify the huge body of Jim Crow legislation passed in the Southern—and, alas, in some of the Northern—states. In essence, Negroes were held to be a different species of man; thus the requirement that they receive "equal protection of the laws" was interpreted to validate *different* treatment from whites. The Court, without knowing it, adopted Aristotle's theory of "proportional equality": to treat men "equally" does not mean to treat them identically; it requires only that all receive their "just deserts." [12]

Since Negroes, according to this racial logic, fell into a different biological category from whites, it was absurd to demand identical treatment. (One might as well argue that a zoo-keeper should feed elephants and lions the same meals!) Again it should be noted that the Supreme Court was following, not leading. In that era, and, indeed, well into the twentieth century, American social science nurtured race theories, concepts built around the hypothesis that there were innate racial differences which affected competence, intelligence, health, and even honesty and diligence. At the top of the evolutionary scale stood the handsome, energetic, intelligent "Caucasian"; the rest followed, their rank depending upon all the intervening stages of pigmentation and their relative merits ("Mongoloid," "Brown," "Arab," etc.). At the bottom was the Negro, member of a primitive "Negroid race" usually exemplified in schoolbooks by a savage with a bone through his nose. [13]

Let the contemporary reader, who may think this picture exaggerated, listen to H. L. Mencken, writing in 1910:

The educated negro of today is a failure, not because he meets insuperable difficulties in life, but because he is a negro. His brain is not fitted for the higher forms of mental effort; his ideals, no matter how laboriously he is trained and sheltered, remain those of the clown. He is, in brief, a low-caste man, to the manner born, and he will remain inert and inefficient until fifty generations of him have lived in civilization. And even then, the superior white race will be fifty generations ahead of him. [14]

The Negro was not only different, he was, on allegedly scientific grounds, certified inferior to the noble Caucasian.

With the decision in *Plessy* v. *Ferguson,* "race" became a legitimate basis for legal category. The states might legitimately establish all manner of special regulations governing the behavior of the Negro (and elsewhere in the nation, the Asian "mongoloid" immigrants, the Mexicans, and the poor American Indians were likewise singled out for special treatment) without infringing his civil rights. To state it differently, the civil rights of the Negro were those defined by his white neighbors and came down in essence to the right to work and keep his nose out of politics. And this was not a situation limited to the former Confederate states; as the Negroes moved North in increasing numbers, they took with them the cross of race prejudice. According to the distinguished Negro historian John Hope Franklin, in the first year of the twentieth century "more than 100 Negroes were lynched, and before the outbreak of World War I the number for the century had soared to more than 1,100." It was a time of savage race riots; symbolic of the new trend was the fact that the two worst—Atlanta (1906) and Springfield, Illinois (1908)—were on opposite sides of the Mason-Dixon Line. Small towns in the Midwest began by municipal ordinance to bar Negroes from residence.[15]

Simultaneously, on the Pacific Coast, anti-Oriental sentiment was reaching a new high. School segregation was instituted for the children of Chinese and Japanese immigrants, and laws were passed by the states designed to prevent Asian settlers from purchasing land. Direct Chinese immigration had been closed off by the Chinese Exclusion Act of 1882, but Japanese had been arriving in increasing numbers, and the admission of Hawaii as a territory in 1899 make it possible for a number of Hawaiian Japanese to go to the mainland. There was constant pressure in Congress from the West Coast Congressmen to bar the Japanese, and in 1907 President Theodore Roosevelt managed to get the Japanese government, in a famous "Gentleman's Agreement," voluntarily to prohibit emigration to the United States. The "Yellow Peril" entered the lexicon of the American racist.[16]

From the ominous forebodings of the nativists, it was difficult to determine whether the greatest peril to the "Aryan Republic" stemmed from the Asian immigration, or from the Jews and Papists. But whichever menace they emphasized, they accepted a common conclusion: the obliteration or (perhaps worse) the "mongrelization" of the Caucasian stock, which had brought the United States to its eminence, was only a matter of time unless drastic action were taken to "Save the Race." A serious text in political science and comparative government put the matter concisely. Said Columbia's Professor John W. Burgess:

the Teutonic nations . . . are intrusted, in the general economy of history, with the mission of conducting the political civilization of the modern world. The further conclusions of practical politics from this proposition must be, that in a state whose population is composed of a variety of nationalities the Teutonic element, where dominant, should never surrender the balance of political power. . . . Under certain circumstances it should not even permit participation of the other elements in political power.[17]

Though there was considerable disagreement among xenophobes as to exactly which races fell within the Teutonic category, and a few dissident voices argued for Celtic supremacy, it was clear that the thrust of the argument was aimed primarily at Jews, Slavs, and Italians. (Perhaps in hopes of achieving honorary "Teuton" status for the unquestionably American Negroes, Booker T. Washington joined in the chorus against the new immigration, somberly warning that it might lead to "a racial problem in the South more difficult and more dangerous than that which is caused by the presence of the Negro.") [18] Henry Adams, with his characteristic pessimism, hoped that the Teutons could at least stage a good *Götterdämmerung* so that "men of our kind might have some chance of being honorably killed in battle" and thus avoid enslavement by the Jews.[19] Other anti-Semites took a more positive view of the possibilities: "No Jew here can go on the street without exposing himself to the danger of being pitilessly beaten," stated an 1899 protest from Brooklyn Jewry.[20]

There was another large minority which almost literally lived under the gun: the industrial working class which the Marxists styled the proletariat. Unfortunately for the Marxists, and for the political movements in the United States which rested their claims and aspirations on dialectical materialism, the American working class never became a proletariat—as did, for example, the French or the German. That is, the American worker ignored his historical mission as the gravedigger of capitalism and refused to accept the Marxist premise that exploitation was simply an ineluctable by-product of the capitalist order. In short, he did not develop a Marxist-style "class consciousness" which in effect would have psychologically entombed him in a sealed room—a room which could only be unsealed by revolution and the "dictatorship of the proletariat."

In other words, the industrial worker, often living in a condition approaching industrial serfdom, did not lose hope. Like the Polish or Italian immigrant (which he often was), he was exploited and degraded, but he was seldom alienated. And if he rejected the Marxist gospel of revolution, it was not in favor of passivity. While the United States had no political insurrections under proletarian auspices, I think it is clear that we had more violence in the conduct of labor disputes in the half-century before the trade-union movement received legitimation than did France and Germany combined.[21]

This must be emphasized. Perhaps because the Marxists have seized the ideological heights in our time, no revolutionary movement can receive accreditation unless it pays obeisance to dialectical materialism. And conversely, a group of sociologists and historians have almost convinced mid-twentieth-century Americans that our tradition has been built on love, fellowship, and *consensus*. These opposites have paradoxically combined to geld the American tradition, to convert a vibrant, dynamic, and violent society, in which men have fought out with all available weapons the crucial issues of their times, into a peaceful, even somnolent, process of brotherhood and compromise, an extended Quaker meeting. It is true that the American working class as a collectivity never lost faith in the American dream. It is equally true that American workers took arms and fought on many an industrial battlefield to attain their rightful place in the free and equal community which the dream postulated. The steelworker who took his pistol in his lunch pail, like the Western Federation of Miners commando who set off 4,500 pounds of dynamite under the Bunker Hill and Sullivan smelter, was hardly testifying to a faith in consensus. Nor were the ubiquitous Pinkertons, or the Pennsylvania Iron and Coal Police.[22]

The situation of the industrial worker has to be understood against the background of the "Age of Enterprise," of the growth of great private governments under the name of "trusts." Massive industrialization began with the Civil War—which Charles A. Beard justly designated "the second American Revolution"—and accelerated at an ever-increasing pace throughout the last decades of the nineteenth century. The railroads led the march. In 1850, there were 7,365 miles of railroad in operation; in 1870, 46,844; *in 1890, 161,276.* In the same period, capitalization of the railroads jumped from $318,126,000 in 1850 to $2,476,893,000 in 1870 to *$10,122,636,000 in 1890.* Accompanying this fantastic transportation revolution was a spectacular growth in industrial production: the contribution of manufacturing industries to national product jumped from an estimated $1,630,000,000 in 1869 to $3,730,000,- 000 in 1889. In 1870, to add another dimension, the agricultural and the nonagricultural work forces were in balance with roughly six million in each category. By 1890, the agricultural force had risen to almost ten million, but nonfarm employment was up to fourteen; the next ten years saw this differential grow: in 1900 the ratio was eleven to eighteen.[23]

Statistics on economic growth are useful, but they do not give any insight into the economic and political forms which this expansion took. The giant corporations, the holding companies, the trusts were not just quantitative expansions of the small business. The United States Steel Corporation, founded in 1901 with capitalization that for the first time passed the billion-dollar mark, was not just the village smithy writ large. The development of the trusts brought a new political and economic universe where the old rules of behavior, designed for a rural nation, were essentially worthless. The old conception of the police power, for example, was based on the assumption that the community as a whole would always be competent to deal with the activities of its parts. But the development of great railroad systems and industrial empires created entities with far greater assets than most states. It was commonly said of the Pennsylvania state government in the 1890's that Standard Oil did everything but refine it. In the 1880's, when the California authorities attempted to domesticate the Central Pacific-Southern Pacific monster—the "octopus" of Frank Norris' muckraking book—the annual gross income of the railroads was *five* times that of the state! [24]

We can hardly take time here to discuss the economic history of the United States, but it is vital to this narrative to appreciate the extent to which the great industrial organizations operated as sovereigns—as private governments—within the geographical limits of the United States. This period is often described erroneously as an age of "free enterprise" or "laissez faire" as if corporate growth had occurred in an economic vacuum. Nothing could be further from the truth: the great trusts flourished in a state-sponsored greenhouse where the cold winds of competition were excluded by the protective tariff. Moreover, it was by state action, often amounting to purposeful inaction, that economic behavior was largely freed from the traditional restraints of the community.

This may sound like a clever play on words, but it is not. Under the Anglo-American legal tradition reaching back to the Middle Ages, economic activity was subject to severe community checks. This view, with some modification, was still implemented in law at the time of the Civil War. Indeed, in many areas it has never been modified: no one can, for example, put an oil derrick in his suburban yard or a chemical factory in his garage without authorization from the community. Zoning laws are a reflection of the tradition that one's private property rights are subject to definition by the body politic. It was simply inconceivable in the common-law conceptual universe for an individual to say: "This is my property and I can do anything I want with it." All private property rights were subject to public definition.

Yet the great corporations effectively escaped from the collectivism of the common law and set themselves up as final judges of their own property rights. The railroads, for example, successfully frustrated state rate regulation with the argument that they alone could properly define their vested rights, that for the state to attempt to set rates was a violation of natural economic laws. But the crucial consideration in the liberation of the railroads from the police power was *favorable state action on their claim!* It was the United States Supreme Court, not the shade of Adam Smith, which broke their shackles and turned them loose. To a close student of political economy, there is no way to avoid the conclusion that, despite all the fine talk about "laissez faire" and "rugged individualism," the great American corporations were nurtured and protected by new public policies—they were "Wards of the State."

To return to the mainstream of the argument, the relationship of the employer to his employees has to be appreciated in terms of public protection of private government. In terms of legal myth, the free American worker bargained as an equal with United States Steel. If he did not like Judge Gary's conditions of employment, he simply took his freedom of choice elsewhere. In the event that he decided to imitate the tactics of the corporation by joining with his fellow workers to corner the labor market, i.e., by organizing a trade union, suddenly the state blew the whistle and called a foul. He discovered that, unlike the employers, he was engaged in an illegal conspiracy in restraint of interstate commerce. This is no exaggeration: while the Supreme Court held that a corporation which (with the aid of a good tariff) controlled over 95 percent of the sugar refining in the nation was not restraining interstate commerce, it also held the unionized Danbury hatters to be an illegal conspiracy in restraint of interstate trade for shutting down a minute proportion of the country's hat production.[25]

This sort of legal maneuvering was, however, child's play. It was in strike situations that the state really showed its knuckles on behalf of its wards, the corporations. In the first place, there were the company police who exercised the state's police power: they were characteristically sworn in as sheriff's deputies, were kept on the payroll of the big corporations as private armies, and they moved directly and brutally against strikers. In the second, the issuance of an antistrike injunction by a friendly judge—which became an automatic event—put the strikers simultaneously in defiance of their employer and the state. If they persisted, as Eugene Debs learned in the Pullman Strike of 1894, the union leadership landed summarily in jail for contempt of court. And finally, in the event that company police and injunctive prohibitions failed to inhibit the free enterprise of the unions, the state militia was available to enforce martial law. Occasionally—as in the great railroad strike of 1877, the Pullman Strike of 1894, or "troubles" in the Coeur d'Alene in 1899—the state militia seemed unreliable and federal troops were called in.[26]

In other words, the whole power structure operated to protect the employer from his employees. The injunction was, in the gleeful phrase of the Chicago railroad executives, "a paper Gatling gun," but in the event that injunctions failed, Gatling guns were also available. It must be emphasized that this had no relationship whatsoever to traditional "laissez-faire" theories. If classical liberal economic views had been adopted, the state would merely have held the ring and let labor and management fight it out. Perhaps the point can be made more explicit by noting that the Supreme Court of the United States solemnly determined that freedom of speech was in no way limited by an injunction which forbade union organizers *even to discuss* with coal miners the advantages of a union! [27]

The great corporations then were not composed of "rugged individualists" fighting their way on their own merits in a "survival of the fittest" universe. On the contrary, their ability to build and triumph was at root founded on their expropriation of governmental power—an expropriation which, it must be added, rested throughout the last quarter of the nineteenth century on public consent, or, at worst, upon public inertia. Thus, no matter how picturesquely or savagely one portrays the raids of the "robber barons," he cannot evade the fundamental political reality that until after the turn of the century they were national heroes, "industrial statesmen." Fundamental reform was not in style, and when the public did get distressed, for example, during the periodic depressions, it rushed off in quest of superficial panaceas such as "greenbacks" and "free silver."

In short, when state power was devolved upon these great private, corporate governments (protective tariffs, for instance, virtually conferred the taxing power: high levels of protection which barred foreign competition gave American producers a statutory right to tax American consumers), the transfer did not take place in secret conclave. It occurred on the legislative floors and in the courtrooms, and, as far as one can determine from political programs and election returns, was done with the approval of the populace as a whole. And the complaints which were registered from dissident elements were more demands for a share of the loot than for a change in the system; the "funny-money" crusades were, for example, designed to break the power of "Wall Street Bankers" and increase rural liquidity, but a shift to greenbacks or to "16 to 1" would in no way significantly have altered the power structure of the economy.[28]

What had occurred in the post-Civil War period was an enormous contraction of the public sector, but this "withering away of the state"—despite much free enterprise rhetoric—had not led to a laissez-faire utopia based on free market competition, but to a quasi-feudal economic polity, to the exercise of public, governmental power by huge, irresponsible duchies which implemented virtually all aspects of sovereignty. About the only thing that Standard Oil, the Southern Pacific Railroad, the American Sugar Refining Company, or Carnegie Steel did not do was issue postage stamps. Typical of this feudal atmosphere was J. P. Morgan's remark to President Theodore Roosevelt when he learned that the United States had instituted antitrust proceedings against *his* Northern Securities Company: "If we have done anything wrong [said the banker], send your man [the Attorney General] to my man and they can fix it up." [29]

But, as the new century dawned, these great exponents and examples of feudal sovereignty were coming under increasing assault. The stage had been set by the passage in the 1880's and 1890's of a series of statutes—Civil Service Bill, Interstate Commerce Act, Sherman Anti-Trust Act—which established a *theoretical* framework for national regulation of various abuses. In practical terms, these measures were, in the Chinese phrase, "paper dragons," but they were on the books and could serve as precedents for measures with teeth. Moreover, almost as if by signal, exposé literature suddenly became popular. While Theodore Roosevelt could angrily draw on his knowledge of *Pilgrim's Progress* to style these journalists "muckrakers," their careful studies of the "trusts" and of corruption took over the pages of most leading magazines. Meanwhile less meticulous but more terrifying analyses were appearing in the form of fiction: the country was literally nauseated in 1905 by Upton Sinclair's devastating, but essentially truthful story of the foul conditions in the meat packinghouses, *The Jungle*. And William Randolph Hearst—who Lincoln Steffens felt was born without morals the way some are born without color vision—was tearing California apart with his lurid crusade against the monopolists, notably against the Southern Pacific Railroad, and expanding his newspaper empire. Indeed, Louis Filler, a careful student of the reform era, has categorically stated that "Hearst, more than any other man, was the absolute expression of the blind need and ignorance and resentment which troubled the worker and farmer." [30] While Ida Tarbell and Lincoln Steffens built an intellectual case for reform, Hearst, "steeped in mire," went for the jugular and slugged it out with the feudal barons on the lowest level of sensational, and effective, journalism.

We cannot pause here to chronicle the rise of the reform movement to its high noon in 1912; this has been brilliantly and sensitively limned by Richard C. Hofstadter in his *Age of Reform*. Our concern is with the impact of this massive public uprising on issues of civil liberty. Unfortunately no clear pattern emerged: the reformers were a varied lot and for a series of special reasons took widely different postures on civil rights. To put the matter differently, each group of reformers lived in its own little world with its own overweening problems; views on liberty thus tended to reflect the immediate needs of the place and moment. A few examples will perhaps clarify this ambivalence. The trade-union movement, living under incredible legal harassments, was, of course, strongly in favor of the right to organize. At the same time, unionists tended to favor both immigration restrictions and various measures designed to keep Negroes and Chinese (to mention two regular targets) out of the labor market. From the viewpoint of the California union worker, the hapless Chinese was a born "scab." Indeed, the radical California Constitution of 1879, written under strong trade-union influence, banned the employment of Chinese in industry and mines. Similarly in the South, organized workers saw the Negroes as perpetual strikebreakers, as the reef upon which all efforts to unionize the section inevitably foundered.

The Southern Populists, too, took a dim view of the Negroes. From their angle of vision, the well-disciplined battalions of Negro voters had been a key weapon in the power of the "Redeemers," the Southern agents of Northern capitalist exploitation who had ruled in Dixie since the end of Reconstruction. This is a complicated story which has been narrated by C. Vann Woodward in his *Origins of the New South* and his biography of *Tom Watson*, the radical turned racist who somehow symbolized the inner tensions of Southern Populism. For our purposes, it is enough to indicate the broad consideration that in the South the demand for economic freedom by the lower-class whites had as its tragic concomitant the further depression of the Negro. And the Populists in the West mixed their reform potion with a sizable shot of anti-Semitism. Curiously, the Jew became the prototype of the Wall Street capitalist; the farmer was the victim of the great Rothschild Conspiracy.[31]

The urban progressives were generally far more "tolerant," in the wide sense of that word, than their rural brethren. While city reformers, often of old native stock, did on occasion curse the clannish and suspicious immigrant communities which frequently supplied the electoral buttress for corrupt machine politics, they also —and Lincoln Steffens is the prize example—became aware that the immigrants were the instruments rather than the sources of corruption. That in fact the men behind the scenes who profited from the franchise steal or the ice monopoly were none other than the pillars of the Establishment, the "industrial statesmen" of the Gilded Age. Moreover, this was a time when settlement house workers, and former social workers, contributed a tremendous impetus to the drive for urban, industrial reform, and the picture of the immigrant which they conveyed—poor, helpless, exploited— gave a humanitarian cast to every sector of reform with which they were associated.

Spurred by fear and resentment as well as by the ideals of self-help which one assimilated with the American atmosphere, and encouraged by liberals, Socialists, and religious reformers both within and without the ethnic communities, the underdog groups began to mobilize for their own defense and welfare. There was nothing new about this—the Germans, Irish, and even Ulstermen had long since founded powerful community groups which did everything from lobbying with Congress (against restrictive immigration proposals) to managing burials, death benefits, and insurance. But with all due respect to the problems faced by the earlier migrations, the "new immigration" confronted afflictions which were both quantitatively and qualitatively of a different order of magnitude. This was particularly true of the Jews who were subjected simultaneously to religious, ethnic, and economic discrimination. While many of the oldsters were willing passively to take this beating as God's chastisement, the younger elements in the Jewish community began to organize the counteroffensive. Outstanding in this respect were the founding in 1906 of the American Jewish Committee and, in 1913, that of the Anti-Defamation League of B'nai B'rith. While the American Jewish Committee had essentially a foreign mission—to aid the Jews persecuted in Russia—the Anti-Defamation League was clearly established as a defense against American anti-

Semitism. Indeed, it may well claim to be the pioneer civil rights group; the initial Anti-Defamation League program as set forth in its charter looked beyond the parochial problems of the Jewish community to the liberties of all Americans: "Its ultimate purpose is to secure justice and fair treatment to all citizens alike and to put an end forever to unjust and unfair discrimination against and ridicule of any sect or body of citizens."

At the same time there were stirrings in the disorganized and depressed Negro community, stirrings which led in 1905 to the Niagara Conference and the foundation, largely under stimulation of white liberals, of the National Association for the Advancement of Colored People. It is hard to realize it, but up to this point, the Negroes had no significant secular organization to advance their claims. What actions were taken in defense of Negro rights— such as the bitter protest in 1906 occasioned by President Roosevelt's dishonorable discharge from the Army of three companies of Negro troops who had clearly been victimized by malicious citizens of Brownsville, Texas—were instituted by Negro religious leaders, notably the bishops of the well-organized African Methodist Episcopal Church.[32] Or they were instituted by white supporters of Negro rights who were at that time few and far between. (The Louisiana Socialists, for example, set up a Jim Crow local for Negroes, presumably endorsing the principle of "separate but radical.") [33]

There was, in short, a sense of ferment in the land. No longer was the sovereignty of corporate government, the corruption of politics, the exploitation of the immigrant and the worker accepted as part of the national landscape. The Gilded Age was over, though the external manifestations of its glory still held center stage. A new epoch was emerging, though few there were who could identify its birth pangs or predict its form. Throughout the nation, from rural Wisconsin to slum-ridden New York City, the trumpets of reform were sounding the Charge. And everywhere there was hope, an almost smug sense of moral optimism, and the conviction that victory was inevitable. By the time the election of 1912 was held, the American voter would be hard put to find a

candidate for President who was not for "Reform": Debs, Roosevelt, and Wilson were all excoriating corruption, and even William
Howard Taft alleged (with considerable justice) that he was a
better reformer than Theodore Roosevelt.

Yet, unnoticed in the reform euphoria and the premature victory celebrations of the reformers, there was also an ominous and
brooding sense of national insecurity. The United States had risen
to the status of a world power with a set of ideals, of social myths
founded on the realities and imperatives of rural life. But by 1910,
the reality had outgrown the ideal: a huge, and truly alien industrial civilization was steadily and inexorably encroaching on the
power and status of rural America and of the traditional Protestant, Anglo-Saxon leadership. Suddenly people who had always
felt "at home" in the United States began to feel like strangers
in their own demesne. An old order was clearly dying, its value
system was moribund and inadequate, but nothing new had emerged
to replace it. Eventually, as we shall see, a new set of values built
around freedom and equality in a multicultural, multiracial urban
society did emerge to provide a focus for American aspiration; but
before this could take place the American people had to live through
the savage turmoil of World War I, the brutal reaction of the
1920's, and the challenges of Depression and War.

II

WALPURGIS NIGHT:
THE "GREAT WAR"

It is always dangerous for the historian to employ the conditional tense, yet I cannot help but speculate in this mood on the possible course of events had the United States avoided embroilment in World War I. As one examines the trends of domestic policy from 1890 to the present, he can hardly escape the conviction that the "Great War" effectively stunted, at least for a generation, the reform tradition and left psychological scars in the American psyche which ache to this day.[1]

The contrasts between prewar and postwar America are clear and compelling. In 1914 reform was in the saddle. Throughout the nation eager optimists were striving day and night to end the abuses of the Gilded Age and establish "Progressive Democracy." Yet by 1920 reform was seemingly at a standstill. Warren Harding was elected President over a conservative Democrat in a campaign more reminiscent of 1880 than of 1912. Perhaps even more symbolic was Mrs. Harding's faith in astrology—the Age of Reason seemed to have vanished without a trace.

Is it possible that if the United States had been able to maintain its traditional isolation from the Old World, the difficult transition from rural agrarianism to urban industrialism could have been mastered without the dreadful travail of the 1920's and 1930's? I suspect so, but this is retrospective wishful thinking; the alternatives of 1914 disappeared, and no one can ever know the conditions or destination of the road not taken. For better or for worse, the United States in 1917 entered the European power complex and our world was never the same again. To say this is not to suggest that isolationism could have remained a viable policy much longer—technological changes were leading willy-nilly to a shrinking of the globe; it is rather to indicate that there were other routes to the present which could have changed radically the domestic consequences of American involvement. Suppose, for instance, President Wilson had chosen to abandon isolationism by bringing the great authority of the United States firmly behind the proposal for a negotiated settlement? Such intervention could have been decisive in breaking the stalemate of butchery, might have made possible the survival of the Russian democratic revolution, and, above all from the angle of vision of this book, would have obviated the savage chauvinism that accompanied American entrance into the war.

Few references were made in the last chapter to the international position of the United States. In fact, before 1914, external affairs were largely irrelevant to the conduct of American life or the crucial decisions of American government. Since the time of Washington and Jefferson, the United States had (in a manner oddly reminiscent of contemporary India) combined nonalignment with high moral self-esteem. American policy-makers could generally be relied upon to sound a righteous note on problems of the day, but they were conspicuously unwilling to gird the sword of righteousness. President Millard Fillmore, for instance, greeted the European revolutions of 1848 with warm sympathy, pointed out to the desperate rebels the fine example that had been set them by the United States, gave full moral support to these liberation movements—and then added the classic postscript:

it becomes an imperative duty [of the United States] not to interfere in the government or internal policy of other nations and although we may sympathize with the unfortunate or the oppressed everywhere in their fight for freedom, our principles forbid us from taking any part in such foreign contests.[2]

The United States, its leaders agreed, could best forward the cause of freedom by showing an example to the benighted and standing aside from the dirty conflicts of the Old World. It was far wiser, as Henry Clay put it, to "keep our light burning on this western shore, as a light to all nations, than to hazard its utter extinction amid the ruins of fallen or falling republics in Europe." [3] The European democrats, in other words, would just have to make their own way in the world; the United States would be pleased to provide them with a paradigm of wise and effective popular government, but no freedom fighters or people's volunteers would carry the burden of liberation from the New World to the Old.

This combination of moral superiority and contempt was as typical of the Democrats as of the Republicans; it pervaded both corrupt and reformed circles. It probably achieved its classic formulation, on the deathbed of the tradition itself, when President Woodrow Wilson proclaimed in 1916 that the United States was "too proud to fight." Thus, despite the brief foray into colonialism represented by the Spanish-American War, the American vision in 1914 was essentially continental. In the same sense that the American businessman wanted high tariffs to insulate the American market from foreign competition, the American progressives had a parochial vision of salvation. Few were interested in saving the world, but tremendous energies were poured into cleaning the rascals out of the statehouse or city hall. On the left, the Socialists —following the thesis of John A. Hobson—asserted that foreign expansion was part of the pattern of capitalist exploitation and were vigorously anti-imperialist. (It is doubtful if any American Marxist at this time had heard of the Russian who would give this theory its most vigorous expression, V. I. Lenin.) For Socialist leader Eugene V. Debs, foreign policy issues were capitalist ruses concocted to divert the attention of the American people from important domestic problems, and to forestall the international power of the working class.

At the same time, as a consequence of the huge immigration of the 1890's and 1900's, there were in the United States great undigested ethnic aggregations. Most of these were non-English-speaking East Europeans, though significantly the largest single national group was German—more than 2.3 million in the first generation alone. The progressives were fond of talking about the United States as a melting pot, but as far as the first generation of newcomers was concerned this was quite unrealistic. While in political terms the immigrants were mostly vigorous in their loyalty to the United States, they understandably retained strong cultural attachments to the old country. (A standard family problem in the immigrant communities arose from the second generation's refusal to learn the old mother tongue and generally to abide by traditions.) It is clear, for example, that a large number of Germans came to the United States precisely to escape from "Prussian militarism" and compulsory military service. They were anything but German *patriots*, but they were Germans, and they organized socially and politically in German-American associations. To the outsider, they were Germans—they talked German, gathered in German beer cellars, sang German songs, and attended German churches. (Even the Catholic Church, which refused to permit ethnic parochialism in theory, allowed the establishment of ethnic succursal chapels, i.e., within a parish and subject to its jurisdiction there could emerge a "German church," a "Polish church," a "French church," and in California, a "Chinese church.")

If the German-Americans had a residual loyalty to German culture, there were other groups which were actively engaged in supporting revolutionary movements in the old country. The classic case was the *Clan na Gael*, the Irish-American organization which largely financed the anticolonial movement in the Emerald Isle and brought tremendous political pressure to bear in Washington in behalf of Irish freedom. But among the immigrants from the Austro-Hungarian Empire, that masterpiece of geographical question-begging, there were numerous groups agitating for Bohemian, Polish, Croatian, and Hungarian independence. Jews in America were similarly organized to aid their brethren in the Pale and to encourage and subsidize emigration from Czarist Russia.[4]

Statistics for 1910 give some insight into the size of the immigrant contingent: there were 13,515,886 foreign-born immigrants and no less than 18,897,837 in the second generation, i.e., the first American-born generation. When we realize that the total population in 1910 was 92,407,000, we see that roughly one-third of the population was no more than one generation from Old World roots. Obviously the problem of the assimilation—or "Americanization," in nativist usage—of immigrations was one which, if sufficiently ignored, would go away. Indeed, the melting-pot theory was in real terms an excuse for not confronting the issue, and it had the pragmatic sanction of history: the history of the United States had chronicled the successive absorption of immigrant waves which, if not painless, had been accomplished without fundamental crisis.

To an extent which has never been appreciated by historians, the isolationist foreign policy of the United States was a necessary condition for the success of this gradual assimilation. While no one can accuse the statesmen who for over a century formulated and maintained this position of noninvolvement of consciously shaping their views in terms of the metabolism of immigration, their viewpoint was completely functional. The unanticipated by-product of isolation was the removal of American foreign policy from the controversial sector: immigrants were not called upon to choose sides in Europe, and their cultural loyalties to former sovereignties led to no conflicts with national policy. True, many ethnic pressure groups agitated in Washington to get help for Kossuth, the Polish rebels of 1863, and the eternally rambunctious Fenians, but they always received the same answer: we sympathize with you, but will not officially intervene in Old World squabbles. In other words, so far as the government of the United States was concerned, the attitudes and loyalties of immigrants to their homelands were nonpolitical in character; given the isolationist foundations of American policy, the immigrant was never called upon to demonstrate his Americanism.

There had been a few brief deviations from this rule: during the Mexican War, for example, Irish Catholics were often accused of sympathy with the Mexicans (and a Mexican Army battalion, the

San Patricio, was formed of Irish deserters from the American Army), and the Spanish-American War had led to some discrimination against Americans of Spanish or Mexican descent. But in general the lofty, disembodied moralism of American policy created no situations in which the immigrant had to stand up and "be counted for America." The fact, for example, that the American government was sympathetic to the British during the Boer War in no sense hindered the pro-Boer agitation of the German and Irish minorities in the United States.

Thus if the United States were to veer from its isolationism toward a policy of intervention in Europe, it might have been predicted that the policy vacuum within which the immigrant exercised his ethnic loyalties would be destroyed. The attitude of a German toward Germany, of an Irishman toward England, or of a Jew toward Russia would now become a component of the political sector, a matter of active concern to the government of the United States. And with roughly a third of the population in the first- and second-generation immigrant category, it might also have been predictable that demands would be made to turn the melting pot into a pressure cooker. The dogged bands of nativists and xenophobes had been asserting this for years, but now events on the world and national scenes suddenly gave their message an appeal it had never previously received. But this is to anticipate later developments, for when the Great War broke out in August, 1914, Americans simply took for granted their traditional insulation. Indeed, in 1915 when an American referred to "the War," he was likely to be describing the internecine brawl then raging in Mexico; current events in Europe seemed a long way off. It was too bad that the European powers were reverting to their old, bad habits, but one could hardly expect much from degenerate monarchies.

To Thomas Woodrow Wilson, the election of 1912 marked the rehabilitation of the Democratic Party as the vehicle of the "New Freedom." Wilson, who considered himself the first *real* Democratic President since the Civil War (he would have said the "War Between the States"), arrived in Washington totally immersed in domestic policy. Accused of being a "rural Tory" by the savage Bull Moose, Theodore Roosevelt, Wilson demonstrated his modernism by riding to his inauguration in an automobile—this despite the fact that in 1906 he had ominously predicted that the auto would spread socialism in the United States! [5] With his inauguration in March, 1913, the Confederacy captured Washington: Southern Democrats controlled key positions in Congress, and Wilson's Cabinet ministers proceeded joyously to institute Jim Crow in the federal administration.[6]

Symbolizing Wilson's absence of a foreign policy was his appointment of William Jennings Bryan as Secretary of State. The Department of State which the "Great Commoner" directed was an insignificant little agency with roughly seventy-five employees in Washington. Bryan promptly made a name for himself by ruthlessly applying the patronage axe both in Washington and in the foreign service. He also achieved temporary fame by opposing the appointment of President Charles W. Eliot of Harvard as Ambassador to Peking on the ground that Sun Yat-sen and his disciples were devout Christians who would be offended by the designation of a Unitarian! [7] But whatever his limitations as a diplomat or administrator, it was clear that Bryan was vigorously anti-imperialist, antimilitarist, and generally anti-interventionist. His great cause was the arbitration of international disputes, and he put Colonel Roosevelt into a classic rage by reimbursing Colombia for T.R.'s stimulation of Panamanian "independence."

The world drifted along through 1913 (a portent of things to come was the passage of the Income Tax Amendment to the Constitution and the institution by Congress of a trivial tax) and into 1914 with great turmoil in Europe and great indifference in the United States. Wilson masterminded his domestic program through Congress in a fashion truly breathtaking and quite casually began an intervention in Mexican politics which made even Theodore Roosevelt look like a "good neighbor." (Awakened at 2:30 A.M. on April 21, 1914, Wilson was told by Bryan, Secretary of the Navy Josephus Daniels, and his secretary, Joseph Tumulty, that the Mexicans in Vera Cruz had seized some American sailors.

"Take Vera Cruz at once," he instructed and went back to sleep.) [8] Americans in ever-increasing numbers were going to the "flickers" as movie houses opened throughout the country—for every citizen who had heard of the Archduke Franz Ferdinand, there were easily a thousand who idolized Mary Pickford, "Little Mary, Queen of the Movies."

The shots fired in Sarajevo on June 28, 1914, echoed but faintly in the United States. Some of Bakunin's more fervent apostles had been assassinating European royalty off and on for half a century. The fact that this time the assassin was a Serbian nationalist rather than an anarchist hardly seemed to justify a crisis of state, particularly since the Serbian government had promptly disclaimed responsibility and offered amends. However, in a fashion which even those most directly involved never pretended fully to comprehend, a minor diplomatic incident generated a European war. In a sense, all the great powers came in by the back door: the Russians went to rescue the Serbs and restore their authority in the Balkans; the Germans joined their Austrian allies and set out to destroy the Entente which, in their paranoidal view, had them "encircled"; the French, nursing memories of 1871 and dreams of revenge, charged to the aid of ravished Belgium and their Russian ally; and the British—well, the British intervened to fulfill commitments to the French which the majority of the cabinet and Liberal majority in Parliament were unaware existed and to protect the integrity of Belgium.[9]

At the risk of oversimplification, it can be said that while the civilian leadership in Germany, France, and Britain was dismayed by the prospect of actual hostilities, the military in each nation were able to cast the dice and determine policy. The Asquith government could assert, as it did, that the British had no alliance with the French, but could hardly escape the consequences of the Anglo-French naval "understanding" that had concentrated the French Navy in the Mediterranean and left the protection of the French Atlantic coast to the Royal Navy. Even the Kaiser could wobble at the last minute at the prospect of invading Belgium, but the German General Staff was not to be denied its long-rehearsed opportunity to implement the Schlieffen Plan. And the French High Command was equally in no mood for compromise: for several years they had been armed for this day with the sure knowledge that the great offensive dictated by their Plan 17 would reverse the verdict of 1871 and put the tricolor on the Brandenburg Gate.

Thus a war that few aside from the military really wanted unrolled before the transfixed stares of the principal diplomats and in an atmosphere of chauvinistic hysteria which made sensitive critics wonder if nineteen centuries of Christian doctrine had left any mark on Western man. One prescient voice in England, deploring the gaiety and patriotic hysteria of August, 1914, expressed a premonition the future would vindicate. "Let us not put on paper caps," said Harold Begbie, "and march through the streets waving penny flags, breathing beer and singing 'Britons never shall be slaves.' Let us not sing boastful songs! Honor may call us to fight, self-preservation may force us into the slaughter-house; but let us wear on our sleeves the crepe of mourning for a civilization that had the promise of joy . . ." [10]

Everyone—whether in London, Paris, Vienna, Saint Petersburg, or Berlin—seemed to assume the war would be over by Christmas. But by Christmas both sides had taken to the earth, soldiers became moles, and from the Swiss border to the English Channel two lines of trenches confronted each other. No one had known quite how the war started; now no one knew how to end it. For four years millions of young men, the hope of the future, were marched into the charnel house that was the Western Front, while in the East the German Army systematically butchered the poorly equipped and disastrously led Russians who were herded against them. The strategy of trench warfare seemed to resemble *Poddavki*, the Russian variation of checkers where the object is to lose all one's pieces before the opponent loses his: if an offensive failed, the solution was to increase the force and try again —through the artillery barrage, the mud, the wire, and finally the enfiladed machine guns and rifles of the subterranean enemy. While the French generals, imbued with the doctrine of *l'offensive à outrance* seemed to win this macabre competition, the Germans and British were not far behind. A generation was sacrificed in this insane homicide pact. And perhaps as terrible as the destruction of human lives was the crippling of human vision—those whom fate spared were spiritually stunted and drained. And fearfully cautious: it was the remnant of this butchered generation which later, in the 1930's, cherished the ideology of appeasement on the ground that even totalitarianism could not be worse than war.

Leaving the European war in the condition that continued through 1918—inertia tempered by sporadic, fearful blooding— let us turn to the situation in the United States and trace the impact of the war on foreign policy, domestic developments, and civil liberty. As was noted earlier, the outbreak of hostilities was greeted with little fanfare in the United States. President Wilson offered his good offices to mediate the crisis, was ignored by the bellicose parties, and on August 18, 1914, made the most far-reaching statement of neutrality that could be undertaken: he called upon Americans to be "neutral in fact as well as in name, impartial in thought as well as in action." At roughly the same time, State Department Counsellor Robert Lansing was drafting the first of an almost infinite series of United States protests against the rigors of the British blockade, and Secretary of State Bryan, who had recently procured a surplus cavalry saber and had it melted down into miniature plowshares, was meditating on ways of keeping American money—the greatest of all contrabands, he felt, because it provided access to the others—neutral.[11]

With no forebodings of the xenophobic future, various national minorities in the United States chose sides: the Germans massed their pressure to support the Central Powers and became the linchpin in an informal anti-British–anti-Russian coalition which included both Irish and Jewish components. (It is hard to visualize this alignment, but in 1914 Germany was to the Jews the most enlightened nation in Europe, one where there had been neither pogroms nor Dreyfus Affairs but rather a seeming integration of the Jewish minority into national life.) [12] To the Irish nationalists, the war seemed like an ideal opportunity to break British power; every British defeat was viewed as one more nail in the coffin of British imperialism and already plans were underway (with German aid) for what became the Easter Rebellion of 1916. On the other side of the street, there was a strong pro-British lobby which had as its most vociferous organ *The New York Times,* and a number of ethnic groups which hoped for the destruction of the Austro-Hungarian Empire and the establishment of independent ethnic states (Czechs, Croatians, Hungarians, etc.). Nobody seemed to be pro-Russian; indeed, the presence of Russia in the Allied camp was a prime source of ideological ammunition for the pro-Germans and an embarrassment to Allied partisans. (Again, we must escape from the ominous historical shadow of Nazi Germany and point out that during World War I there was *at least* as much respect for civil liberty in Imperial Germany as there was in France, Russia, or the United States.)

If the United States had remained neutral "in fact as well as in name," these manifestations of cultural attachment to various European nations would have had little political significance. But despite Wilson's rhetoric and Bryan's prayers, American opinion began to solidify on the British side. There is no point in reexamining the reasons for this alignment in any detail, except to note that the combination of pro-British sympathies among the "old Americans" and German stupidity was almost unbeatable. I confess that it is impossible for me to draw any moral boundary between the Central Powers and the Allies: German conduct in Belgium was surely no less moral than the activities of the French in Tonkin or Madagascar, or of the British in Ireland or India. (It would be pointless to compare the Germans with the Russians in this regard; even militant spokesmen for the Allies avoided discussions of Russia.) To say this is in no sense to justify the outrages committed by the Germans in Belgium, or those perpetrated by the Foreign Legion in Indochina; it is simply to argue that there was no open-and-shut case against Germany in the First

War as there was in the Second. However, the Germans seemingly did their best to contribute to the Allied propaganda picture of the brutal, iniquitous "Hun"; their spokesmen had an unbelievable talent for sadistic rhetoric.

As the stories of the "Rape of Belgium" came flooding into American newspapers (and British propaganda specialists invented the "crucified Canadian" and impaled Belgian children on Uhlan lances), the German-American community mobilized to stem the tide. Beginning with a campaign in the winter of 1914–15 to embargo arms shipments (which, given the blockade, were all going to the Allies), the German-Americans brought their campaign to a climax with a great meeting in Washington on January 30, 1915.

The very success of the German-American Alliance in effectively mobilizing its pressure led to violent counterattacks; suddenly the government, and the press, realized the size of the *Verein* and the threat it posed should the United States take a strong line against Germany. *The New York Times* led the assault:

Never since the foundation of the Republic has any body of men assembled here who were more completely subservient to foreign influence and a foreign power and none ever proclaimed the un-American spirit more openly.[13]

The German government played into the hands of the Americanizers in a fashion which must have brought tears to the eyes of honest, sincere German-Americans: almost immediately after this conference, the Kaiser announced submarine warfare against Britain, and within a week official German attempts to sabotage American ships and munitions factories were revealed to the, by now, semihysterical press. As John Higham states in his splendid study of nativism, *Strangers in the Land*, "through popular thinking there spread an image of the German-American community riddled with treason and conspiring under orders from Berlin. As early as February [1915] wild rumors told of German-American intentions to invade Canada. By August there was common talk that German-Americans were rejoicing over the death of American citizens on torpedoed ships; and whispers told of a mysterious multiplication of German street bands spreading propaganda by playing 'The Watch on the Rhine.' " [14]

The insanity was beginning, that incredible spy mania and apparent willingness to believe any tale of espionage and sabotage however inherently improbable which reached epidemic proportions once the United States entered the war. And while it is easy to make glib social psychological generalizations about such phenomena—generalizations which are by their nature immune either to verification or refutation on an empirical basis—it seems safe to suggest that the absence of social homogeneity in the United States played a crucial role in these waves of hysterical insecurity. Or, to put the matter more precisely, the *realization* of fragmentation served first of all as a rationale for demanding Loyalty to the United States in political terms, and then as the foundation of measures designed to destroy ethnic pluralism and "Americanize" the population. Having lived through World War II with hardly a quiver, it is difficult for later generations to appreciate the mood of terror, the sense of mutual distrust, which infected American society during the First World War; there had been nothing to match it since the "Great Fear" which swept France in 1789. But if we are to understand the savage violations of basic civil rights which occurred when we set forth to "make the world safe for democracy," we have to realize that perfectly normal, decent people (like our parents and grandparents) simply lost their grip on common sense and literally went berserk in the face of imagined, and largely nonexistent, perils.

To state the matter differently, American society was built around a myth of unity, an assumption of a common faith in the democratic credo and a common loyalty to the symbols of political community. This ideal had survived a ferocious civil war, and despite the clamoring of racists and nativists, appeared to be surmounting the problems of mass immigration. As was suggested earlier, the process was essentially pragmatic: Believe in the melting pot and wait a generation. But this could only succeed in the absence of an interventionist foreign policy (except perhaps in areas of slight immigration such as the Far East), and now as 1915 became 1916 and the United States became more and more deeply involved with the fortunes of the Allies (Secretary Bryan, true to his star of antimilitarism, resigned in June, 1915, convinced that the United States had in its reaction to the sinking of the *Lusitania* deserted the course of neutrality), a great loyalty crisis was precipitated. Led by that leather-lunged jingo Theodore Roosevelt, an increasingly large segment of the American public began to demand an end to "hyphenated" Americanism: "America for Amercans" said the former President, denouncing as "moral treason" any division of allegiance. Roosevelt may by the fervor of his anti-German statements have cost the Republican candidate for President, Charles E. Hughes, the election of 1916. But whatever the private reactions of German-Americans in the security of the polling booth, he had a tremendous impact on public opinion generally.

Indeed, nothing like this had ever happened in the history of the United States. The Civil War had been occasioned by, and led to a temporary formalization of the existence of, two quite homogeneous communities; in the spring of 1861 the Southerners hived off and everybody knew just about where he stood. In other words, except for some ambivalence in the Border States, there was little *personal* insecurity: Robert E. Lee and even ex-President John Tyler took for granted loyalty to Virginia and albeit reluctantly "went out" with their state. The nation divided because, on the fundamental level of myth, and social structure built on myth, it was not a viable community; it could not, in Lincoln's phrase, exist "half-slave and half-free," and a terrible conflict was the instrument for determining which principles of community should dominate.

The problem in World War I was significantly different. The old bases of community founded on a rural, white, Protestant society of farmers and small businessmen had been sapped at their foundations by urban, industrial, Catholic, and immigrant explosions. An old society, to paraphrase Matthew Arnold, was dying, and a new society was powerless to be born. Community values were in flux and the old sense of security in jeopardy—and into this anomic, disturbed universe came the ultimate disruption: the fear of treason. At the time of the Hungarian Revolution against Soviet tyranny in 1956, a young freedom fighter was asked why, after years of oppression, he and his comrades had suddenly dared to raise the banner of revolt. Why had they not remained intimidated and cowed by the regime? He replied simply: "One day, for the first time, we trusted each other and we trusted our neighbors." [15] Forty years earlier, the people of the United States lived through the converse situation: one day they awoke and distrusted their neighbors. In the same way that the Hungarians—alas so briefly—discovered a sense of community and trusted, the Americans lost their identity and hated.

This led to eccentric behavior. The public who reelected Woodrow Wilson to the Presidency in 1916 on the slogan "He Kept Us Out of War," was equally capable of making the eagle scream, particularly in support of "Preparedness" for war. And the worst of it was that the public got no effective leadership from the President; indeed, Wilson seemed to incorporate in himself precisely the tensions and ambivalences that racked the society as a whole. Perhaps it was this quality which gave to Wilson's career the elements of Greek tragedy: he seemed eternally damned, both in Princeton and in Washington, to destroy by his hands the ideals of his intellect. Despite his knowledge, clearly set forth in *Congressional Government* and other works, that politics is controlled by decision-making, he relied on rhetoric to preserve neutrality and permitted subordinates such as Secretary of State Robert Lansing, Ambassador Walter Hines Page in London, and his confidential advisor Colonel E. M. House to act in a decidedly pro-Allied fashion. (House, the special envoy of the "neutral" President, casually related in his diary that the British ship—the ill-fated *Lusitania*—which took him to Europe on his mission for Wilson in January, 1915, ran up the American flag on entering dangerous waters off Ireland! She was carrying a load of munitions and was armed.) [16]

Wilson was a strange man. John Maynard Keynes, observing

the President at the Peace Conference, put his finger on the crucial flaw:

His thought and his temperament were essentially theological, not intellectual, with all the strength and weakness of that manner of thought, feeling, and expression. . . . It was commonly believed at the beginning of the Paris Conference that the President had thought out [a program for implementing the Fourteen Points]. But in fact the President had thought out nothing; when it came to practice, his ideas were nebulous and incomplete. He had no plan, no scheme, no constructive ideas whatever for clothing with the flesh of life the commandments which he had thundered from the White House. He could have preached a sermon on any of them or have addressed a stately prayer to the Almighty for their fulfillment, but he could not frame their concrete application to the actual state of Europe.[17]

On the one hand a man of stirring vision, Wilson could also display qualities which simply put Theodore Roosevelt into profane rages and led former President Taft to refer to him as "the greatest opportunist and hypocrite ever in the White House." His ex-Secretary of War, whom he sacrificed to the Congressional wolf pack, observed bitterly that the President was a man of high ideals but no principles.[18]

There is a large element of truth in these remarks, but they also reflect the naïvete of quite simple men in coming to grips with an intricate and convoluted personality. Wilson had that potent combination of operational ruthlessness with impersonal dedication to high aspirations which has for sixteen centuries been the hallmark of political Augustinianism in both Catholic and Protestant manifestations. An enemy once labeled John Calvin a "holy opportunist"; Wilson fell into the same category. Essentially he transmuted political imperatives into dogma; as Keynes noted, confronted with the necessity of compromise, Wilson would wrestle manfully with his conscience and, winning, would immediately convert the expedient solution into Holy Writ. This passion for autohypnosis had a mystifying impact on normal political men —who never confused the Sermon on the Mount with a political platform. Perhaps only an Erasmus could possibly comprehend the chilling loneliness of a man who in his hour of victory could honestly say "I am so constituted that . . . I never have a sense of triumph." [19] Certainly Wilson would have felt more at home in the sixteenth century.

While this is hardly the place for an extended biographical analysis of Woodrow Wilson, it is impossible to understand the events of 1917–20 without appreciating the strange amalgam that gave his character its distinctiveness. Georges Clemenceau in cynical dismay remarked that Wilson thought he was Jesus Christ; the tragedy of Wilson was that, however high his aspirations, he rather followed in the footsteps of the Grand Inquisitor. When in April of 1917 the United States entered the war, the President foresaw, without seeking to forestall, the greatest wave of suppression of fundamental liberties in the history of the United States.

On April 1, 1917—a week before the declaration of war—Wilson called in his friend Frank Cobb, editor of the *New York World* and, obviously distressed by the situation, launched into a remarkable prediction of future events:

"Once lead this people into war," he said, "and they'll forget there ever was such a thing as tolerance. To fight you must be brutal and ruthless, and the spirit of ruthless brutality will enter into the very fibre of our national life, infecting Congress, the courts, the policeman on the beat, the man in the street." . . .
He thought the Constitution would not survive it; that free speech and the right of assembly would go. He said a nation couldn't put its strength into a war and keep its head level; it had never been done.[20]

The scholarly President who had as a boy lived through Sherman's "March to the Sea," whose birthplace lay in that Virginia valley where Sheridan announced that his devastation would require crows to pack rations, who had grown up in the bitter wreckage of the Confederacy, was not one to underestimate the potential savagery of his constituents. Nor, to his eternal shame, was he prepared to follow Abraham Lincoln's majestic precedent by throwing the great moral force of the Presidency into the scales against chauvinism, fear, hate, and bestiality.

The pressure for Americanization and an end to "hyphenated Americanism" had been growing; with the United States in the war, it overflowed all restraints. Moreover, since sentiments of this sort are seldom accompanied by logic, the internal enemy was visualized as one compact category which included German-Americans, Socialists, Wobblies, pacifists (known commonly as "slackers"), and militant trade unionists. The one optimistic note that emerged from this undifferentiated process—and one has to look pretty hard—was the decline of racism: the Teutonic master-race theory suffered instantaneous attrition, though ingenious racists attempted to demonstrate that the Germans were bogus Teutons. But the main line of discrimination became political rather than ethnic: it was the presumptive political views not the ethnic origin of the German-American which led to suspicion.

Harold Hyman and others have chronicled the shambles of civil rights in detail. However, certain aspects of the situation should be limned, particularly for purposes of comparison with World War II. First of all, the *positive* oppressive role of the federal government was limited: only 877 people were actually convicted under the Espionage Act of 1917, though indictments were lodged against 1,956. The real crime of the federal authorities was one of omission. They stood aside and permitted, where they did not encourage, the domination of the United States by one vast vigilante organization. The Department of Justice, led by an Attorney General who stated publicly the view that opponents of war should ask mercy from God "for they need expect none from an outraged people and an avenging Government," officially sponsored the largest of the vigilante groups, the American Protective League.[21] Equipped with badges and calling themselves "Secret Service," 250,000 members of the APL were on the snoop by 1918. The quest for juvenile sedition was in the capable hands of the Boy Spies of America.

Wilson became disturbed by the mob-rule aspects of the APL and asked Attorney General Gregory if it should not be curbed, but the latter stood his ground, maintained his support, and the President dropped the matter. But Wilson's intuition was correct; the APL was nothing less than a government-sponsored lynch mob which proudly took the law into its own hands in summary and brutal fashion. Its specialty was not arrest and trial in courts duly appointed for that purpose; it specialized in direct prophylaxis: tar and feathers, beatings, and flag-kissing. (No one seemed to sense the irony of forcing suspects on their hands and knees to kiss the symbol of American freedom.) The official apology for the APL, Emerson Hough's *The Web*, claimed—with perhaps some exaggeration—that the league "brought to judgment three million cases of disloyalty." This has to be glossed, however, to read that the APL used direct action against three million people whom it defined, by whatever processes of deduction or divination, as "disloyal." [22]

With the APL, and a dozen or more similar organizations (the Sedition Slammers and the Terrible Threateners were, with the Anti-Yellow Dog League, the most picturesque) whooping up the search for disloyalty, with the conviction spreading that German spies and saboteurs were everywhere, with Theodore Roosevelt shrieking for the blood of "half-hidden traitors," and the circumspect Elihu Root announcing that there were men on the New York streets "who ought to be taken out at sunrise tomorrow and shot for treason," it was not surprising that the American people simply went mad. And it was not long before any who opposed the spy hunt on libertarian or common-sense grounds were themselves automatically consigned to the category of the disloyal. The constitutional right not to speak became the protection of the astute at a time when a federal judge could in deadly earnest define freedom of speech as protecting only "criticism which is made friendly to the government, friendly to the war, friendly to the policies of the government." [23] And even then suspects were on occasion forced to kiss the flag for showing insufficient enthusiasm, i.e., for keeping their mouths shut.

First to be engulfed by the great wave were the residual evidences of German culture. As towns changed their names, streets were rebaptized, and hamburgers became liberty sandwiches, many patriots celebrated July 4, 1917, by consigning German books to bonfires. German opera was banned, and not only was the speaking of German in public forbidden in many areas, but state legislators set to work to bar the teaching of that tongue in public or private schools. As usual Theodore Roosevelt was leading the charge; while the colonel waited impatiently for Wilson to permit him to organize a division of volunteers—a species of feudal levy —for duty in France, he took up the slack of disloyalty at home. (That Roosevelt could have imagined for one minute that the President would provide such a publicity vehicle for a political and personal opponent indicates the extent to which he misjudged Wilson.)

It would be pointless to continue a bill of particulars which could fill several volumes. The suppression of dissent affected every sector of American life: books, films, newspapers were censored and banned; teachers and ministers were disciplined or dismissed; lawful opposition to conscription was extirpated by methods both legal and illegal. (The difficulties of labor and radical groups were legion and have been reserved for separate treatment in the subsequent chapter.) Everywhere one went, he found the gospel of "Positive Americanism" preached as the highest truth and enforced by the indiscriminate and savage sanctions of the patriotic mob. Freedom of speech, press, petition, or assembly had no standing in competition with this truth; the "disloyal" had no rights. As the Governor of Minnesota noted with regard to meetings called to discuss the constitutionality of the draft (a matter not determined by the Supreme Court until the following year):

If anti-American meetings cannot be stopped by local officials, every resource at our command will be used to punish the offenders and prevent such meetings from being held. If, by means of this action on our part, bloodshed and loss of life will result, the responsibility therefor will rest on those who are back of and support, by their presence, these un-American demonstrators.[24]

And what of the Constitution, that "law for rulers and people, equally in war and in peace [which] covers with the shield of its protection all classes of men, at all times, and under all circumstances"? Justice David Davis, friend and campaign manager of Abraham Lincoln, had stated the ideal in these words in the very shadow of the Civil War. Elsewhere in the same decision—*Ex parte Milligan*—he had observed that "By the protection of the law human rights are secured; withdraw that protection, and they are at the mercy of wicked rulers, or the clamor of an excited people. . . . The power of punishment is alone through the means which the laws have provided for that purpose, and if they are ineffectual, there is an immunity from punishment, no matter how great an offender the individual may be, or how much his crimes may have shocked the sense of justice of the country, or endangered its security."

In the sense that Justice Davis formulated its imperatives, the Constitution went into hibernation during the war. It should be recalled that at that time, indeed, until 1925, the Supreme Court refused to exercise constitutional oversight in the area of state intrusions into freedom of speech or opinion. Thus there was no basis for appealing most state actions to the high tribunal; the state courts, generally composed of elected judges, had the last word on wartime infringements of individual rights and rarely stood firm against the sentiments of King Mob. (Oddly the Supreme Court did protect economic rights from state limitation: the Nebraska law forbidding the teaching of German in the grade schools, public or private, of the state was declared unconstitutional in 1923 on the ground that it deprived German teachers of their right to make a living!) [25]

Consequently the important civil liberty cases of the war period were all concerned with the power of the national government to limit freedom of opinion; the question was the scope of the protection guaranteed to the citizen by the First Amendment's seemingly absolute pronouncement that "Congress shall make no law . . . abridging the freedom of speech, or of the press; or the right of the people peaceably to assemble, and to petition the Government for a redress of grievances." When one examines the relevant sections of the Espionage Act of 1917 and the Sedition Act of 1918, it is immediately apparent that a constitutional question was incorporated in their prohibition of certain broad classes of speech. It was, for example, a felony—punishable by a fine of

$10,000 and/or 20 years' imprisonment—to discourage the sale of Liberty Bonds. Interestingly enough, stockbrokers, giving bona fide pessimistic advice to clients, were specifically exempted from the scope of this interdict.[26]

The best historical evidence indicates that the authors of the First Amendment did not intend to deprive the United States government of all jurisdiction over sedition or seditious libel, that in fact they took the existing common-law restraints on speech and press for granted. Indeed, when the Jeffersonians denounced the Sedition Act of 1798 as unconstitutional, it was on states' rights, not First Amendment, grounds. Thus the so-called "absolutist" interpretation of the First Amendment, endorsed vigorously in recent years by Justice Hugo Black, has no firm historical foundation.[27] But having said this, and admitted that the problem confronting federal judges in 1917–19 was one of determining *where* the line should be drawn between authority and individual liberty, the conclusion seems inescapable that, with a few grand exceptions such as Learned Hand, his cousin Augustus Hand, and C. F. Amidon, the federal district judges simply refused to try to draw any lines. They seemed unaware that there was any possible conflict between constitutional guarantees of freedom of opinion and the vigorous enforcement of the sedition statutes.

The Supreme Court, led in this direction by Justice Oliver Wendell Holmes, Jr., and Louis D. Brandeis, at least made the effort. Holmes was no civil libertarian—as he put it in a letter to a friend, he had no use for "jaw about free speech"—and had no respect on principle for minority rights: "What proximate test of [governmental] excellence can be found except correspondence to the actual equilibrium of force in the community—that is, conformity to the wishes of the dominant power?"[28] But if he expressed some contempt for those who tried to resist the verdict of history, his contempt for grown men who were acting like hysterical children was even greater. The old Union captain, thrice wounded in the Civil War was not prone to panic. When the great authority on evidence, J. H. Wigmore, who had served out the war in the security of Washington as an officer in the Judge Advocate General's Department, launched a bitter and puerile attack on the unpatriotic character of Holmes's dissent in the Abrams Case, the Justice laconically observed, "Colonel Wigmore may be a better lawyer than I am, but I think I know a little more about war than he does." [29]

Although by the standards of our time Louis Brandeis would undoubtedly be considered a "conservative" on civil rights problems, judged by the criteria of his time he was a militant liberal. Arriving on the Court in 1916 after a ferocious Senate and public battle over confirmation (some opposed his appointment because he was a "radical," some because he was a Jew, and probably most for both reasons), Brandeis soon developed a very close relationship with Holmes and was clearly the major factor in prodding the latter—who was both skeptical and inert—to take a stand on the wartime civil liberties issues. In short, Brandeis convinced Holmes to abandon his olympian detachment from the follies of the time and enter the fray; the result was the famous "clear and present danger rule." [30]

Promulgated by Holmes for a unanimous Court in the Schenck Case (1918), the "clear and present danger" formulation attempted to delimit speech which was protected by the First Amendment from that which the United States legally could suppress. In the classic analogy, Holmes pointed out that the First Amendment would not protect a man falsely shouting "Fire!" in a crowded theater—some words, he suggested, were direct incitements to action which created a "clear and present danger" of successfully accomplishing an illegal end. Schenck, the secretary of the Socialist Party, whose conviction the Court affirmed, had by his opposition to conscription created what reasonable men could believe to be a "clear and present danger" to the victorious prosecution of the war; his words were therefore outside of the area of discourse protected by the Constitution. Although no evidence had been adduced to indicate that Schenck had influenced the actions of a single American, and one might therefore suggest that he was, if anything, shouting "Fire!" in an empty theater, Holmes still deserves great credit for at least emphasizing that the powers of the government were not plenary, that the First Amendment did have meaning if only abstractly, that the citizen was not wholly stripped of his rights of speech, press, and opinion by wartime legislation.

Moreover, in the 1918 cases, the Supreme Court sustained all the convictions brought to it on appeal—in every case unanimously—but in 1919, with the war effectively, if not legally over, the solid bench split. Then, as will be seen shortly, Holmes and Brandeis found themselves in dissent, voicing vehement disagreement with the hysteria of the age.

To sum up then, the First World War led to an ignoble and disgraceful defacement of American ideals: a black mass celebrated by the elected leaders of the American people. In this chapter we have examined only one aspect of the period—the chauvinism; in the next we turn to the additional dimension, the suppression of economic and political radicalism in the name of national security. But as background for the whole epoch we must accept the tragic fact that the American Dream had become a nightmare.

III

THE RED HUNT

"Such is the unity of all history," wrote the great British historian Frederic W. Maitland, "that anyone who endeavors to tell a piece of it must feel that his first sentence tears a seamless web." [1] In examining the impact of the First World War on civil liberty, it has been necessary to tear the web more drastically than usual. The last chapter focused on nationalist hysteria and its roots. Here we will concentrate on the simultaneous, or at least overlapping frenzy against radicalism. Discussion of racial conflict, which largely grew out of the great migration of Southern Negroes to wartime work in the North, is reserved for analysis in the chapter on the revival of tribalism which follows.

But the fact that writing is inexorably unilinear should not be allowed to conceal the multidimensional character of reality. Events did not occur in compartments, nor did they arrive on the scene by categories. To employ an analogy, the United States in the war period was suffering from several acute diseases of the body politic—concurrently. From a simplistic viewpoint, the country was just "sick," but a political diagnostician can try to single out the particular ailments. In short, the Great War precipitated a massive political, social, and economic malaise, and our task here is to sort out and examine the various components of this agonizing seizure. It should always be kept in mind, however, that each series of events has to be fitted into the perspective of the whole atmosphere of repression. And that events in one category were often meshed with those in the others: Bolsheviks were denounced as German agents; scurrilous attacks were made on Jews as Russians, hence Bolsheviks; and the Prohibition movement thrived on the slogan that beer was a German device to undermine the efficiency of the American worker.[2]

It is hardly possible here to recapitulate the history of American radicalism except to point out that during the first decade of this century the Socialist movement was, by both earlier and later standards, well-organized and flourishing. Formed in 1901, the American Socialist Party was an amalgam of urban Marxists, radical trade unionists, municipal reformers, and agrarian underdogs. While it had in its ranks the usual complement of priestly sectarians who spent their time glossing Marxist texts and hammering out theoretical pronouncements, the great strength that the party accumulated in this era was hardly the outgrowth of its abstract profoundity. When in 1912 its candidate for President, Eugene Victor Debs, polled almost a million votes, and the National Secretary could report that 1,039 Socialists had been elected to various offices in the nation,[3] there were those both within the party and without who saw the United States on the verge of a Socialist revolution. But the opposite was in fact the case. The Socialist Party, far from being a nucleus of revolutionaries, had in many areas become accepted as a traditional political organization, one which represented the left wing of the reform movement but which stood firmly in the reformist tradition.

The German Socialists of Milwaukee, for example, brought clean, honest municipal government to their city. In Victor Berger they had a political boss (a *bonze* in the colloquial German of his constituents) who would at a later date have felt thoroughly at home in such a reform political machine as La Guardia's in New York City. To Lenin is attributed the sardonic observation that before German revolutionaries would seize a railroad line, they would buy tickets. Berger and his organization would have confirmed Lenin's bias: they were meticulously legalistic.[4] In hundreds of other cities throughout the country (the South excepted), the Socialist Party provided the launching pad for reform movements which found themselves blocked by the corrupt, undemocratic character of the traditional parties. The supporters of this "gas and water" Socialism were generally uninterested in the labored formulae of the national Socialist platform. They merely wanted to clean up Haverhill, Reading, Schenectady, or South Siwash.

Thus, while the Socialist Party at the outbreak of the war presented a dynamic exterior (it had thirteen daily newspapers and almost three hundred weeklies, with significant foreign language representation [5]), it was actually schizophrenic. The great mass of those who supported its candidates were not in any ideological sense "socialist," and yet the national destinies of the party were in the hands of dedicated ideological activists, men who unlike the leaders of the German Social Democratic Party or the British Labour Party were unwilling to trim their sails to the nationalistic will of the "masses." A number of analyses of American Socialism have been written in the attempt to explain the collapse of this once-thriving movement, but not one has sufficiently emphasized this basic consideration. The party was a war casualty because its leaders *refused* to betray the ideals of proletarian internationalism.[6] Under the impact of wartime chauvinism, the electoral rank and file simply vanished or went into hiding; the Bolshevik Revolution and subsequent splits in the party merely shattered the militant remnant.

Had the American Socialist leadership imitated their European comrades and become "social patriots," the party might well have survived, have adjusted itself to wartime exigencies, and retained its reform constituency. But from the moment the Emergency Conference in St. Louis, meeting the day after war was declared, adopted a firm antiwar position, Socialism became, in the public eye, a front for the Hun. The statement, presented by Morris Hillquit, the great Socialist leader from New York, still has a ring of grandeur about it:

The Socialist Party of the United States in the present grave crisis reaffirms its allegiance to the principle of internationalism and working class solidarity the world over, and proclaims its unalterable opposition to the war just declared by the government of the United States. . . . We brand the declaration of war by our government as a crime against the people of the United States and against the nations of the world.[7]

This position was endorsed by 80 percent of the delegates and, in a referendum, by an overwhelming vote of the membership.[8] But this is deceptive in terms of real support. Party membership reached a high point of about 125,000 in 1912 and had by this time probably dropped to the neighborhood of 75,000.[9] The members may have stood firm, but the nonmembers who had been voting Socialist and providing the party with its broad constituency, which could possibly have developed into a permanent electoral base, took to the hills. Under withering attack from all sides (traditional politicians disturbed by Socialist growth took maximum advantage of the situation), suffering constant desertions (most of the Socialist leaders in the AFL, for example, repudiated the party [10]), these courageous internationalists marched into their private Armageddon. From this point forward, the Socialist Party was to be an instrument of radical protest, not a political movement.

The American Federation of Labor, with Samuel Gompers in the vanguard, went vigorously to war, but there was a segment of the labor movement which took a vociferous and revolutionary antiwar position: the Industrial Workers of the World. The IWW has by now become so clothed in myth that it is difficult to reach a realistic appraisal of either its strength or its objectives. Ostensibly standing for "One Big Union" and the militant class struggle, the "Wobblies" were also curiously akin to European syndicalist movements which subsequently merited the designation of "fascist." There was the same romanticization of violence, the same antirationalism which expressed itself in contempt and hatred of politics. In short, there was a total rejection of "bourgeois values" which often in practice amounted to an endorsement of revolutionary gangsterism. When Big Bill Haywood sent Harry Orchard out to murder the Governor of Idaho or to dynamite a mine shaft full of "scabs," he was less concerned with building a new world than destroying the old.[11] Thus to rob a grocery store was hardly a sin; it was merely expropriating the goods of a "class enemy." There was a classic Wobbly handbill which conveys the essence. "Don't drive copper tacks in fruit trees—it kills them!" it informed agricultural workers. It was distributed with a bag of copper tacks! [12]

In terms of members, the IWW was never large. The United States government alleged in 1917 that there were 200,000 in the organization, but this was part of the case for suppression and was fantastically exaggerated.[13] In the same year, the IWW leader Vincent St. John claimed 60,000 dues-paying unionists. If we add to this a substantial body of non-dues-paying sympathizers, a figure in the neighborhood of 100,000 seems reasonable.[14] It is difficult to get meaningful statistics in part because the IWW took an existential approach toward administration. Keeping records and the like was a bourgeois fixation which they left to the "stool pigeons" of the "American Fakiration of Labor." No true revolutionary would ever waste his subversive potentialities on bookkeeping. Moreover, there was tremendous turnover both of members and locals. In a typical case, an IWW organizer would pop up in a lumber camp where grievances were rife, sign up the loggers, stage a strike. When, as was usually the case, the lumber operators invoked lynch law to break the strike, the organizer was lucky to escape with his life and the freshly baptized local simply vanished. The workers, for their own protection, hid or destroyed their Red Cards—but often remained strong fellow travelers of the IWW and waited for their next chance. Whole locals disappeared in this and other more colorful fashions. One group in San Diego disbanded in 1911 and gave as their rationale "Mexican Revolution"! [15]

The resemblance of the IWW to later syndicalist-fascist movements was also noticeable in its appeal to what Marx and Engels called the "lumpenproletariat," the dregs of society. Unlike the Socialists, who were as followers of Marx pretty much committed to being the heirs of capitalism, the Wobblies were consumed by a ferocious nihilism; they were capitalism's assassins. Like Mussolini's *squadristi* and the early cadres of the National Socialist Party, they built their constituency on the revenge of the alienated, those who could find no hope of a future in bourgeois society.[16] (Any who would deny this charge on the basis of the IWW *Program* should spend a few minutes reading the platforms of the Italian Fascists or the Nazis *before* the latter seized power.) [17] The Socialists, even the so-called revolutionaries of the left wing, were always sustained by a vision of the future; they envisaged bourgeois society as an intermediate station on a historically routed journey. In short, their commitment was to a future *in* history, while the IWW saw history as a plot against the disinherited and defied both past and future in the name of their appalling image of the present.

And from their position at the bottom of the heap, there was a good deal of rough justice in the IWW evaluation. It is all very well to suggest that the Wobblies were not sterling characters, and it is equally important to note that history can grant no absolution —no amount of Allied stupidity at Versailles could *justify* the barbarism of Nazi Germany. But at the same time, the dispassionate observer is torn with shame when he reads the bloody chronicle of the suppression of the IWW. The power and the constituency of the IWW were created by conditions of blind, savage exploitation of the helpless, by that perversion of American ideals which passed as the free enterprise system in the first decades of this century. To repeat, this situation of near-peonage could not provide moral validation for the excesses of the IWW, but it does help to explain the basis of Wobbly power. While in any historical period one can find brave men who in the name of one nihilistic credo or another engage in daemonic resistance to the status quo (the European Secret Army in Algeria is a recent example of this phenomenon), the question which must be asked is not *why* are these men so committed (a problem for psychiatrists) but *what* rottenness in society threw leaders of this sort to the top?

In the case of the IWW, the answer is not hard to find. The organization was nourished by a ruthless system of economic and political exploitation which had made impossible the development of any decent code of human relations. Let us take one instance of the IWW in action, a case discussed in the following terms by an official publication of the United States Department of Labor: the "Wheatland Riot" of 1913.

Following a practice not unusual among large-scale growers, E. B. Durst, hop rancher, had advertised in newspapers throughout California and Nevada for some 2,700 workers. He subsequently admitted that he could provide employment for only about 1,500, and that living arrangements were inadequate even for that number. Workers of many racial stocks from many areas poured into the community . . . A great number had no bedding and slept on piles of straw thrown on floors . . . many slept in fields. There were no facilities for sanitation or garbage disposal and only 9 outdoor toilets for 2,800 people; dysentery became prevalent . . . The water wells were insufficient for the camp . . . workers were forced to buy what supplies they could afford from a concession store on the ranch.[18]

Above and beyond these physical conditions, the pay was appalling and was kept that way by Durst's homemade version of the "reserve army of the unemployed," the surplus labor he had recruited. The workers simply would not take this, and a spontaneous demonstration occurred. At this point, the IWW—in the persons of Blackie Ford and Herman Suhr—moved in to organize a "camp local," and Durst struck back. The strikers, after a fruitless attempt to negotiate with Durst, called a second meeting.

The meeting, which the county sheriff later testified was entirely peaceable, was invaded by a band of armed deputies who came to arrest Ford. One of the deputies on the fringe of the crowd fired a shot to "quiet the mob." This precipitated a riot, in the course of which the district attorney, a deputy sheriff, and two workers were killed and many more were injured.

Hysteria apparently gripped the authorities after the outbreak. Mass arrests of "wobblies" or sympathizers were carried out. Many of the arrested men were severely beaten or tortured, and many others were held incommunicado for weeks. Ford and Suhr, the two leading I.W.W. organizers in the camp, were convicted of murder and sentenced to life imprisonment.[19]

Throughout the country, IWW organizers inevitably turned up in the areas of worst labor-management relations; if the AFL had been beaten, or had been unwilling or unable to provide organization, desperate union militants would turn to the Wobblies for one last chance. Sometimes it worked—as in the Spokane area lumber mills or the famous Lawrence, Mass., textile strike of 1912—but more often IWW intervention simply provided an excuse for decisive brutality by police and Pinkertons.[20]

Before we turn to the details of wartime suppression of Socialism, the IWW, and related radical movements, tribute should be paid to the IWW for a great contribution to the civil liberties tradition, the "free speech fight." By now it should be clear that I am not sympathetic toward either the character or the methods of the IWW—too many social historians seem to have assumed that because the Wobblies were rough they were diamonds—but, however motivated, their struggles for freedom of speech merit the respect of those who have profited from their feckless courage. Characteristically, the free speech fight had that spontaneous, *ad hoc* quality which was the bench mark of the IWW. Like the anarchists of Barcelona, who allegedly awake in the morning with supernal knowledge that *this* is the day to strike, there was minimal organization. An IWW delegate in, say, San Diego would be arrested for making a street-corner speech, then the word would drift up the Southern Pacific line, and at every stop local Wobblies with time on their hands would start for San Diego. Vincent St. John noted that the national headquarters had little to do with what followed. It merely notified the locals of the free speech fight and suggested that "if they have any members that are footloose to send them along." [21]

Soon every freight car coming into San Diego would deposit a few free riders with Red Cards, and the latter would head for the street corners to make their IWW pitch and join their "Fellow Worker" in the calaboose. Shortly, groups of Wobblies would short-cut this procedure by simply going to the jail and demanding admission! In this fashion, hundreds of militants would clog the machinery of justice, turn the jail into a shambles, sing rebel songs—"Dump the Bosses off Your Back," "Solidarity Forever," "Paint 'Er Red," "Hallelujah! I'm a Bum!"—day and night, and live off the bourgeois taxpayers until their demands were met. They were beaten, shipped out of town, soaked with hoses, starved in their cells, but to no avail. The nastier the treatment, the more Wobblies "joined the party," coming to San Diego or Spokane from as far away as Chicago. Sometimes the local authorities held out a week, sometimes as long as six months. Their sentiments were tersely put by the San Diego *Tribune:* "Hanging is none too good for [the Wobblies], they would be much better dead, for they are absolutely useless in the human economy; they are the waste material of creation and should be drained off into the sewer of oblivion, there to rot in cold obstruction like any other excrement." [22] But generally the IWW came out ahead, and the twenty or more free speech battles that they mounted between 1909 and 1913 were a noble contribution to the libertarian tradition. Whatever may have been the content of their philosophy, in these encounters they were struggling for a key proposition of the American Dream: the right of unpopular people to express dissenting views.[23]

As can easily be imagined, both the Socialists and the IWW had built up a residue of bitterness against them in the years before 1917. When the United States entered the war, the time had come for settling some long-standing scores, and the opportunity was seized to maximum advantage. The Socialist Party opposed American intervention in measured but hardly "disloyal" terms; the IWW excoriated the war and all things connected with it in its usual slam-bang fashion. (The Socialists, for example, challenged the constitutionality of the draft; the IWW urged all and sundry to refuse military service.) This left them easy targets for the chauvinistic counterattack: they were betraying the United States in its hour of crisis, agents of the Hun. As the *Sacramento Bee* put it, "There must be no leniency to the damnable IWW. They are traitors to the Government. There is evidence that they are in the pay of Germany. . . . The safety of the nation itself demands their extermination." [24] Senator Henry Ashurst announced that IWW stood for "Imperial Wilhelm's Warriors."

The key word here, the word which provides the *leitmotiv* of the great Red Hunt, is *extermination*. The events which occurred between April of 1917 and the time when savage wartime fears

THE RED HUNT 59

expired in the banalities of the Harding Administration can only be understood as a campaign of extermination. No holds were barred, no logic was too absurd, no constitutional or moral values were permitted to intrude when the United States and the state governments set out to extirpate "treason" and "sedition" and joyously loosed an angered populace upon its "radical" neighbors.

The period can be divided, for the sake of convenience, into two stages: wartime suppression, and the postwar follow-up led by Attorney General A. Mitchell Palmer. The major difference between the two is not one of technique, but rather the additional lurid dimension provided to the postwar repression by the Bolshevik Revolution and the emergence of international Communism. Thorough treatment of either is obviously impossible here; what is significant in the scope of this work is the collapse of American ideals which accompanied the extermination of radicalism—and the dogged, feeble, but indomitably courageous efforts of individuals and organizations like the National Civil Liberties Bureau to stem the tide of legal lawlessness.

In the last chapter we examined the atmosphere of government-sponsored mob violence, with particular reference to those Americans who were allegedly disloyal for ethnic reasons, and need hardly reemphasize this vigilantism in the radical context. Keeping in mind this background of surging crowds of superpatriots endlessly in search of pro-Germans, "slackers," or even the merely unenthusiastic, let us turn to the legal proceedings which were instituted during the war against the Socialist Party, its newspapers and leaders, and against the IWW. Of the three top leaders of the Socialist Party—Eugene Victor Debs, Victor Berger, and Morris Hillquit—only Hillquit emerged unscathed, possibly because for a good part of the time he was in a sanitarium for the tuberculosis which sapped his life, possibly because he had run for Mayor of New York in 1917, receiving one-third of the vote, and his arrest would therefore have looked too much like sheer political reprisal.

Debs, a complex man of deep internal torments, had taken an ambiguous position, at least publicly, on the war. He refused to attend the party convention in St. Louis which endorsed the anti-war position, but gradually, as the second echelon of the Socialist leadership fell before the sedition laws, Debs became less circumspect in public statement, particularly in regard to the gross violations of civil rights involved in the prosecutions.[25] In the summer of 1918, Debs apparently crossed his psychological Rubicon and, at age 62, set out to join his comrades behind federal bars. There is evidence that the Washington authorities did not relish a courtroom encounter with this great tribune,[26] but the matter was taken out of their hands in June, 1918, when a local United States Attorney in Cleveland, Ohio, presumably building his own reputation as a sedition hunter, brought an indictment against Debs for obstructing the recruitment of military personnel, inciting insubordination and disloyalty in the armed forces, and of uttering words which would encourage resistance to the authority of the United States.[27]

It would be pointless to recapitulate the substance of Debs's speech to the Ohio Socialists, which was the basis of the indictment, or of his speech to the hand-picked jury (made up of citizens whose average age was 70 and average income at least $50,-000) [28] which convicted him of sedition. Suffice it to say that Debs took his stand on the First Amendment—"I look upon the Espionage Law as a despotic enactment in flagrant conflict with democratic principles and with the spirit of free institutions," he told the court before being sentenced to ten years in Atlanta [29]—and that no evidence of any sort was introduced by the United States to verify the specific charges of the indictment. The essence of the government's case was that *if* a soldier had heard Debs, it was reasonable to believe he *might* have been influenced toward insubordination. A year later, the Supreme Court unanimously sustained the conviction; Justice Holmes (who was privately not impressed with the menace of Socialism) suggested in the Opinion that the evidence against Debs was sufficiently strong to convince reasonable men that he did in fact intend to obstruct recruiting.[30] The old fighter went off to jail, and Woodrow Wilson sternly rejected pleas for executive clemency. As late as January, 1921, the President rejected a recommendation from A. Mitchell Palmer (of all people) that the sentence be commuted. "This man was a traitor to his country," Wilson told his private secretary, "and he will never be pardoned during my administration." [31]

Victor Berger's adventures were somewhat more colorful. The Milwaukee Socialist boss was one of the least lovable figures in the movement—an authoritarian, he had also built up a reputation as an anti-Semite by his unrestrained attacks on the New York Jewish wing of the party, and was an unabashed white supremacist (he once warned, in supporting Chinese exclusion, that "this country is absolutely sure to become a black-and-yellow country within a few generations" unless strong action was taken [32]). There is also good reason to believe that Berger, like his constituents, was strongly pro-German in his antiwar sympathies, and his personal organ, the *Milwaukee Leader*, was barred from the mails in September, 1917, for its outspoken opposition to war measures. In February, 1918, Berger was successively nominated by the United States Attorney for incarceration in federal prison for sedition and by the Wisconsin Socialists for the United States Senate. Even though under indictment, he polled over 100,000 votes in the special April election, and as a consolation prize was elected in November to the United States House of Representatives. With one dissenting vote, the House refused to seat him and called for a special election to fill the vacancy. Berger won this election too, and was again refused his seat. He was finally defeated at the polls in November, 1920, though in 1922 he won the place again and this time was at last seated. [33]

Meanwhile, back at the federal courthouse, after a trial which even by the standards of that time was judged extraordinary, Judge Kenesaw M. Landis sentenced Berger and four associates to twenty years' imprisonment. Landis we will meet again when he presides over the trial of the IWW. A judicial mountebank, he specialized in sensationalism (he once fined Standard Oil $10,-000,000 in an antitrust case) and made a career out of combining the functions of judge and prosecutor. In disposing of Berger and other "Reds," he was in his element and never permitted the total lack of concrete evidence of criminal conspiracy against the Socialists to slow down the trial. Unfortunately, in this case (as in the Standard Oil decision mentioned above), his addiction for "people's justice" took Landis too far out of the bounds of procedural regularity. In 1921 the Supreme Court held that Landis by his bitter attacks on German-Americans before the trial began had revealed "prejudice" and should have granted the Socialist request for a change of venue to another court.[34] By this time the judge had moved to a more appropriate setting for his talents—as "Czar of Baseball."

These were the trials granted to the *leaders* of the Socialist Party. The rank and file leadership received a brand of justice even more summary. "Our judges," wrote Zechariah Chafee, Jr., "condemned at least eleven persons to prison [under the Espionage Acts] for ten years, six for fifteen years, and twenty-four for twenty years," and he noted that this figure covered only reported cases (in an unreported decision in Sacramento, twenty-six were sentenced to ten years' imprisonment) and excludes the mass trial of the IWW leadership in Chicago.[35]

Moreover, this discussion of trials does not take into consideration the tremendous administrative harassment that radicals were subjected to in their efforts, for example, to keep their newspapers going. No one has ever done a careful study of the impact of censorship and the denial of mailing privileges on the radical press, but the attrition was fierce, and the death rate of publications, particularly among the foreign language weeklies, was very high. The New York *Call*, the Socialist Party's leading daily paper, lost its mailing privileges in November, 1917. It managed to stagger on with a makeshift distribution system until the privilege was restored in June, 1921,[36] but few of the other journals under attack had either the resources, the dedication, or the geographically compact readership of the *Call*. The denial of mailing privileges by the Postmaster General, a decision made without trial of the charges or even a hearing by an official vested with great discretionary authority, was a deathblow to most radical papers. Postmaster General Burleson, for example, denied privileges to the

Call because it was inciting the people to "arson, murder or assassination"—even though its editors were never indicted for this offense, or any other—and the Supreme Court sustained his decision as a legitimate and unreviewable exercise of discretion.[37]

If the authorities were unrestrained in their campaign against the Socialists, they went literally berserk in the wartime assault on the IWW. In the fall of 1917, United States officers raided the various headquarters of the IWW, and 166 alleged leaders of the organization were indicted for conspiring to obstruct the war effort. Subsequently 113 were brought to trial before Judge Landis in Chicago, and later two other mass trials were launched in Sacramento and Kansas City. Although the fiction was maintained that only individuals were on trial, Landis soon made it clear that it was the IWW in its collective capacity that was in the dock. Huge masses of irrelevant material, some of it going back a decade, were introduced into evidence even though no connection existed between this data and any individual on trial, and it bore no relation to the war effort.[38] The real offense that called for legal retribution was membership in the IWW, and the outcome was a foregone conclusion. After 55 minutes of deliberation, the jury returned with verdicts of guilty in ninety-six cases and Landis took over sentencing. The top leaders uniformly got twenty years, thirty-three received ten-year terms, and another thirty-three were sent down for five; the remainder got one year or less. In addition, the judge fined the guilty an aggregate figure of $2,300,000! For some time to come it appeared that the main locus of IWW activity woud be Leavenworth Prison.[39]

While these trials were under way, action of an even more direct sort was common throughout the country. Any suspected of IWW sympathies were dealt with under local, often lynch law. It became, for example, very risky to organize or participate in IWW defense activities, to try to raise funds to aid the defendants. While courageous civil libertarians such as John Dewey, Carlton Hayes, Thorstein Veblen, and the leaders of the embryonic American Civil Liberties Union called for fair play, the Department of Justice (according to the ACLU) "arrested the active members of

I.W.W. defense committees at many points in the country, stopped their meetings, and seized their funds." The national defense committee in Chicago discovered that its appeals for aid were piling up in the post office, undistributed.[40] Everywhere fund-raisers were given a standard treatment by the American Protective League: they were beaten up and/or arrested for sedition. A recommendation was made in the United States Senate that disloyal organizations be forbidden to solicit funds through the mails.[41]

Even this was child's-play by comparison with the handling of IWW locals, and alleged members, in the Western states. Now, cloaked in high patriotic garb, the enemies of the IWW moved in for the kill; the consequence was a state of vigilante martial law. Listen to the advice of the Tulsa *World*, November 9, 1917:

If the I.W.W. . . . gets busy in your neighborhood, kindly take the occasion to decrease the supply of hemp. A knowledge of how to tie a knot that will stick might come in handy in a few days. It is no time to dally with the enemies of the country. . . . The first step in the whipping of Germany is to strangle the I.W.W.'s. Kill 'em just as you would any other kind of a snake. Don't scotch 'em; kill 'em! And kill 'em dead! It is no time to waste money on trials . . .[42]

The *Sacramento Bee* plugged the firing squad as the cure for IWW "poison," [43] and *The New York Times*, while deploring the hanging of IWW organizer Frank Little in Butte, Montana, noted in partial exculpation that "I.W.W. agitators are in effect, and perhaps in fact, agents of Germany." [44]

It would be fruitless to devote more space to the "extermination" of the IWW—a chronicle of brutality becomes dulling after a while as one, in psychological self-defense, takes refuge in disembodiment and refuses to empathize with the victim of the lash. However, there is one episode which can be used to close this saga, one which starkly delineates the degree to which wartime hysteria against the IWW was employed to destroy a legitimate labor organization: the Bisbee Deportation.

Bisbee, Globe, and Miami were small, isolated communities in the Arizona desert wholly dominated by copper mining. Labor troubles had been endemic in the area, the IWW had been active, and in the summer of 1917 things came to a head when the dominant union, affiliated with the American Federation of Labor, called a strike. The situation was complex. The IWW immediately jumped into the strike and attempted to take the leadership away from the AFL, the latter retaliated by denouncing the IWW organizers as stool pigeons and extremist provocateurs in the pay of the bosses, the federal government attempted to mediate, and antilabor groups began to denounce the whole enterprise as IWW-sponsored treason against the United States. Although there had been no violence, the Globe Loyalty League—"a militant body organized to fight the I.W.W. without compromise or quarter"—on July 6 issued a fire-eating manifesto:

. . . terrorism in this community must and shall cease; that all public assemblies of the I.W.W., as well as other meetings shall be suppressed; that we hold the I.W.W. to be a public enemy of the United States; that we absolutely oppose any mediation. . . .[45]

At this point, one of the mine operators, Walter Douglas of Bisbee, threw a match into the powder magazine: "You cannot compromise with a rattlesnake . . . that goes for the International Union [AFL] and the I.W.W. . . . I believe the government will be able to show that there is German influence behind this movement. . . . It is up to the individual communities to drive these agitators out." [46] (An Arizona judge had already suggested a more direct course: "I would like to go up there [to the picket line] and mow those sons of bitches down with a machine gun.") [47] On July 12, Sheriff Harry Wheeler of Cochise County and the Bisbee Loyalty League picked up the cue from Douglas: at dawn about 1,200 men organized into posses, rounded up *all* local labor militants, 1,186 in all, loaded them into boxcars and shipped them off to Columbus, New Mexico. Authorities in Columbus refused to accept the shipment, so it was taken back and dumped at a remote, virtually abandoned army post in the desert, and, in the words of President Wilson's Mediation Commission, the deportees were "left to shift for themselves" in a situation where they "were wholly without adequate supply of food and water." [48] After two days, the United States Army went to their rescue, and the refugees were established in a camp near Columbus. The *Bisbee Daily Review* chortled over the purge: "no longer does a blot remain on the escutcheon of Bisbee. 'Wobblyism' has passed into the labyrinth of things discarded." [49]

Although, as the President's Mediation Commission pointed out in its careful and detailed report, the action had been taken by the sheriff after consultation with the leading local mine operators, it had involved illegal censorship of outgoing telegrams and telephone messages, and its instigators had grossly violated the constitutional rights of the deportees, those responsible justified their act by invoking the doctrine of anticipatory retaliation ("we had to defend ourselves from certain attack") and escaped punishment.[50] Needless to add, the deportation, in which there had been no attempt to discriminate between IWW and AFL militants, destroyed the trade-union movement in Bisbee: the Loyalty League set up its own union, the Workingmen's Protective League, and refused to permit bona fide trade unionists even to enter the town.[51]

The events which we have been describing all occurred while the United States was actively participating in the First World War. This is no justification, but it does provide some insight into motives when one realizes that decent people in wartime often become consumed with patriotic fervor and lose their perspective. Sheriff Wheeler of Cochise County, for example, had been known as a fair, prolabor man before the war; among the miners it was said that "if you were opposed to Wheeler you got a beating before you got home" [52] (a remark which in itself provides a sharp *aperçu* into frontier democracy). With the Armistice in November, 1918, and the subsequent surrender of the Central Powers, one might assume that the frenzy would have abated, that a return to sanity would have left the American people, like the victim of a hangover, with a feeling of sheepish guilt. Yet, for reasons which have never been adequately probed,[53] the opposite was the case. The antiradical sentiments of the wartime years became, if anything, more intense after the Armistice and reached a somber climax of indignity in the Palmer Raids of 1919 and 1920.

The background of the Great Red Scare was provided by a number of objective historical factors—the Bolshevik Revolution and formation of the Comintern; a wave of vicious bombings or attempts at assassination of public officials attributed to the "Reds"; a tremendous surge of strikes as labor abandoned the restraints of wartime and attempted to have wages catch up with prices; demobilization and accompanying uncertainty (and, as John Dos Passos superbly limned in *1919*, which should be required reading for historians of the period, *boredom* with Victorian America); the constitutional absurdity of the Eighteenth Amendment, the Maginot Line of moribund Puritanism; a depression in which everything dropped but prices (in 1919, 2.3 percent of the work force was unemployed; by 1921, this had leaped to 11.9 percent); a reunited Republican Party savagely mauling President Wilson (who collapsed under the strain) and employing the motif of disillusionment with the war to castigate the whole reform tradition. These are the main threads the historian can trace, but there was a deeper social basis for the madness of the immediate postwar years: a generalized but largely unarticulated recognition that the country and the world had been transformed, and an equally widespread inability to comprehend the premises of the new, emerging social order. It was, in the phrase of the time, "a cockeyed world," but only the Dadaists and a few other artists of extraordinary cultural sensitivity faced up to the fact and tried to adjust their standards to the reality.

Most Americans simply got frightened and looked for the villains, the daemonic agents of insecurity who had destroyed the nice, comfortable world of 1914. Some rushed to eliminate strong drink, others saw jazz, or modernistic theology, or Darwinian biology, or the League of Nations as the enemy. But the simplest answer, one which fitted neatly into a long tradition of nativism, was to blame foreign influence, and specifically the impending conquest of America by foreign radicals. This attack, of course, meshed beautifully with the antiradical campaign of the war years, but was potentially far more inclusive. American Jews, for example, who had distinguished themselves in supporting the war effort, could be netted by the equation of Jews and Bolshevism; the American Federation of Labor could be lambasted along with the IWW as a radical, foreign conspiracy against the freedom of the American workingman. (The preamble to the AFL Constitution announced that "a struggle is going on in the nations of the civilized world between the oppressors and the oppressed of all countries, a struggle between capital and labor, which must grow in intensity from year to year and work disastrous results to the toiling millions of all nations. . . ." and Gompers was a British-born Jew.)

Unquestionably some who employed this slippery logic did so quite cynically—it provided them with a splendid demagogic basis for destroying their opposition and, say, instituting the "American Plan" (the "open shop") in their factories. However, the evidence suggests that an overwhelming percentage of those who seized upon this amalgam theory were quite sincere, even desperately sincere, people striking out blindly at the seeming protagonists of a novel and terrifying *Zeitgeist*. Essentially the fundamental ideals of the Democratic Dream were repudiated in the name of preserving the American status quo ante 1914. One set of institutions and folkways were fossilized as the "American Way," and spokesmen for change (as well as innocent symbols of change such as the Southern Negroes, who, migrating North during the war years, were greeted with fierce hostility by their new neighbors—but this will be discussed in the next chapter) were castigated as traitors. This is a not uncommon historical phenomenon—Oswald Garrison Villard once observed at a Republican Lincoln Day dinner that an American conservative was one who worshipped a dead radical, and each generation attempts to impose its standards on its children, even its pattern of revolt. What made the 1918–21 period distinctive was that this conflict

between generations was both uniquely multidimensional and conducted in the atmosphere of lynch law which had encased wartime
patriotism.

Three episodes must suffice to buttress the proposition that the
American Dream had degenerated into a wild, flailing effort to
restore the *ancien régime:* the Abrams Case, the refusal to seat
the Socialists in the New York legislature, and the Palmer Raids.
The first illustrates the theory of amalgam in judicial operation;
the second, the repudiation of the key technique of the democratic
political process, the will of the electorate; and, the third, the employment by the national government of authentic police state
procedures against alleged subversives. In addition, it should be
recalled that the actions of national, state, and local authorities
against Socialists and Wobblies, described above, did not stop at
the Armistice: the Kansas City trial of IWW activists did not get
under way until December 1, 1919.

In August, 1918, Jacob Abrams and six anarchist-Socialist associates were arrested for sedition. The indictment charged that
by distributing some leaflets on the lower East Side of New York,
they had threatened to impede the war effort. The throwaways,
written in English and Yiddish, were a bitter denunciation of
President Wilson's decision to intervene against the Bolsheviks in
the Murmansk area and called for a general strike to prevent shipment of munitions to the anti-Soviet forces. The leaflet in English
contained a postscript: "P.S. It is absurd to call us pro-German.
We hate and despise German militarism more than do your
hypocritical tyrants. We have more reasons for denouncing German militarism than has the coward in the White House." [54]

It could, perhaps, have been put more courteously, but one
may doubt whether the best political manners would have made
much difference. The Abrams circle was brought to trial in October—before a federal judge borrowed from Alabama who patently
looked on the defendants as exhibits in a museum of un-American
horrors—and despite their assertion that nothing they had said
could be construed as favoring a disruption of the war *with Ger-*

many, three were sentenced to twenty years' imprisonment, one
to fifteen, and one to three. In delivering sentence, Judge Clayton
performed the mystic act of amalgamation:

> . . . we are not going to help carry out the plans mapped out by the Imperial
> German Government, and which are being carried out by Lenine [*sic*] and
> Trotsky. I have heard of the reported fate of the poor little daughters of the
> Czar, but I won't talk about that now. I might get mad.[55]

One may speculate on what sentences Clayton would have given
if he had gotten "mad"; twenty years was the maximum. As
Chafee pointed out in his masterful analysis of this episode, "If
they had actually conspired to tie up every munition plant in the
country, and succeeded, the punishment could not have been
more." [56]

We may leave the Abrams litigation here. The Supreme Court,
only Holmes and Brandeis dissenting, confirmed the conviction
in 1919; [57] in 1921, the sentences were commuted on condition
that the radicals go to Russia.[58] Note the proposition that has
emerged: a radical in New York who supported the Bolsheviks
was not only un-American, but pro-German. Only one ingredient
was missing on the overt level, though it was implicit in the
Abrams case: the pro-Bolshevik radical was also a Jew. The possibilities of this racist slogan were not lost on the nativists—who
pushed vigorously the thesis of pro-German Jewish Bolshevism.
Nor was it taken lightly by American Jewish defense organizations. In the spring of 1920, the Anti-Defamation League sent to
the editors of five hundred leading newspapers a series of articles
by Isaac Don Levine, former Chicago *Daily News* correspondent
in Russia, highlighting the opposition of Russian Jews to Bolshevism. The letter of transmittal noted that Levine's writings
contained "a conclusive answer to the many libelous stories recently appearing in the press of this country which . . . charge
Jews with responsibility for Bolshevism in Russia and for social
and economic unrest in other countries . . ." [59]

It is interesting to note the key role of New York, both
state and city, in the events of the Great Red Scare. The enormous

polyglot metropolis, full of aliens, Jews, Catholics, atheists, "wets," Bohemians, Bolsheviks, anarchists, DeLeonists, and God knows what else, symbolized in itself the antithesis of the *ancien régime*. It was in New York that a frightful bomb exploded on Wall Street, killing thirty-eight and injuring hundreds; it was in the New York Post Office that sixteen dynamite bombs, each disguised as "Sample—Novelty" from Gimbels, were discovered bearing the addresses of, *inter alios*, Justice Holmes, Judge Landis, Attorney General Palmer, Postmaster General Burleson, and J. P. Morgan; it was New York's distinction to serve as the locale for the most massive of the Palmer Raids and for the first of the three-ring circuses that resulted when state legislatures established committees to investigate "Revolutionary Radicalism" —the Lusk Committee of 1919–20.

New York State achieved additional notoriety in 1920 when the State Assembly expelled five Socialist members on the ground that they had "been elected on a platform that is absolutely inimical to the best interests of the State of New York and of the United States." President Wilson made no comment. Indeed, in one sense the expulsion could have been considered as a response to his Congressional message of December 2, 1919, demanding stronger action against Reds.[60] To his eternal credit, Charles Evans Hughes, former Governor of New York, Justice of the Supreme Court, and Republican candidate for President, immediately and in hard, cold phrases which could not be misunderstood castigated the Assembly's action:

If there was anything against these men as individuals, if they were deemed to be guilty of criminal offenses, they should have been charged accordingly. But I understand that the action is not directed against these five elected members as individuals but that the proceeding is virtually an attempt to indict a political party and to deny it representation in the Legislature. This is not, in my judgment, American government.[61]

And Alfred Emanuel Smith, that tragic hero of the winter war for American ideals, whose nobility and courage in the hard campaigns of the twenties has been obscured by his later bitterness at

Roosevelt, echoed Hughes's condemnation. "It is inconceivable," said the Governor, "that a minority party, duly constituted and legally organized, should be deprived of its right to expression so long as it has honestly, by lawful methods of education and propaganda, succeeded in securing representation, unless the chosen representatives are unfit as individuals." [62] Smith had enough experience with the rurally dominated legislature to know that the bucolic solons were not just attacking "Reds"; their real target was *The City*, the new Babylon.

The Assembly was unmoved. It conducted a farcical investigation, refused to permit Hughes to testify, denounced the iniquities of Socialism, and then in effect disfranchised 60,000 New York City voters by confirming the expulsion. For good measure, it passed a series of repressive acts against "revolutionary radicals," one of which would have barred the Socialist Party from the ballot entirely, and adjourned in an atmosphere of patriotic euphoria —it had been "a victory for undivided Americanism" the Speaker announced.[63] Governor Smith caustically vetoed all the antiradical statutes, asserting in essence that "Americanism" should be defined as a dedication to certain ideals and that the measures passed by the legislature were consequently a greater threat to the cause of American freedom than the alleged subversion of the "revolutionary radicals." Nonetheless, the deed was done. In the name of protecting the state from unproved subversion, the majority of the State Assembly had expelled duly elected opponents from the chamber. The next logical step was to drive them from the political community entirely—which brings us to the Palmer Raids, the "Red Ark," and the deportations of 1920.

In an ironic passage of *The People, Yes*, Carl Sandburg wrote of the Irish cop in Denver who was heard withering a Pawnee Indian Wobbly with the observation, "If you don't like it here, go back where you come from!" [64] It was not, however, until the Bolshevik Revolution (with perhaps a brief exception during the frenzied anti-French politics of 1798–1800) [65] that the notion got abroad that radicals, whatever their degree of disaffection with the United States, bore allegiance to a foreign power. As was

noted in the last chapter, the United States had before the turn
of the century taken a very free and easy legal approach to aliens.
There were few restraints or disabilities arising from alienage, and
in some states those who had taken out first papers were given the
right to vote.[66] In the early years of this century, the laws governing aliens were tightened up and expanded in coverage at the same
time, and as another facet of, the systemization of immigration
procedures. Most of the restrictions were designed to prevent the
United States, in the phrase of the time, from becoming a "dump-
ing ground" for convicts, paupers, and diseased foreigners. But
after the assassination of President McKinley, provisions were en-
acted to bar anarchists or "criminal syndicalists" from entry, and
to facilitate their deportation if apprehended on American soil.[67]

During the war, this statute was further expanded to authorize
the deportation of a wide range of radicals, but the crucial point
was the method of procedure against an allegedly deportable
alien: he had absolutely no constitutional protection. There was
(and still is) no trial at law of the charges, no jury, no appellate
recourse against an administrative determination of guilt: "the
decision of the Secretary of Labor shall be final." [68] In other
words, the Secretary of Labor (who has been superseded in this
function by the Attorney General since 1940), and in fact his
subordinates, who handled the day-to-day work of the Immigration Bureau, were given the authority to exile human beings from
the United States on the basis of decisions made by themselves,
decisions which were subject to no significant external check. Perhaps on occasion a determined federal judge (Judge George Anderson of Massachusetts was a notable example) [69] could intrude on
this plenary exercise of power by determined procedural attrition,
by holding, for instance, that the immigration officers had not
lived up to *their own rules* in denying an alien a "fair hearing."
But in general the government was unhindered by the Constitution or the courts in its purgative endeavors. What Assistant Secretary of Labor Louis Post, who saw the operations from the inside, called the *Deportations Delirium of Nineteen-Twenty* [70]
was conducted in utter disregard of traditional concepts of justice.

As a footnote to the handling of "subversive" aliens, it should be mentioned that undesirable naturalized citizens could also be disposed of in this handy fashion if they were first denaturalized. The classic instance of this procedure concerned Emma Goldman, the matriarch of American anarchists, who was deprived of her citizenship and deported to Russia in 1919. The ground for denaturalization was that she had received her American nationality on marriage to a man later denaturalized for fraud, and it seems clear that Jacob Kersner, her former husband, was deprived of his citizenship just to make it possible for the government to "get" Red Emma.[71] Emma was shipped off in December, 1919, on the "Red Ark"—the army transport *Buford*—as part of a cargo of 249 subversives bound for Soviet soil. *The New York Times* gleefully bid good riddance to this "pernicious soldier of disorder." [72]

The story of the Palmer Raids and deportations can be briefly told.[73] In the summer and fall of 1919, against a background of labor unrest and bomb threats, the clamor increased for decisive government action against radical aliens (Senator Kenneth McKellar had earlier suggested that the United States establish a penal colony on Guam for native-born subversives [74]). The Senate on October 19 unanimously passed a resolution demanding that the Attorney General get about the business at once, and Palmer —whose Washington home had recently been blasted by a bomb —took the hint, got himself a sizable appropriation, set up an antiradical unit in the Department of Justice, and the wheels of injustice began to turn.[75] On November 7, 1919, the offices of the Union of Russian Workers, an anarchist-Communist group, were raided and 250 members of the organization arrested. Local authorities, notably in New York, took a hand in the game and conducted their own raids and arrests: over 500 alleged alien subversives were held in New York City alone.[76]

The Congress and the newspapers expressed their gratitude to the Attorney General for saving the country from a "gigantic plot." [77] Palmer overnight became a national hero, and it has been suggested that he reached the conclusion at this point that antiradical notoriety could be his ticket to the White House.[78] With this

Presidential bee buzzing in his bonnet, Palmer then set out to organize a *real* dragnet. On December 27, 1919, the Acting Secretary of Labor signed more than three thousand arrest warrants and turned them over to Palmer, and on January 2, 1920, almost five thousand suspected alien members of the Communist Labor Party and the Communist Party (the two factions which had emerged when the pro-Bolsheviks split from the Socialist Party in 1919) were arrested. The raids occurred simultaneously in thirty-three cities—those seized were held in deplorable, makeshift prisons, denied the right to communicate with their families, and often treated brutally.[79] Many understood little English. In Lynn, Massachusetts, thirty-nine Yiddish-speaking bakers were arrested as they gathered in revolutionary strength on the night of January 2—no one present was able to communicate to the police that they were engaged in organizing a bakery.[80]

Palmer reached his zenith in early 1920, and then, at first imperceptibly, the Red Scare began to lose its potency and degenerated into anticlimax. Most Americans were tired of the whole business of living in crisis and only asked for a chance to change the subject. Senator Warren G. Harding undertook to lift the burden, and with a sigh of nostalgic relief the electorate voted for "normalcy." Most of those arrested by Palmer were eventually released (less than a thousand were actually deported), and as the Republicans took over the government it became apparent that the frame of political reference had been fundamentally altered. For radicals the season of active terror was over. But this was not a consequence of the new administration's dedication to the ideals of liberty. Rather, it was a function of the dominant Republican view that *all* ideas were un-American. Wilson kept Debs in jail because, in his perverse way, the President respected the force of ideas. Harding freed the old Socialist because he viewed him as a harmless nut.[81] The American Dream, with all other dreams, had become irrelevant.

IV

TRIBAL
AND RELIGIOUS WARS
(1914–1921)

In the last two chapters, we have examined the fate of American ideals, of the American Dream of a free community of diverse individuals and variegated groups, under the shattering impact of the First World War. While we have suggested the role that the lynch mentality played among the people at large, the emphasis has been on those deviations from the ideal standard which grew directly out of national policy. In this chapter, the concern shifts from the consequences of high policy on the fortunes of Germans, radicals, or pacifists to the ethnic and religious convulsions which rocked the country during the war years and on through the beginning of the 1920's. They were not necessarily a consequence of the war, but at the same time the atmosphere of government-sponsored lawlessness which enveloped the Wobbly or the conscientious objector could not be prevented from spreading into all areas of tension. The citizen who had, for instance, been encouraged by his government to beat hell out of a Socialist could hardly be blamed if he assumed that this was the American Way of dealing with troublemakers—and lynched a Negro.

It might be worthwhile to repeat a point made earlier about the history of intergroup relations in the United States: violence was a standard ingredient whenever a dominant group confronted an emerging subculture. Perhaps this was a perverse function of the fervent faith in democracy and equality: by majoritarian standards, a lynching is thoroughly democratic (there is usually only one dissenter); and if equality meant anything, it meant that nobody was any better than (i.e., *different from*) the majority. Yet, while the howls of the mob could always be heard in counterpoint, there was also a constant and vigorous assertion of the aspiration, of the ideal of a government of laws where even the worst member of the community could find justice and, if necessary, protection against the summary intentions of his neighbors.

In January, 1838, this claim of the American conscience received classic expression in a talk by a young lawyer of 28 before the Young Men's Lyceum of Springfield, Illinois. The background was supplied by a wild vigilante campaign in Mississippi where, in the words of this speaker, "this process of hanging, from gamblers to negroes, from negroes to white citizens, and from these to strangers [continued] till dead men were seen literally dangling from the boughs of trees upon every road side . . . to rival the native Spanish moss . . . as a drapery of the forest"; a brutal lynching in St. Louis, where a mob burned a free Negro accused of murder; the murder in Alton, Illinois, of Elijah Lovejoy, the abolitionist editor, by a proslavery gang; and the ominous portents of civil war in Missouri between the "Gentiles" and the Mormons—a war which broke out in pitched battles and sieges that fall. Most politicians and political aspirants then (and far too many in our time) bent before this gale and took refuge in clucking sadly about "public passion" while explaining that, of course, bad men indubitably merited retribution.

Abraham Lincoln, however, took a different course. While expressing himself with that tactful humility which always characterized his statements, Lincoln drew the line with luminous precision:

As a nation of freemen, we must live through all time, or die by suicide. . . . There is, even now, something of ill-omen amongst us. I mean the increasing disregard for law which pervades the country; the growing disposition to substitute the wild and furious passions, in lieu of the sober judgment of Courts; and the worse than savage mobs for the executive ministers of justice . . .

. . . thus it goes on, step by step, till all the walls erected for the defense of the persons and property of individuals, are trodden down, and disregarded. But all this even, is not the full extent of the evil. By such examples, by instances of the perpetrators of such acts going unpunished, the lawless in spirit, are encouraged to become lawless in practice; and having been used to no restraint, but dread of punishment, they thus become, absolutely unrestrained . . .

The question recurs "how shall we fortify against [this suicidal thrust]?" The answer is simple. Let every American, every lover of liberty, every well wisher to his posterity, swear . . . never to violate in the least particular, the laws of the country; and never to tolerate their violation by others. [Under no circumstances] is the interposition of mob law, either necessary, justifiable, or excusable.[1]

To put the matter a little differently, the American ideal has always been that while majority rule is necessary to the existence of a free society, it is not a sufficient definition of freedom. And while the reality of life in the United States has—as we have seen —deviated from the ideal all too often, the key notion of the self-denying majority, the majority which limits its own power in the name of certain procedural principles, has remained as a fundamental proposition of American constitutionalism. Some have justified this autolimitation on the basis of natural law: the power of the state or the community must not trespass on man's God-given rights. Others have founded their formulations on pragmatic grounds: human rights and a high level of "juridical defense," which was the term used by the great Italian sociologist, Gaetano Mosca, for what we would call "due process of law," are essential to the efficient operation of a civilized community.[2] But however this view of minority rights was justified, it ran into rough water in the war and postwar periods, an era characterized by constant and often ferocious tribal and religious conflicts in American society.

The groups which suffered most acutely from the whip of social and religious intolerance were the Negroes (on ethnic grounds), the Roman Catholics (on religious grounds), and the Jews (on a combination of both). In each instance, persecution was not new, but the tremendous changes that occurred in the United States during the first quarter of the twentieth century gave it a new range and intensity. Take, for example, the impact of geographical mobility on the position of these minority groups. As long as a Jew remained in the ghetto on the lower East Side of New York City, or in Boston's Dorchester, he had a high degree of psychological security. He was among his people, and, while the world outside might be hostile, he made it his business not to stray outside the warm and hospitable atmosphere of the ghetto. And the converse effect was that to most Americans the Jew was an abstraction, and anti-Semitism was merely incidental fallout from primitive religiosity ("the Jews crucified Christ"), bucolic anticapitalism ("the Jewish bankers run the world"), or antiradical nativism ("the Jews are agents of an international radical conspiracy"). However, once the younger generation of American Jews began to leave the ghetto and the call for "assimilation" went out from various Jewish intellectuals, this stabilization based on ethnic separatism broke down. When Jews began to demand their rights as Americans, a large number of Americans surged into action to deny them this status, to keep them at best in their ghettos, at worst to drive them from the land. And anti-Semitism descended from the clouds of abstraction to the concrete level of defamation and persecution.

First the case of the Negro should be examined—it presents in starkest form the impact of mobility on social relations. A few statistics point up the issue: in 1900 there were roughly nine million Negroes in the United States and almost eight million lived in the South. Lived, it should be emphasized, in a traditional and highly stable pattern of white supremacy. In essence, their condition was that of the prehistorical peasantry. They had no past and no future, only a grinding present of poverty, malnutrition, and disease. Life was seldom brutally oppressive. There was little need for constant oppression because the lines of authority were so clearly drawn, and the power of the white community so overwhelming, that only a hero or a madman would challenge the status quo. The average Negro lived out his marginal existence in a world without time. It was a white man's universe, and, if in a reserved corner of his consciousness he bitterly resented his degradation, the Negro had no basis for hope. His will to action was destroyed by his premise of impotence—it is the shared assumption of mass powerlessness, more than the guns of the elite, which maintains the mold of traditional societies.

Thus in 1900 the Negro seemed immured in the mold of traditional society; he was a fixed element in Southern society. If we look at the figures for other areas of the nation at that time, we find only 385,000 Negroes in the Northeastern states, 496,000 in the twelve North Central, and only 30,000 in the nine Western. Then the Great Migration began—a migration which has been so extensive that in 1962 over half of the nation's 18,000,000 Negroes lived *outside* of the South. The industrial revolution and the transportation revolution hit the South; the Negro, living as he did in a semicomatose historical condition, began to realize that there was another possible form of existence, and started to leave the farms for the cities and towns. *Stadt luft macht frei* ran the medieval German saying: "city air nourishes freedom," and while the Negro did not find much freedom in Atlanta, Birmingham, Mobile, or Montgomery, he did gain an awareness of its meaning, a sense of historical aspiration. Then the move to the North, to the Negro version of the Golden Cities of Cibola: Chicago, Detroit, Philadelphia, Washington, Baltimore, and distant New York. The railroads probably carried the bulk of these pilgrims, but the introduction of the automobile and the development of road systems (it seems that of all the Southern states only Kentucky could boast in 1914 of the presence of a macadam road) eased the task of the Negro emigrant heading North.

In the first decade of this century, the Southern states had a net loss of 122,000 Negroes. Then came World War I, the Boom, the auto, and, between 1910 and 1920, a 50-percent increase in Negro emigration to 180,000. In the 1920's the dam broke. The South lost 525,000 of its colored inhabitants. The process has, of course, continued, but we can stop at this point and shift to the other side of the page, the impact on the states (in fact, the large cities) where these migrants settled. Here the figures are equally spectacular.

Recalling that the Negro population of the whole North Central region in 1900 was roughly half a million, we find that between 1900 and 1930 Illinois (largely Chicago) had a net immigration of 213,000 Negroes; Michigan (mainly Detroit) added 127,000. The Northeastern increase was equally notable: with a 1900 base figure of 385,000 *for the whole region,* New York in these three decades gained 272,000 and Pennsylvania 217,000! This is the statistical background of the "race problem" as it emerged in the aftermath of the Great War.[3]

To the Negroes leaving the South, the cities of the North and West may have seemed like the Promised Land, but any illusions they had were swiftly shattered by the welcome they received. Some communities, as was noted earlier, simply barred them by law from remaining. In most instances, particularly in the large cities, they were left to fend for themselves in slums and shanty-towns subject to brutal police control. As far as employment went, they were always the "last on, first off." Essentially the Negroes thus became pariah communities, living in the most broken-down —and overpriced: there were rich profits to be made in slum rentals —housing in the great cities. Moreover, while the martial law of Southern race relations no longer existed, they discovered that their new white neighbors accepted the same racist views as their old masters.

The truth of the matter is that Northern communities were totally unprepared for an "invasion" on this scale, and when it came the churches, welfare organizations, and social agencies were sometimes unwilling, more often incompetent, to cope with the problems that arose. And the objective problems were formidable. The Negroes suffered from disease; they were "immoral" by the standards of white society, having a high illegitimate birthrate, a high crime rate; their slums were appalling. A sensitive observer with historical perspective would argue that one can hardly condemn a man for being dirty if he has been held down in the gutter, but the citizens of Tulsa, Chicago, Washington, and countless other cities were not interested in history. Moreover, when the Negroes arrived, they displaced and competed with other groups at the bottom of the social ladder, and these groups—often foreign immigrants—reacted with blind violence and organized in the name of their one great asset, white skin.

The "best" elements in society, who were seldom unwilling to collect slum rents, looked down with contempt upon the Negro as a member of an inferior race who needed firm guidance from his white mentors. The "worst" elements in society were quite prepared to take on the task of instruction, of "keeping the nigger in his place." The consequence of this pragmatic united front was a horrible series of race riots which rocked the nation throughout the summer of 1919. Distinctive about what James Weldon Johnson called the "Red Summer" was not only the extent of the violence—there were twenty-five separate race riots—[4] but also a new dimension in the Negro reaction. However pathetically and ineffectually, however blindly and vengefully, Negroes were fighting back, were breaking out of the chrysalis of time to an active role on the stage of American history. They were no longer part of the scenery, animate objects of subhuman status who could be overlooked as the watchman ignores the prowling cat. They had, for better or worse, become participants in the drama.

Initially it was for the worse. Negro veterans, just returned from making the world "safe for democracy," formed the core of the home guard (notably in the cities), and their resistance brought fearful white retaliation. In the vanguard of the white avengers was the recently revitalized Ku Klux Klan, which had begun its revival in the South during the war and subsequently spread with incredible vigor and venom throughout the Middle West and rural sections of the East. The Klan capitalized on all the problems we have been discussing in this and earlier chapters: it was an S.S. Brigade of frightened, alienated, and vicious white Protestants which applied its perverted sanctions of "Americanism" to aliens, Jews, Asian immigrants on the West Coast, foreign-born citizens, Negroes, and Roman Catholics. Kleagles also got a good deal of prurient pleasure out of lashing naked whores in the name of Christian morality, and during Prohibition went on occasional crusades against bootleggers, crusades in which piety was tempered by considerable caution. Unlike prostitutes, bootleggers were usually handy with dangerous weapons. They also tended to stay out of unfriendly territory; although invited to Boston on several occasions by the Knights of Columbus for a discussion of the issues, New England Klansmen burned their crosses in the bush rather than on the Common.

When in May, 1919, *The Crisis,* the organ of the National Association for the Advancement of Colored People, spoke for the Negro veterans, it stated flatly *"We return. We return from fighting. We return fighting.* Make way for Democracy! We saved it in France, and by the Great Jehovah, we will save it in the U.S.A., or know the reason why." [5] The response to this spirit of militance was terror, repression, and brutality. Beginning on July 27, 1919, Chicago had a 13-day race conflict with 38 dead and 537 injured, the bulk of them Negroes. There were unchecked lawlessness, burning, and looting which left over 1,000 Negro families desolate and homeless. In other cities the conflagration broke out full force, as in Knoxville and Omaha (where a Negro accused of assaulting a white woman was "shot more than a thousand times, . . . was mutilated beyond recognition . . . [and] finally hanged downtown at one of the busiest intersections"),[6] and there were numerous less sanguinary encounters. The nation's capital was not immune from this epidemic. For several days in June, 1919, Washington, D.C., was racked by racial strife. In 1921 there was a "race war" in Tulsa, Oklahoma, in which over a million dollars worth of property was destroyed. Everywhere the storm troopers of the Klan were much in evidence, urging the mobs to greater feats of racial savagery.

And, as might be expected, Bolsheviks were immediately identified by the Klansmen and other guardians of American culture as the focus of Negro infection. A tiny Negro radical organization, the National Brotherhood Workers of America, and fiery pronouncements by Negro Socialists in such journals as *The Messenger* and *The Emancipator* (both published in New York for a small band of the Negro faithful) were seized upon by racists as evidence of the "foreign" inspiration of the "New Crowd

Negro," the designation employed by Negro radicals to distinguish themselves from the "Uncle Tomism" of Booker T. Washington and his generation of colored leaders.[7] The nativists had the answer, one which would dispose of the whole syndrome of unrest. It was put at length in a full-page advertisement in the Seattle *Post-Intelligencer*, November 18, 1920, but the first paragraph will make the point:

We must smash every un-American and anti-American organization in the land. We must put to death the leaders of this gigantic conspiracy of murder, pillage and revolution. We must imprison for life all its aiders and abettors of native birth. We must deport all aliens. . . .[8]

In the specific area of race relations, the rhetoric was similarly unrestrained. Senator Thomas Watson of Georgia, for example, devoted a good deal of space in his weekly journal, *The Jeffersonian*, to the Negro problem. The Negro, he noted, simply had no comprehension of "virtue, honesty, truth, gratitude and principle," and on occasion one had to be lynched or flogged "to keep him from blaspheming the Almighty, by his conduct, on account of his smell and his color." Watson even rose to theoretical heights when he insisted that *"Lynch law is a good sign: it shows that a sense of justice yet lives among the people."* He denounced Woodrow Wilson in 1912 as *"ravenously fond of the negro,"* and in evidence asserted that Wilson had "SENT BOOKER WASHINGTON A MESSAGE OF CONDOLENCE AND CONFIDENCE WHEN THAT COON WAS CAUGHT AT A WHITE WOMAN'S BEDROOM DOOR, AND WAS DESERVEDLY BEATEN FOR IT."[9]

Watson admittedly was an arch-Yahoo—we shall see him again demanding the lynching of Leo Frank, and he also made a fine art of vilifying the Catholic Church—but even at the center of the political stage there was little sympathy for the Negro. One can gain an appreciation of the "moderate" opinion of the day by reading the debates in the House of Representatives on the anti-lynching bill introduced in 1921 by Congressman L. C. Dyer of Missouri. Lynching had become a national scandal—the Report from the House Judiciary Committee which accompanied H.R. 13 stated that between 1889 and 1921 there had been 3,377 lynchings in the United States, 2,658 of them Negro victims, that there had been 83 in 1919, 65 in 1920, and 63 so far in 1921—and there had been demands for national action. In 1920, the Republican Platform urged "Congress to consider the most effective means to end lynching in this country, which continues to be a terrible blot on our American civilization." President Warren Harding, with his characteristic crispness, stated in the course of the campaign that:

Some of the difficulties might be ameliorated by a humane and enlightened consideration of [the lynching problem], a study of its many aspects, and an effort to formulate, if not a policy, at least a national attitude of mind calculated to bring about the most satisfactory possible adjustment of relations between the races and of each race to the national life.[10]

This statement had a certain quality of open-endedness—an unkind critic once described a Harding speech as a mass of wandering platitudes in search of an idea—but later Harding did ask Congress for an antilynching statute, and the Republican leadership brought one into the House. The Democrats rushed to preserve Southern womanhood and states' rights. Few defended lynching *per se*, but they consistently justified the situation which made it inevitable—the defiling of Southern maidens by black monsters. Here, for instance, is Sumner of Texas: "We people who believe we understand the situation are convinced that you men are fixing to cut the cord that holds in leash the passion of race conflict in the South." [11] The figure of speech appears to be accidental, but it is worth noting that while the "cord" may have been figurative to Sumner, it was literal to many a poor Negro: the lynch mob's rope.

Tillman of Arkansas picked up the theme, arguing that the measure would make the·situation in the South even more tense by giving the "illiterate, lewd, vicious, criminal black man" a sense of authority.[12] Generally the Southern Democrats picked up this theme. Not only was the bill an unconstitutional intrusion into the jurisdiction of the states, it was also an effort by "Yankeedom" to tell the Southerners how to live with "their" Negroes. It was also a cheap effort by the Republicans to pick up the votes of Northern Negroes—several participants charged that Congressman Dyer was fawning before the Negroes in his St. Louis constituency who allegedly held the balance of power.

However, the Democrats did not have a monopoly on racial prejudice. Few spokesmen for the bill emphasized the virtues of the Negro. Indeed, they tended to agree that the Negro was well below the white man on the evolutionary ladder, and concentrated on defending the high ground of due process of law. One Maine Republican, however, matched anything that the Southerners offered. "If there are more Negroes lynched than whites," said Hersey, "it is because of certain monstrous crimes committed by the Negro that arouse the blood of the white man. The terrible crime of rape was a legacy left to the South after the destruction of slavery." Hersey joined his Southern friends in their concern for the sexual protection of white women and ominously warned his G.O.P. colleagues that the antilynching law would give the Negroes "the opportunity in large cities to hide up dark alleys and in crowded buildings and shoot up innocent men, women, and children." [13] The bill eventually passed the House, but died in the Senate. One may speculate on the political, to say nothing of the moral, benefits that could have accrued to the Republican Party had it continued thus to support Negro rights. It was estimated in 1960 that 80 percent of all Northern Negro voters endorsed Kennedy.

We can leave the Negro at this point, at the bottom of the pile but beginning to struggle upward toward the light of freedom and equality, though note should be made of the emerging role of the National Association for the Advancement of Colored People as the champion of Negro rights. Organized in 1909, on the centenary of Abraham Lincoln's birth, at the instigation of a distinguished group of white liberals—the same honor roll turns up time and again throughout those desperate years: John Dewey, Jane Addams. Oswald Garrison Villard, Rabbi Emil Hirsch, Rev. John Haynes Holmes, Helen Phelps Stokes, Lillian Wald (to

name only a few)—the group amalgamated with the "New" Negro
leadership that had been groping for direction and cohesion since
the Niagara Conference of 1905. In 1911 a program was adopted
stating the Negro claim to complete political and social equality,
but emphasizing an evolutionary approach which would concentrate on attaining legal and educational parity.

A monthly magazine, *The Crisis*, was launched with W. E. B.
Du Bois, the Negro scholar and instigator of the Niagara movement, as editor.[14] Ironically enough, in the light of Du Bois' later
career as a "radical" and Stalinist apologist, *The Crisis* was a vigorous supporter of American participation in the First World War
and spent a good deal of time cataloging the heroism of Negro
soldiers; indeed Du Bois was attacked by Negro Socialists for endorsing segregated officer training schools for Negroes during the
war. After the war, in the face of the events we have described,
Du Bois tacked sharply, and the NAACP initiated a strong
campaign against racial brutality and lynching and labored to
strengthen its legal department. But it was still essentially a white
organization, dominated and financed by white liberals, with a
membership of only 100,000 in 1920. As late as 1938 its annual
budget was less than $57,000.[15]

The Jewish community in the United States was neither as vulnerable nor as defenseless as the Negroes when the great wave of
tribalism struck in the first decade of this century. It was mentioned
earlier that in 1906, as a response to the massacre of Jews in the
Russian town of Kishinev and other Czarist pogroms, the American Jewish Committee was formed to assist their suffering comrades overseas. In 1913, the B'nai B'rith—"Sons of the Covenant,"
a large Jewish fraternal organization—launched the Anti-Defamation League with the major assignment of combating racial and religious discrimination in the United States. The A.D.L. was initially particularly concerned with checking the virulent anti-Semitism that was endemic in American popular culture: in newspapers,
magazines, songs, vaudeville performances, plays, school textbooks,
and silent movies. During the war, the American Jewish Committee also began to devote some of its energies to domestic anti-

Semitism, and occasionally the organizations sponsored combined protests.

All authorities agree that there was a steady growth of anti-Jewish prejudice, though there is little agreement on the reasons. I have already suggested that the Jew was a singularly exposed target for the slings and arrows of prejudice. He could be denounced on allegedly Christian grounds as a "Christ-killer," he could be excoriated with the curse of Rothschild as the prototypal capitalist, and he could be stigmatized as the carrier of Bolshevism. (Lenin, no Jew, was enrolled as one by many anti-Semites; they usually spelled his name Lenine, presumably to rhyme with Levine.) On the level of myth, one might also risk the suggestion that to the embattled rural mind the Jew was somehow symbolic of The City, that metastasizing cancer on the American body politic.

Anti-Semitism was no novelty in American life, but in 1913 an event occurred which made it national news and supplied a focus for all the brimmed-up aggressions of parish-pump nativists. The murder trial of Leo M. Frank in Atlanta, Georgia, had much the same impact as the Dreyfus Case a generation earlier. Like the French treason trial, the Frank case polarized national opinion. On the one hand, anti-Semites organized to demand vengeance for the blood of Mary Phagan, an innocent child corrupted and murdered by a "lecherous Jew"; on the other, liberal opinion mobilized to prevent a manifest frame-up, a lynching in judicial guise.

Frank, who had grown up in Brooklyn and attended Cornell (Class of 1906—Mechanical Engineering), had settled in Atlanta in 1907 and had become manager of a pencil factory owned by his uncle Moses Frank, a Confederate veteran and leader in the local, somewhat hermetic but yet respected, Jewish community. Leo had settled in, married a local girl, Lucille Selig, and rapidly made a reputation for himself as an able, ambitious young businessman. At the time of his arrest, he was the president of the Atlanta Chapter of the B'nai B'rith.[16]

This is not the place to recount in detail the tragic sequence of events which began on April 26, 1913, with the disappearance

of Mary Phagan and the discovery of her defiled corpse in the
cellar of Frank's pencil factory, and terminated with the kidnap-
ping and lynching of Leo Frank on August 16, 1915. Frank's guilt
or innocence of the charge of rape-murder soon became irrelevant
as Tom Watson and his following turned the legal process into an
anti-Semitic shambles. "Our little girl—*ours* by the eternal God!"
screamed Watson in *The Jeffersonian*, "has been pursued to a
hideous death and bloody grave by *this filthy perverted Jew of
New York*." Frank's lawyer was told bluntly, "If they don't hang
that Jew, we'll hang *you*." When the noted, if somewhat talkative,
detective William J. Burns was hired by the Frank defense, he
narrowly escaped being mobbed in Marietta when a crowd came
after him for "selling out to the Jews." (The Burns Agency immediately had its license revoked in Atlanta.) [17]

Frank was sentenced to hang, and, while Watson editorially
licked his chops at the prospect of vengeance on this "lascivious
pervert," protests poured in from elsewhere in the nation. William
Randolph Hearst, in particular, took the Frank case into his jurisdiction and thundered against Georgia justice. Apparently the
Hearst movie enterprise even brought out a film which vividly
depicted the injustice of the verdict.[18] Although new evidence appeared, the Georgia courts rejected all requests for a new trial,
and finally Leo Frank took his plea to the United States Supreme
Court, claiming that he had been denied "due process of law."
Louis Marshall, one of the great constitutional lawyers of the
era and a leading spokesman of the Jewish community, took the
brief to the Justices of the High Court. He lost 7–2, but had the
partial satisfaction of a trenchant dissent from Justice Oliver
Wendell Holmes, Jr., joined by Justice Charles Evans Hughes.
Said Holmes: "Mob law does not become due process of law by
securing the assent of a terrorized jury. . . . it is our duty . . .
[to] declare lynch law as little valid when practiced by a regularly
drawn jury as when administered by one elected by a mob intent
on death." [19] Unfortunately the majority of the Court refused to
intervene on the ground that this was not a matter within federal
jurisdiction.

The rest of the story has a nightmare quality. Governor John M. Slaton, who had grave doubts about the evidence and the character of the trial, meditated on a request for commutation of sentence. Watson fumed and shrieked, arousing his following to a fever pitch with questions—*"How much longer is the innocent blood of little Mary Phagan to cry in vain to heaven for vengeance?"*—and battle orders—"RISE! PEOPLE OF GEORGIA." [20] At the last minute Slaton commuted Frank's sentence to life imprisonment, ordered him secretly transferred from Atlanta to Milledgeville Prison Farm, and braced himself for the storm. It hit. Only the intervention of troops prevented a frenzied mob from hanging the Governor and dynamiting his home, and when Slaton left office and Georgia three days later, his once promising political career was over. His final message deserves memorialization: "Two thousand years ago another governor washed his hands of a mob and turned a Jew over to a mob. For two thousand years that governor's name has been a curse. If today another Jew were lying in his grave because I had failed to do my duty, I would all through life find his blood on my hands, and must consider myself an assassin through cowardice." [21] John M. Slaton was a man, one likes to think, of whom Abraham Lincoln would have been proud.

For Frank the prison farm was no haven. He was hardly there before a half-crazed fellow convict sliced his throat with a razor, and, as he was slowly recovering from this attack, the pressure was rising outside his sickroom. Watson was raving and demanding direct action. The August, 1915, issue of *Watson's Magazine* was one barbaric call for retaliation against Leo Frank, and the Jews, who had, he claimed, bought the Governor. "Are the old lessons lifeless? Are the old glories gone? Are there no feet to tread the old paths? Once there were *men* in Georgia . . . men who caught the fire from the heavens to burn a law which outraged Georgia's sense of honor and justice." [22] There were feet to tread the "old paths" and affirm the "old glories." On the night of August 16, 1915, twenty-five men took Leo Frank from his sickbed and hanged him on an oak tree near Marietta.

The Marietta *Journal* defended the act—"We regard the hanging of Leo M. Frank as an act of law-abiding citizens."—and Tom Watson chortled with savage glee: "A vigilance committee redeems Georgia and carries out the sentence of the law on the Jew who raped and murdered the little Gentile girl, Mary Phagan. . . . Jew libertines take notice." [23] To their credit, most of the leading newspapers in the South and in the nation could only express their profound sense of shame. All over the country the committees which had rallied to aid in the Frank defense went into mourning. There could be no appeal from the verdict of the mob. For Watson, however, the Frank case was the beginning of a new career as an anti-Semite. He had discovered that attacks on the Jews greatly improved his newspaper circulation and income, which had been falling off as his readers got bored with his endless anti-Catholic tirades. And his political stock rose: in 1920 he was elected to the seat he had held thirty years before in the United States Senate and soon became the leading supporter of the Soviet Union and opponent of "red-baiting," militarism, and the "trusts"! It perhaps gives us an insight into the curious political configurations of that time to note that, when Watson died in 1922, Eugene V. Debs sent a letter praising this "heroic soul who fought the power of evil his whole life long," and the Ku Klux Klan sent a huge floral cross! [24]

As one who has read the trial record half a century later, I might add, almost as a footnote, that Leo Frank was the victim of circumstantial evidence which would not hold up ten minutes in a normal courtroom then or now. And subsequent testimony by men who were highly placed in the Georgia government and associated with the case strongly supports the defense contention that the principal prosecution witness, Jim Conley, was himself the murderer.[25] So much for the objective universe—it had little impact on the myth of the evil Jew which was conjured up by anti-Semites whenever they discussed the case.

Fortunately there were no more episodes like the Frank trial, but there were plenty of less serious, but nonetheless degrading matters for the Jewish defense organizations to deal with. From

1914 to 1920, the Anti-Defamation League files indicate,[26] there was never a quiet moment in the offensive against anti-Semitism. Half a dozen examples will give the range of anti-Semitic expression—Streicher-like in quality—that pervaded American entertainments and reflected popular views of Jews—and will also remind the present generation of the extent to which the United States is now free of such gross, commonplace evidences of anti-Jewish sentiments.

ITEM: "SHAKEY" AND "JAKEY" PLAY TERRE HAUTE, INDIANA

"Shakey the tailor to his son Jakey: 'Jakey, stop playing with matches. Jakey, do you hear? If you must play, come inside at least. There you can make a good fire.'" *A boffo.* The hoosier audience collapsed in mirth at the humor of the vaudeville team of Weston and Young, *alias* Shakey and Jakey. One member of the audience, the A.D.L.'s "Vaudeville Vigilante" I. E. Marcuson, was not amused. Writing A.D.L. headquarters on November 24, 1916, he observed, "There is hardly a week that there is not a Jew impersonator . . . prejudice is already so bad here I hate to let anything continue which might in any way increase it." A public campaign was launched by the A.D.L., protest was made to theater managers and vaudeville book circuit managers, and private discussions were held with the comedians, most of whom, alas, were Jewish. It took time, but gradually the League reported the decline of "Shakey" and "Jakey."

ITEM: "JEW ROSENSTEIN" IN "THE MISSING DIAMOND"

In the early days of the movie industry, when an ever-increasing audience was flocking to the "flickers," the "Jew comedy" became a staple. It was estimated that about once every two weeks a film was produced featuring "Izzy," "Moe—the fence—Green-stein," "Moneybags Solomon," "Sam Loewenstein, the Railroad Raider," or "Jew Rosenstein," the diamond smuggler. As an A.D.L. study noted, "Whenever a producer wishes to depict a betrayer of public trust, a hard-boiled usurious money-lender, a crooked gambler, a grafter, a depraved fire-bug, a white-slaver or other villains of one kind or another, the actor was directed to rep-resent himself as a Jew." From the viewpoint of the movie watcher, it must have appeared as though the Jews had a monopoly on American crime. The producers could not yet inject a Jewish dia-lect—these were silent films—but they used every stereotypical device at their command, notably the hawk nose, earlocks, and long, sloppy-tailed coat. The A.D.L. tried to get the National Board of Censorship, the voluntary agency set up by the movie industry, to bar these defamatory movies, but the board—which was the industry's response to demands for government censorship because of the brash lasciviousness of many early films—took no interest. Then the League, with the cooperation of Jewish community groups throughout the country, took direct action by urging indi-vidual theater owners not to book pictures which caricatured Jews. When in 1916 a theater owner refused to show *Rebecca's Wedding Day* in Chicago, and exhibitors in many other cities fol-lowed suit, the producers began to rethink their comedy roles. Several large companies promised that they would abandon the "Jew Comedy," and the genre soon fell into general disrepute.

ITEM: THE CASE OF THE "MALINGERING" JEWS

After the United States entered World War I and conscrip-tion was introduced, the Army drafted a *Manual* for the use of draft board medical examiners which included a section on the de-tection of malingerers: "Foreign born, and especially Jews, are more apt to malinger than the native born." The Administrative Committee of the A.D.L. immediately protested to President

Wilson. The President expressed his dismay and ordered the entire edition recalled and destroyed. Similarly, Secretary of the Treasury McAdoo agreed to expunge some anti-Jewish remarks from Liberty Bond brochures.[27]

ITEM: "YIDDISHA ARMY BLUES"

In 1918, a California songwriter had an inspiration—one which happened to coincide with a number of nasty stories about Jewish efforts to avoid war service. The result was the song "Yiddisha Army Blues":

> Jake tried to sell his business
> But he couldn't give it away
> So he set the place on fire
> In a business way.
>
> It's true I saved my money
> Till I got a little start
> Now for the battle-fields
> I'm going to depart.
>
> My head it starts a-reeling
> I get such a sickish feeling
> When I hear them sing that song
> Over There. . . .
>
> Oi, Oi, Oi vey, I'm shaking in my shoes . . .

The A.D.L. asked its West Coast representatives to intervene with the publisher, and threatened to ask the Postmaster General to use his wartime powers to close the mails to the publisher's shipments. The publisher, however, agreed to destroy the entire edition and recall all unsold copies.

ITEM: SHAKESPEARE'S SHYLOCK

Probably no "small" issue has caused more discussion and debate within Jewish organizations—and between Jewish and non-

Jewish civil liberties groups—than the determination of a proper position toward "objectively" anti-Semitic episodes in great literature. The three classic instances are Chaucer's tale of the ritual murder of little Hugh of Lincoln, Shakespeare's Shylock, and Dickens' Fagin. (In the summer of 1962, the matter was again in the headlines when some Jewish organizations in New York protested against a live television performance of *The Merchant of Venice*, and Alec Guinness' superbly malign performance as Fagin in the movie version of *Oliver Twist* has been a perennial source of controversy.)

It is quite clear from the records that the ADL and other Jewish organizations were vigorous supporters of "censorship" in their campaign to eliminate anti-Semitism from popular culture. In part, this was accomplished by unofficial group protest, as in the effort to clean up vaudeville and the movies; in part, it also utilized, as the threat to get the Postmaster General to close the mails against the Los Angeles song publisher indicates, more formalized, official sanctions. The assault on *The Merchant of Venice* raises in classical form the problem for civil libertarians that is created when various religious or ethnic groups attempt to bar literature which they find harmful to their status or insulting to their beliefs.

The theoretical issue is a good deal stickier than militants on either side are prepared to admit. To take one dimension: at what point does the exercise of freedom of speech, say by Negroes who inform a magazine it will lose its colored circulation if it refuses to support desegregation, become "censorship"? Moreover, the notion that a work of art is an independent entity in time which can always be appreciated on its intrinsic merits assumes that, for example, ninth graders reading *The Merchant* will appreciate the architectonic splendor of Shakespeare's creation and ignore the seemingly anti-Semitic delineation of Shylock. A similar thesis would support the showing of Griffith's "great" movie, *The Birth of a Nation*—with its savage portrayal of Negro behavior—in Southern grade schools. Art, after all, is art.

In short, the "no censorship" extremists refuse to admit that a society can draw *any* lines in terms of exigent situations. Censorship is a proposition with no halfway stations between Yes and No. On the other hand, the advocates of censorship have never, in my judgment, been able to establish categories which do not delegate arbitrary power to administrators and, in practical terms, leave the normally inert public at the mercy of "Watch and Ward" activists, those curious types who for reasons that lurk on the margin of psychopathology dedicate their lives to ferreting out sedition, pornography, and the like.

The real problem, in other words, comes down more to standards than to abstractions. (That standards often vary is shown by the case of the psychologist who had administered the Rorschach inkblot test to some youngsters and was accused of showing children "dirty pictures.") Anyone who has read with care the attempts by the Supreme Court to define pornography can only throw up his hands in dismay at the categorical chaos that ensued; and he must resent the standard forms of "private" censorship where a police chief, a body of local clerics, or some self-appointed saviors provide a "seal of approval" to newsstand dealers who accept their judgment of the merit of paperback books or "girlie" magazines and sell only those with the informal *imprimatur*.

What this adds up to is a rather curious position—I accept the *principle* of censorship, but can find no acceptable administrative techniques for implementing it, techniques that do not supply a cure that is worse than the disease. Frankly, however, I am convinced that most opponents of censorship in fact share my ambivalence. The anti-censorship stalwarts of the A.C.L.U., for example, are also busy trying to bar (censor?) religious practices from the public schools. If one can agree that the ambiguities of the First Amendment serve as a barrier to religious activities in public education, he could equally well make the point that the somewhat less ambiguous phraseology of the Fourteenth would prohibit the showing of *The Birth of a Nation* or the assigning of any work that would tend to bring into disrepute the "equal protection of the laws." At any rate, one man's "censorship" is another man's "separation of church and state."

Whatever may be the theoretical dimensions of the censorship issue, the nub of the problem is that however much I may sympathize with the groups who feel affronted, *my* sympathies are irrelevant. While I may want to vent my censorious rage on *The Birth of a Nation* or *Advise and Consent*, there are Arabs picketing *Exodus* in Boston and Nazis protesting *Sergeants Three* in Chicago. (Indeed, my last book *Courts and Rights* was not greeted with enthusiasm in the South.) Thus, what we must strive for is the maximum area of freedom, even for racist and Communist spokesmen, sustained by self-restraint and maturity. This means the Jews, the Negroes, the liberals will have to take their lumps like big boys and fight back not by attempting to suppress, but by presenting their counter views with vigor and clarity.

Now this is said in the context of 1963, a time when—as we shall see—American attitudes toward racial and religious prejudice are radically different from those of 1910. No responsible Jewish group would today attempt to bar *The Merchant*, though half a century ago it was a prime target of the A.D.L. and other defense organizations. (When the issue arose over a TV performance of *The Merchant* in 1962, for example, the A.D.L. reiterated the stand it has taken in recent years that "a work of great artistic quality . . . cannot be subject to censorship.") What must be recalled here is that for minorities in the United States of 1910 it was *sauve qui peut*. There was no civil liberties tradition; censorship was taken for granted in a society run on Victorian principles of conspicuous, if deceptive morality. Jews were on their own in a hostile universe, and, if their methods strike us today as less than utopian, it might be noted in explanation, if not extenuation, that they were not living in a democratic utopia. They did not create the jungle, and it is hardly surprising that they took refuge in jungle warfare. (Nor were the Jews alone in their direct action approach to discrimination and prejudice: on January 17, 1923, the Chicago City Council, by a vote of 56–2, called for the dismissal of all Ku Kluxers from the municipal payroll.)

The initial campaign against Shylock was begun by the Central Conference of American Rabbis well before the A.D.L. was founded, but it ran into the barrier of the College Entrance Examination. *The Merchant of Venice* was one of the plays which the examiners listed to be "intensively studied" as preparation for the test. The Central Conference in 1912 took its concern to the College Entrance Examination Board, and in 1914 the play was removed from the required list. The A.D.L. took charge of the campaign at this point, laboring to get individual superintendents of schools to remove *The Merchant* from the curriculum. Between 1917 and 1920 every state commissioner of education and every school superintendent in cities of more than 10,000 people was circularized and, if necessary, approached in person. (Along the same line, the children's *Book of Knowledge* was persuaded to replace a horrendous illustration of Shylock with one from *The Taming of the Shrew*.)

ITEM: "NO HEBREWS OR DOGS WANTED"

In 1916, in response to numerous complaints, the A.D.L. undertook a study of hotel advertisements and discovered that a large number of resort hotels openly listed Jews, or "Hebrews," in the category of undesirables along with dogs, consumptives, "spoiled children," and the like. A national program was mapped out essentially along three lines of action. First, A.D.L. and other Jewish spokesmen would visit the hotel owners and ask them to delete the offensive reference; second, similar protests would be made to tourist agencies to remove from display the circulars of those hotels which discriminated; and, third, a political campaign was instituted to obtain passage of legislation barring such discriminatory practices. With the cooperation of other Jewish groups considerable influence was exerted on various state legislatures, and seven responded immediately with "Anti-Discrimination" statutes (Illinois, Colorado, New Hampshire, Connecticut, Pennsylvania, Maine, and Minnesota).

All this was work directed at what might be called "routine anti-Semitism"; there was nothing comparable to the witch's brew which poured out of the Frank Case, although the identification of Jews with Bolsheviks had ominous potentialities. By 1920 the Jewish community could congratulate itself on the results of its counterattack on prejudice. What no one could know was that in Detroit a twisted genius was preparing an anti-Semitic bomb which when it exploded made even the Frank Case pale by comparison. On May 22, 1920, the bomb went off. A headline appeared in Henry Ford's Dearborn *Independent* announcing the eccentric manufacturer's latest enthusiasm—"THE INTERNATIONAL JEW: THE WORLD'S PROBLEM." Soon would come the *Protocols of the Elders of Zion* and a national campaign of Jew-baiting unlike anything ever seen before in the United States.

But before we move into the 1920's, it would be well to summarize the position of civil liberties in the United States. The picture was bleak: the ideals of freedom and justice, though affirmed abstractly, were in practice defiled all too often by that surging tradition of mob rule which has been delineated in the preceding pages. Moreover, the national judiciary—which in our time has played so vital a role in asserting the fundaments of the American Dream—was in judicious hibernation. Despite the Fourteenth Amendment's mandate that "No State shall make or enforce any law which shall abridge the privileges and immunities of citizens of the United States; nor . . . deprive any person of life, liberty, or property without due process of law; nor deny to any person within its jurisdiction the equal protection of the laws," an individual's rights were in fact defined by his neighbors. If he got along well with his neighbors, he had no problems. If he was a nonconformist, either by choice (a Wobbly) or by inadvertence (a Negro or Catholic or Jew), he had little legal recourse against neighborhood "people's democracy." He could suffer in silence, or fight back and take his beating. Few elected state officials, including judges, were prepared to imitate Jack Slaton of Georgia and stand up against the "People" (and Slaton did not return to Georgia for many years on the advice of friends who feared for his safety).

There was, in short, no nationally enforced doctrine of "due process of law," no body of precedent bearing the *imprimatur* of the Supreme Court which authorized the federal judges to impose fundamental rules of "fairness" on state trials or to strike down vicious state laws or municipal ordinances. For years the aging lion, Justice John Marshall Harlan had filled the Supreme Court chamber with his denunciations of judicial emasculation of the Fourteenth Amendment, but Harlan went to his grave in 1911 and seemingly took the original ideals of the Fourteenth Amendment with him. The former Kentucky slaveholder, a colonel of volunteers in Mr. Lincoln's army, had registered the *only* dissent in the Civil Rights Cases of 1883, the *only* dissent in *Plessy* v. *Ferguson* in 1896, the *only* dissent in *Hurtado* v. *California* in 1884 (which held in essence that state criminal procedures were not restricted by the Fourteenth Amendment), and the *only* dissent in *Twining* v. *New Jersey* in 1908 (reaffirming the *Hurtado* ruling by holding that the states might require alleged criminals to incriminate themselves). Leo Frank was fortunate to get two Justices to endorse his plea; Sacco and Vanzetti were later unsuccessful in even getting a hearing.

Yet there was another aspect that gave some justification for hope. Gradually there was developing an ideology of civil liberty, largely as a consequence of the work of defense groups. Minorities were fighting back, and quite properly they incorporated in their counteroffensives the attainment of those ideals which when put into practice would eliminate prejudice and inequality. In doing this they put a compelling burden upon the finest elements in the old society and upon the American conscience (for however the American Dream had been degraded in practice, it retained its abstract purity as the inspiration of national purpose; even the worst Red-hunter never repudiated freedom of speech—he merely excluded "Red agitation" from the category of "speech"). When Oliver Wendell Holmes and Charles Evans Hughes supported Leo Frank's appeal, when John Marshall Harlan declared that the Constitution was "color-blind," when Judge Learned Hand ruled for the editors of *The Masses*, the conscience was manifested if not vindicated.

And as we enter the "roaring twenties," another vindicator of the American conscience deserves introduction. We have already noted the rise of Jewish and Negro defense organizations, but we hardly mentioned the birth of the American Civil Liberties Union. Growing out of the wartime National Civil Liberties Bureau (which was itself a creation of the American Union Against Militarism), the Union initially concerned itself largely with pacifists and their problems. However, by 1920 the A.C.L.U. was beginning to concentrate on what we think of as "First Amendment Freedoms": speech, press, assembly, and religion. Although it put in a good deal of time protecting radicals from the wrath of the state, the Union never became identified with any specific group of sufferers. It went to bat for anybody whose constitutional rights were under attack and sometimes got involved in almost Byzantine imbroglios. It investigated and strongly condemned, for instance, the Communist practice of breaking up Socialist meetings at a time when the police were industriously breaking up *all* radical assemblies. (The Communist reply was blunt and should have been given more attention; bad people, the party indicated, had no right to hold meetings and spread reactionary lies!)

The A.C.L.U. was able to concentrate on civil liberties and their legal defense in a fashion that no defense group for a specific ethnic or religious group could manage. It organized vigorously, initiating what one who was directly involved later called the libertarian version of "Big Brother Is Watching." All over the country its volunteer representatives kept their eyes open for free speech issues and reported infringements of constitutional rights to headquarters and the Union's indefatigable *deus ex machina*, Roger Baldwin. A.C.L.U. resources were meager, but if a local situation could be properly nurtured and supporters mobilized, Baldwin could put on a civil rights spectacle wondrous to behold. Protests would pour into newspapers; lawyers materialize with writs of *habeas corpus;* ministers chastise their flocks; stories appear in national journals; Congressmen and Senators of liberal convictions excoriate the local authorities; demonstrators picket statehouse, courthouse, town hall; and, if necessary, a few nationally known figures appear and invite arrest. And the Union played no favorites with constitutional rights. One can only imagine the reaction of James Michael Curley, Mayor of Boston and no mean defender of the faith, when in 1923 he received a severe chastisement from Baldwin for banning meetings of the Ku Klux Klan *and* the Birth Control League.[28]

There was a joyous commitment to the American Dream in Baldwin, Norman Thomas, and the other militants of the A.C.L.U. Despite heavy, often overpowering, odds they returned to battle year in and year out for the lineaments of the free society. Like the cadres of the Anti-Defamation League and the NAACP, the men and women who carried on the work of the A.C.L.U. had no time nor inclination for historical paranoia. A contemporary generation of intellectuals, which has won the battles it never fought and sometimes seems borne down with self-pity and despair because it lives in a risky world, can learn something from these fighters whose repudiation of the easy escape route of cynicism and alienation made possible our freedom to reject. These were activists with a mission of liberation and a great impatience with high-flown theory. It was Morris Hillquit, Socialist, trade unionist, civil libertarian, who once gave his generation's answer to introspection and intellectual narcissism—after listening to a young Socialist explain at great length why he thought he *might* become a Communist, and why he thought he might *not*, Hillquit put his hand on the boy's shoulder and said, "Just whatever you do, *Zay a mentsh*": Be a man.[29]

V

THE YEARS
OF THE LOCUST

It is a curious fact that the 1920's have yet to receive the historical analysis they merit. The 1930's—the "Age of Roosevelt"—have attracted a number of serious historians; there was a dynamism about the New Deal and a charismatic elusiveness about its central figure which have stimulated the historical imagination. In contrast, the 1920's have traditionally received the historical brushoff. To the extent that historians of the New Deal, such as Arthur Schlesinger, Jr., discuss the previous decade, they tend to treat it as the first act of a medieval passion play. Satan and his imps run rampant over the forces of righteousness, but—as the curtain drops —are seen quaking at the sound of a distant trumpet.

This is not to say that the twenties have been wholly overlooked—there are splendid specialized studies such as Irving Bernstein's *The Lean Years*, Andrew Sinclair's *Prohibition*, George Soule's *Prosperity Decade*—but rather to note that the synthesis remains to be done. Arthur Schlesinger's *Crisis of the Old Order, 1919–1933* is in many ways a fine book, and an extremely useful one, but it is written from the perspective of the winner. From the vantage point of the 1960's, the 1920's *were* the first act in a great drama of liberal reform and social redemption, but if one manages to escape from the historical trap that automatically springs when we approach the past from the present (having read the last chapters in the mystery first), one can get a sense of the twenties which is terrifying: as an age of hate, disaster, and repression *totally lacking in omens of impending succor.* A Marxist could perhaps cherish his faith in the future victory of the proletariat, but the average non-Marxist liberal or progressive went forth to battle with no cosmic assurances, indeed with the guarantee of almost certain defeat. In retrospect we can agree that the "old order" was crumbling, but by the objective criteria of *that* era it was the liberal and progressive tradition that was on the ropes. In 1926, the *Annual Report* of the American Civil Liberties Union noted morosely that only 21 meetings had been broken up by mobs as compared with 40 in 1925 and 225 in 1922. This decline brought no joy to the A.C.L.U., since it appeared to them not to reflect a growth in libertarian sentiment, but an unwillingness on the part of dissenters to hold meetings which might provoke disruption.

In fact, the "old order" was riding high. The hysteria of the war years had been employed effectively to discredit and disinherit American radicalism; Progressivism went into limbo with Woodrow Wilson; the trade-union movement was in full retreat before the offensive launched in the name of the "American Plan," or "open shop"; nativists were at last in 1924 to incorporate racial and ethnic restrictions in American immigration law; Henry Ford was committing his immense reputation and resources to a vile campaign against the Jews; and anti-Catholicism was to reach a fearful pitch in the Presidential campaign of 1928. Perhaps the best symbol of the "old order's" total vision and implacable determination was Prohibition. Although supported by alleged "conservatives" and advocates of the "night watchman state," the Eighteenth Amendment was the most far-reaching attempt to impose "stateways" on "folkways" (to use William Graham Sumner's categories) that the United States has ever seen. Few Socialists had ever conceived of state intervention in the lives of the populace on this scale, but in the name of "American morality" these ruthless social engineers put into execution an immense piece of sumptuary legislation, destroyed whole industries, and in the process brought American law enforcement and the Constitution into cynical disrepute. In short, in 1925 the "old order" looked anything but shaky and moribund; it had no knowledge that its death certificate had already been signed, perhaps because the historians who were to authenticate the document were then in grammar school.

We have no time here to play with the fascinating question of historical "inevitability," but it might be well to point out that industrialization and urbanization have influenced different societies in different ways. In Germany and Japan, for example, the "old order" managed to retain its political authority despite social transformation—and this seems to be the pattern in contemporary France. In Britain, on the other hand, after much travail, the "old order" retired to the Riviera or the House of Lords and was replaced by a new elite representing the urban, industrial interests. Marxist historians have gone to great efforts to explain Fascism as the last despairing effort of the capitalist "old order" to retain its sovereignty over the emerging proletariat, and have argued that whenever the "old order" confronts defeat, it will automatically destroy democratic institutions rather than yield power. This is open to many criticisms: historically Fascism has been a mass movement of both alienated workers and alienated businessmen (in Germany, of unemployed workers and small businessmen and shopkeepers) with an irrational, nihilistic thrust; its outcome was never "capitalism" in any accepted definition of the term, but rule over the economy by institutionalized, party gangsterism.

Moreover, in the area of direct concern to us, this interpretation of modern history assumes the subservience of political authority to economic power. The "political forms" of a society are instruments of the "ruling class"; the state, in Lenin's phrase, is the "executive committee of the bourgeoisie." There is no room here for cultural differentiation or variations in national development arising from what might be called (to avoid the slippery ice of "national character") national traditions and habits. A nation such as the United States with a long, militant tradition of responsible government, i.e., of an elite responsible to the electorate, is tucked by the Marxists into the same historical pigeonhole with a Japan or Germany, where the principles of equality and representative government were virtually inoperative.

True, the reality in the United States hardly fulfilled the ideal: it generally amounted to the equality of white, male citizens, with women beginning to intrude in the last quarter of the nineteenth century. But the ideals were enshrined in the American tradition and needed only to be expanded to include the disfranchised. The liberals—those fighting for full equality—could, in short, demand the implementation of *traditional* ideals. In France, Germany, or Japan, those with similar objectives had to destroy the *ancien régime* and create from scratch a competing set of ideals. And the fight goes on from century to century: as late as 1940 the Pétain government in France repudiated "liberty, equality, fraternity," the tocsin of the French Revolution, in the name of "state, church, family"; and there is an underground rumor in France today (significant even if untrue) that Charles de Gaulle plans to pass on his authority to the Count of Paris, the monarchist pretender.

I have gone into this issue because there has developed in recent years a school of American historians which treats the growth of the modern United States as the unfolding of "consensus." In violent reaction against the "class struggle" historiography of Marxism, they play down the schisms in American life in favor of the continuities, characteristically skip over the Civil War and the status of the Negro, and generally make American political history into an exercise in good manners and fair play.[1] It is quite clear that Marx's "class struggle" doctrine, which emerged from his analysis of French politics, had little relevance to events in the United States, but it is something else again to argue that since Marx's class theory was inapplicable, there was no struggle. And the virtue of abstract consensus should not be exaggerated: Protestants and Catholics, who shared essentially the same theological framework, fought for centuries about little matters of definition. (Indeed, the Puritans in old and New England were far nicer to

Jews than to Catholics or Unitarians!) Just as Thomas Jefferson could believe in freedom of thought and yet demand the elimination of Federalist books from the curriculum of the University of Virginia (Federalist principles did not fall into the category of thought; they were, in Jefferson's word, "poison" [2]), so in the 1920's distinguished Protestant churchmen could assert in the name of religious freedom that a Catholic was disqualified for the Presidency.

In the 1920's the future was not inevitable—it was up for grabs. Far more than anyone has appreciated, this was the transitional decade, the crucible, in which the value system and power structure of the old society would either adapt to the new urban realities or declare war *à l'outrance* and snap the bonds of community. The 1920 Census displayed the omens of the future; the watershed was passed, and for the first time the urban population outnumbered the rural (54,157,973 to 51,552,647). And there could be no turning back from industrialization. The First World War had provided a tremendous stimulus to economic growth and placed the nation permanently in the first rank of industrial powers.

The key question, seldom articulated in this form, was: What shape would this new colossus take? Would the antique institutions of freeholder democracy survive the journey and provide the fundament for a democratic mass society? Or would American politics degenerate into a congeries of racial, religious, or economic brawls with the end product a "Balkanization" of American political life? Some may feel this is overdrawn, that it underestimates the cohesion of the American community, but such a judgment is largely based on selective memory. To this day the Southern white subcommunity asserts its right to deal by treaty with the rest of the nation, and one can only imagine the problems that would have emerged had a Catholic Party been formed in the late twenties (and the notion was actively canvassed). [3] As we shall see, a number of noted Americans were anything but prepared to accept a Catholic President. Listen to the distinguished editor and

author George Fort Milton, in a personal letter to William Mc-
Adoo where he would have no reason to engage in rhetorical
flourishes:

. . . the Smith decision is to make the most brazn [*sic*] and frantic attempt possible to win the east [with an appeal] primarily to appetite, and
secondarily to every sort of group complex, inferiority attitude, and resentment to *American standards and ideals* [my italics] which could be con-
trived. To the aliens, who feel that the older America, the America of the
Anglo-Saxon stock, is a hateful thing which must be overturned and humil-
iated; to the northern negroes, who lust for social equality and racial dominance; to the Catholics who have been made to believe that they are entitled
to the White House, and to the Jews who likewise are to be instilled with the
feeling that this is the time for God's chosen people to chastise America yes-
teryear. . . . If the dominance of such groups represent the new America
which Smith is seeking to arouse, the Old America, the America of Jackson,
and of Lincoln and Wilson, should rise up in wrath and defeat it.[4]

William Allen White, the Republican Sage of Emporia, cut
neatly to the heart of the issue: "It is not that Governor Smith is
a Catholic and a wet which makes him an offense to the villagers
and town dwellers . . . The whole Puritan civilization which
has built a sturdy, orderly nation is threatened by Smith."[5] On a
different level, the "whole Puritan civilization" had undertaken
with striking efficiency and success to destroy the trade-union
movement. As Irving Bernstein has shown, by the end of the
1920's, unionism seemed to be a dying cause and the American
Federation of Labor a pathetic, embattled remnant.[6] Despite the
assurances of retrospective prophets, the establishment of a revolutionary working-class movement was not beyond the range of possibilities. One may wonder, for example, what might have occurred had that brilliant mass organizer William Z. Foster not
abandoned authentic industrial unionism in favor of the seductions
and ideological sterilities of the Comintern.[7]

To sum up, the 1920's were a time of testing for the fundamental ideals of American community. There were great centrif-
ugal tendencies in our society which, if institutionalized (as those
in the South have been), could have led to a situation of perma-

nent political tumult. We are not talking here of a possibility of civil war in any formal sense—that was a technological impossibility for one thing, and for another, the memory of our terrible internecine conflict inhibited any tendencies in that direction—but rather of the United States becoming an oversized Belgium (where all key decisions involve negotiation between the Flemings and Walloons) or an Austria (where Socialists and Catholics distribute power on the basis of an elaborate protective formula). The problems created for the United States by one militant and entrenched subcommunity—the South—have been difficult enough to confront; can one conceive of the difficulties that would exist if there were also a Catholic Party, a Farmer-Labor Party, and possibly a businessman's "Conservative" Party?

Although the Republican Party—forgetting Mark Hanna's wise counsel—did in the 1920's abandon the worker, the Negro, and even the farmer, to become the narrow spokesman for the business community (thus sealing its death warrant as the majority party), the Democrats, against terrific odds, maintained the principle of coalition. Perhaps reflecting on the disaster that overcame their party and their region when they split the Democratic Party in 1860 on the slavery issue, the Southern Democratic magnates refused in the twenties to march off into splendid isolation with Prohibition and Protestantism. When Senator Joseph Robinson of Arkansas, a Bible Belt "dry," emerged from the Democratic Convention of 1928 in Houston as Al Smith's running mate, it was symbolic of this fear of fragmentation. And, as Samuel Lubell has emphasized, the election of 1928—at the height of a prosperity which made the victory of *any* Democratic presidential candidate unlikely, least of all a Catholic "wet"—signaled a new alignment in presidential politics.[8] If we exclude the special circumstances of the election of 1912, in which two candidates—William Howard Taft and Theodore Roosevelt—split the Republican vote and gave Wilson the Presidency, 1928 showed Republican strength in the big industrial states faltering for the first time in the twentieth century. Where John W. Davis had lost New York by roughly 900,000 votes in 1924, Smith lost by only 100,000; in 1920, New

York City had cast 30.5 percent of its votes for the Democrats, but in 1928 Smith received 62.1 percent. In fact, in every major city outside of the South (and Los Angeles), the Democratic percentage jumped enormously. For the first time in the history of the United States, Massachusetts gave an "honest majority" to a Democratic presidential candidate (no slur on the Commonwealth is intended: in the freak situation of 1912, Wilson had received Massachusetts' electoral vote with only 35 percent of the electorate behind him). In 1920 Boston was 61.5 percent Republican, in 1928, 67.3 percent Democratic.[9] And it was not that the character of these cities had significantly altered in eight years (there was little new immigration). Rather the cities were becoming *conscious* political entities; the "big city vote" that was to provide the core of Democratic strength was mobilizing. The City was about to become a major force in American presidential politics.

The Democratic Party contained such inner contradictions that only a miracle, it seemed, could keep it intact. Yet despite the 1924 Democratic Convention's rejection of a forthright denunciation of the Ku Klux Klan, and in the face of the Northern Democracy's frank willingness to "nullify" the Eighteenth Amendment (and refusal to participate in the Protestant Reformation), the Democrats held together. Not only did they sustain the coalition, but when the prestige of the G.O.P. disintegrated in the Depression, the Democrats—for all their intestine brawling—were there to present an alternative to the American people. An alternative, interestingly enough, who was neither an Irish Catholic graduate of the East Side nor an evangelical Protestant prohibitionist, but a rural, Episcopal aristocrat of unimpeachable "American" antecedents who looked on both wet and dry crusaders as somewhat uncouth fanatics and considered racial and religious prejudice to be in extremely poor taste.

Because American life was so schizophrenic in the 1920's, it is difficult to convey in a few pages the essence of the era. It was a time of startling contrasts: in a nation which prided itself on its scientific spirit, the three-time Democratic candidate for President, William Jennings Bryan, threw his prestige and talent into de-

fending a Tennessee law which forbade the teaching of evolu-
tion.[10] Victorian morality still held the commanding heights of
rhetoric, but venereal disease took a fearful toll (in 1936 the
Surgeon General of the United States estimated that one American in twenty-two had syphilis [11]), narcotics addiction was rife
(when the first federal regulations of narcotics were instituted in
1915, it was estimated that one American in four hundred was an
addict—the ratio today is one in four thousand [12]), and Prohibition virtually institutionalized gangsterism. While on one hand
the enforcement of the Volstead Act became a shambles (President Harding and his poker-playing cronies were the most distinguished examples of nonviolent civil disobedience), on the other,
the dry leadership became increasingly frenzied and ruthless in its
efforts to salvage the moral law from the boozy swamp of public
indifference and evasion. This fantasy of Ends and Means surely
reached its apotheosis when the Anti-Saloon League urged that
poison be added to industrial alcohol. Wayne B. Wheeler, the
Savonarola of Prohibition, gave this singular proposal the sanction
of higher law by explaining that any who drank the poisoned
stuff would be deliberately committing suicide! [13] It was hardly
surprising that a number of talented and sensitive American writers
abandoned the United States to George Babbitt and, in Mencken's
word, the "booboisie" and headed for Paris.[14]

There were deep fissures in the body politic, but it would be a
mistake to suggest that the average citizen was distressed, or even
conscious, of this inner crisis. At the same time that the business
community was assaulting the autonomy of the worker, real wages
were increasing. Thus, despite the fact that he was barred from
joining a union, spied upon by plant police, bullied by foremen,
and generally treated as a commodity in a fashion that might lead
one to suspect that the employers had been briefed by Karl Marx,
the wageworker did have more to spend and more things to spend
it on. If he was prepared to live by bread alone, the worker could
rejoice in his living standard and assure himself that the total
arbitrary power of the "boss" would never affect him. If "white
supremacy" aggrieved 10,000,000 Negroes, it created few per-

sonal tensions for 81,000,000 whites. Eighteen million Catholics and perhaps 2,000,000 Jews could bitterly resent the religious bigotry of the Ku Klux Klan, but the remainder of the white population emerged unscathed.

Thus a social historian with a wide frame of reference could evaluate this decade in a quite different fashion, suggesting, for instance, that there was unparalleled prosperity until the fall of 1929, and that *most* people in the United States were prosperous, satisfied, and unpersecuted. He would be essentially correct, but his view would be irrelevant to the central thesis of this work, namely, that in terms of key democratic values the United States in the 1920's was undergoing a fundamental metabolic crisis. In strictly mathematical terms, the greatest good of the greatest number—Jeremy Bentham's famous definition of the common good— might have been attained by the physical suppression of all non-white, non-Protestant elements in the population. The bulk of the populace might thereafter have been quite happy and content: Spanish Catholics have seldom seemed distressed over the centuries by the absence of Jews and Protestants.

The issue, then, was not would the United States survive—that could be taken for granted in the pre-Hiroshima world—but would it emerge from the travail and shock as a democratic nation, one in which the power of the majority would be tempered by respect for the rights of minorities, and the parochialism of minorities would be mitigated by their dedication to the common goals of a free community. This requires a delicate equilibrium and rests on the willingness of the majority to restrain its power in the name of certain intangible and often infuriating values. It is, for example, no mean feat for a community of Believers to allow militant atheists the right to propagate their "blasphemies," or for those enraged by a particularly brutal crime to withhold direct retribution. Yet these are the imperatives of the democratic ideal, the principles which had to be implemented on a scale never before attempted in human history and with a highly diversified population, geographically, ethnically, and religiously. An underestimate of the roadblocks that lay ahead in the 1920's and 1930's leads to a grievous inability to appreciate the extent to which the United States in the past forty years has in fact struggled toward the Dream. Modern intellectuals, suffused with ethical relativism, often find it difficult to understand how a man can kill—or die —for an ideal. This undoubtedly keeps down the homicide rate in intellectual circles, but it also throws up an enormous, virtually impenetrable barrier between these observers and the frontier code that dominated the American past, that tradition of direct action ironically symbolized by the story of a Colorado Populist who wound up a bitter attack on the death penalty by urging that anybody who favored capital punishment be taken out and hanged.

From the viewpoint of minority rights and civil liberties, the 1920's had the same uneven, topsy-turvy quality. The great Red hunt degenerated into an infinite series of harassments; the national government abandoned the sedition trail, but state governments (under criminal syndicalism statutes) and local authorities ("breach of the peace," "incitement to riot," "vagrancy") kept up a steady stream of arrests. Occasionally the federal government would help out with a deportation, or improvise an indictment against some particularly sticky radical—in 1925, for example, a federal judge sentenced the famed Italian syndicalist Carlo Tresca (later to be murdered in New York by either a Communist or a Fascist gunman, or perhaps a nonpolitical member of both payrolls) to Atlanta prison for a year and a day for publishing a two-line advertisement of a book on birth control (*L'Arte di Non Fare I Figli*) in his journal, *Il Martello*.[15] But the stormy years were over and were replaced by a time of steady, but eccentric attrition: now here, now there, without rhyme or reason, the net would suddenly fall. It might be triggered by a strike, or by a Sacco-Vanzetti protest meeting, or by the aspirations for higher office of a local prosecutor. Tresca claimed that he was arrested on the demand of the leaders of the New York Italian community, whose pro-Mussolini sentiments he had been regularly excoriating.

Little need be said about the status of the Negro; although from time to time the NAACP raised a legal issue, or protested to a public official or legislative body, the Negroes remained outside of the political community. There were rumblings in the disorganized, poverty-stricken black ghettos: in the first years of the decade, the "Negro Zionism" of Marcus Garvey swept through the Negro community, offering the haven of Africa and a promise of status and integrity as black men, but Garvey was jailed as a swindler and the Universal Negro Improvement Association disintegrated.[16] More significant for the long run than the messianic escapism of Garvey's "Back to Africa" was the growth of a new Negro elite, an able, perceptive, and articulate body of intellectuals which created, mainly in Harlem, the "Black Renaissance" of the twenties and thirties. Their contribution was less political than cultural, but there was a politics implicit within it. Essentially they provided the American Negro with the crucial historical prerequisite of effective political action: a sense of identity, a consciousness of solidarity, an authentic self-image. (No group can ever expect to receive respect unless it takes itself seriously.) By proudly asserting their personality as Negroes, these writers and poets discovered—as other ethnic groups have also—their integrity as Americans, as Negro Americans who had to carve out their own destiny, not become imitation white men. In sum, they rejected the image of the Negro that had been foisted upon them by white society, and with anger, bitterness, joy, pride, and some ingenuous chauvinism set forth to chart their own future.[17]

While the struggle for the fulfillment of democratic principles took place on many fronts—the unions were trying to break out of the straitjacket of "shotgun" injunctions, the Jewish community was engaged in a relentless seven years' war with Henry Ford, advocates of birth control were fighting against constant harassment, and even such quiet and respectable people as the Christian Scientists were forced to deny widespread slanders that they advocated "free love"[18]—the main line of endeavor in the 1920's was clearly the efforts of Catholics to gain their right to full membership in the American community. As was indicated above, religion happened in this instance to coincide with a series of other criteria which divided American society. A publication of the Anti-Saloon League of Ohio put the matter neatly:

If you believe in Anglo-Saxon Protestant domination; if you believe in the maintenance of that civilization founded by our puritan ancestors, and preserved by our fathers; if you believe in those principles which have made this country what it is; if you believe in a further restricted immigration rather than letting down the bars still lower, then whether you are a Republican or a Democrat, you will vote for Hoover rather than Smith.[19]

In fairness to Herbert Hoover, it should be noted that the Republican candidate repudiated religious intolerance, but as he remarked—with some understatement— "the lower rank and file of party workers on both sides did not show the elevation of spirit one could desire." [20]

There were those, including distinguished Catholics, who felt that Smith was a bad choice—that inadvertently his nomination would aggravate the whole range of rural prejudices. On this basis, they argued that the first Catholic to go forward for national office should hail from the countryside rather than Fulton Fishmarket and rested their hopes on Senator Thomas J. Walsh of Montana, the indefatigable investigator of the scandals of the Harding Administration who was a dry and (in the sardonic summary of the New York Irish) "almost a Protestant." [21] The choice of Walsh—a fine man who became permanently embittered by the consequences of his efforts to bridge the gap in the Democratic Party (bridges get walked on)—might have eased the tensions. While Walsh could have been attacked as a tool of the Pope, he was not open to the charge of being a *shammes,* an agent, of the New York Jews. Smith, who included among his closest political advisors Judge Joseph M. Proskauer and Mrs. Belle Moskowitz, was regularly accused of running a Catholic-Jewish political syndicate; when in 1928 James W. Gerard, treasurer of the Democratic Party, sent out appeals for funds, he included on the back of the supplication a list of Smith's New York appointments broken down under religious headings to demonstrate the falsity of this charge.[22] But, after the bitterness, and 103 ballots of the 1924 Democratic Convention (a two-thirds vote was still required for nomination), Al Smith had become a symbol of the aspirations of urban Democrats. So in 1928 the campaign became a total engagement, an across-the-board confrontation between two images of America.

Those who have studied the 1960 campaign, where an almost wholly subterranean religious issue demonstrated great potency,[23] will find the 1928 campaign a virtual circus of bigotry. All the latent anti-Catholicism, which had blazed up from time to time in the past, came to a head, but it would be a mistake, I think, to treat all anti-Catholicism as undifferentiated bigotry. The Catholic Church has been criticized on two levels, and the tragedy of the matter is that often those who have raised serious intellectual critiques have, willy-nilly, found themselves carrying spears in an opera of bigotry. For example, the Catholic Church, unlike the Protestant churches which clung to their rural orientation, made a superb institutional adaptation to urbanization. The key instrument was the parochial school. While Protestant religious cohesion, built around the sanctions of a personal, face-to-face village congregation, largely disintegrated in the impersonality of urban life, the Catholic Church took steps to overcome urban anomie by requiring Catholic children, wherever possible, to attend parochial schools.

This obviously ran in the face of the strong American public school tradition, and also of the long-standing notion that "Americanization" rested on assimilation, and that the public school was the mold that would impress upon unformed youngsters the key American characteristics. Thus there was nothing inherently slanderous about criticizing the Catholic Church (or the Lutherans in the Middle West) for injecting a divisive force into American society when they established confessional schools. The point is one of considerable cogency; it has been advanced by some distinguished liberal educators, and it merits exploration and debate.

Moreover, there were ambiguities in Catholic doctrine on the relationship of church and state which disturbed many thoughtful Americans. In particular, was Catholic acceptance of the First Amendment principle of separation of church and state principled or merely expediential? Unfortunately, in 1899 Pope Leo XIII had chosen to condemn a French liberal Catholic manifestation, which had powerful support, under the name of "Americanism" [24] (similarly Khrushchev denounces the Albanians when he means the Chinese), and to many this condemnation seemed to imply a rejection of the path American Catholics had taken, seemed to suggest that no Catholic could *on principle* accept the separation of church and state. If one added to this the concluding observation in Pope Leo's 1895 Encyclical, *Longinqua oceani*—that the American Church "would make far greater gains if, in addition to freedom, she were to enjoy the favor of the laws and the patronage of the public power" [25]—one could in good faith raise compelling and in no way bigoted questions about the democratic character of American Catholicism.

These are valid arguments—but rarefied ones. They cannot be conducted in the public square in the loaded vocabulary of politics, but must take place in the calm atmosphere of the university or divinity school where scholars converse, where fine glosses on the canon law can be elucidated and examined, where learned priests can digress on papal fallibility without bringing scandal to their faith. The terrible aspect of the 1928 campaign was that the two levels of argument were melded into one, that two universes of discourse were merged, and any intelligent effort to examine the thrust, or the relevance, of canonical pronouncements on church and state was swept up in the tide of primordial prejudice.

The fact is that Alfred E. Smith was caught in a trap. A good loyal Catholic whose religion was an integral part of his Irish-American culture, he had never worried about the abstract consequences of papal infallibility or the fulminations of Pius IX or Leo XIII. "The Italians," so the general line went (and there was some resentment in it; the Irish never quite got used to an Italian Papacy), "were always arguing about something," but it had no immediate and tangible implications on daily life. Smith, in short, was a Catholic and an American democrat, and the thought that there was any inner contradiction between these two faiths never occurred to him. Suddenly he was hit by elaborate citations from the *Corpus Juris Canonici*, papal encyclicals, and sundry ecclesiastics he had never heard of before, and asked to

Take a Stand. To say what he probably felt—namely, that he listened with respectful indifference to the views of the Church hierarchy on matters outside of its jurisdiction: faith and morals, narrowly defined—would have sounded like disloyalty to his faith. One might say this to trusted Jewish and Protestant confidants or, of course, to other Catholic politicians, who held similar views, but it would be a source of scandal in a public pronouncement. (And would surely have brought lightning bolts from touchy prelates.)

Like the American Jew who is accused of "dual allegiance" by the anti-Semite on the basis of statements by David Ben-Gurion that all Jews owe a loyalty to the State of Israel, Smith was caught on the horns of a dilemma. Despite his conviction that the dilemma was false, that there was no need to choose between his father and his mother, he could do little but choke down his rage and with dignity and hope ask that he be judged on his record as an American, and on the record of his people as Americans. Yet, as Edmund A. Moore has shown in his perceptive analysis, *A Catholic Runs for President*, every step Smith took carried him farther into the quagmire. When he fought back, as in his famous Oklahoma City speech, he was accused of dragging religion into the election. When he refused to reply to outrageous charges, he was damned for cowardice, or his silence was construed as proof of guilt.[26]

There would be little value in wading through the mire of the 1928 campaign, but certain aspects of it are important for long-range perspective. The forces of rural bigotry clearly overplayed their hand and in so doing mobilized not only the stalwarts of the Ku Klux Klan, but also an influential counterforce, those significant elements of the "old order" whose dedication to the American Dream was far greater than their concern for political hegemony. American politics had always been pretty rough, but there were limits, and the anti-Smith offensive was passing beyond the "boys will be boys" stage. For example, in 1928 Senator Joseph Robinson of Arkansas—a fine, conservative, Democratic magnate who ran with Smith and was later to be F.D.R.'s loyal majority leader in the Senate—arose in sheer disgust and lashed Senator Tom

Heflin, the Alabaman who against stiff competition must be considered the most worthless, banal, unimaginative demagogue of the era. Heflin had a standard five- or six-hour vilification of the Catholic Church and all its manifestations which, as Robinson sharply noted, he had delivered once a month to his suffering colleagues. Robinson announced that he was "sick and tired of it." Heflin was on his feet:

"I would like to have the Senator make that speech in Arkansas."
Robinson: "I will make that speech in Arkansas, and I will make it in Alabama too."
Heflin: "If you do, they will tar and feather you." [27]

Furthermore, the excesses of fundamentalist Protestantism helped to create a resurgence of liberal Protestantism, particularly among those clergymen and laymen who felt that the anti-Catholic activities of the Methodist Board of Temperance, Prohibition, and Public Morals, and its organizing genius Bishop James Cannon, Jr.,[28] were more dangerous to the principle of the separation of church and state than Al Smith. In this connection, *The New York Times* had already thundered against the aspirations of a "Methodist Pope," [29] and many thoughtful Protestants (including influential Methodists such as Warren A. Candler, senior Bishop of the Methodist Church, South, and President James L. McConaughy of Wesleyan University) were deeply distressed by the efforts to mobilize the pulpit for political ends.[30] Thus when the Moderator of the Presbyterian General Assembly, Dr. Hugh K. Walker, in the *Presbyterian Magazine* urged his constituents to oppose Smith's election "to the bitter end," vehement protests were lodged by various distinguished Presbyterians, including the influential former Moderator Dr. Henry van Dyke.[31] These Protestant spokesmen—and others such as Reinhold Niebuhr—made it clear that, whatever their reservations about the religious content of Roman Catholicism, they stood in the tradition of Christian charity and brotherhood, not of "Anglo-Saxon Protestant domination"; they redeemed the "old order." [32]

Thus the very depravity of the 1928 campaign may accidentally have served a useful purpose, creating in liberal Protestantism an increased concern for interfaith reconciliation, and in sensitive Catholic circles a realization that the Church should spend more time and energy cultivating its neighbors. That Smith was the victim of a vicious assault should not conceal the unfortunate fact that the average Catholic was hardly a model of religious toleration. The Catholic child was seldom aware that, from the viewpoint of canon law, Protestant children were innocent victims of "invincible ignorance" rather than automatic candidates for damnation, and rarely recalled in his relations with Jews that Christ upon the Cross had absolved all who participated in his condemnation. All concerned had a lot to learn about living in a genuinely pluralistic society (rather than a society of variegated, suspicious pluralities). The 1928 debacle triggered a recognition of this, and efforts were made to cope with the new problems by such bodies as the Federal Council of Churches of Christ, the National Catholic Welfare Conference, and the National Conference of Christians and Jews.

While the Catholics were, because of their political visibility, the major recipients of the blast of prejudice that swept out of the South and West in the 1920's, the Jews were also caught up in the whirlwind. It was their misfortune to incur the wrath of that paradigm of the virtues and vices of village America, Henry Ford. Keith Sward has indicated in his savage biography, *The Legend of Henry Ford*, the eccentric, and still somewhat puzzling, origins of Ford's virulent anti-Semitism.[33] Obviously influenced by close associates such as Ernest Liebold and W. J. Cameron, Ford, a cracker-barrel sage, saw the Jews as symbolic of the whole modern syndrome, as a cosmic scapegoat for America's lost youth. In essence, the modern world and all its evils, smoking, drinking, jazz, sex, finance capitalism, trade unions, foreigners, international relations, urbanism, were attributed to the sinister machinations of an International Jewish Conspiracy.

With his national weekly newspaper, the Dearborn *Independent*, Ford set out to turn the tide. There were, and still are, a number of weekly periodicals in the United States with similar ambitions, but the Dearborn *Independent* was in a category all by itself: it began life with a tremendous captive audience and eventually reached a peak circulation of about 700,000. All Ford dealers, who lived in a state of dependence on Ford that only a Kafka could adequately portray, were automatically subscribers and were assigned quotas; hopefully every purchaser of a Model T would take the paper as unthinkingly as he took a spare tire. Rejecting all advertising, the *Independent* announced its mission as the "Chronicler of the Neglected Truth" and went forth to "spread ideas." The central idea was the corruption of city life; as the paper stated, "The real United States lies outside the cities. When we stand up and sing, 'My Country! 'Tis of Thee,' we seldom think of the cities." [34]

Keith Sward has etched in acid the aberrations of the *Independent*—its passion for "funny money," its attacks on the theater and movies, its antimonopoly fulminations—but our concern is with a narrower aspect of the paper's policy, its "discovery" of the master key to the Jewish Conspiracy, the so-called *Protocols of the Learned Elders of Zion*. It is hardly necessary here to recount once more the origins and history of this somber forgery; suffice it to say that the document, part of a book by a Czarist *agent provocateur*, Serge Nilus, written in 1905 to try to deflect social unrest into anti-Semitic channels, purported to be the Jewish battle plan prepared by the general staff of seven "Learned Elders of Zion" for the conquest of the world. Peddling it to gullible foreign anti-Semites had long been a source of steady income for the Russian *aficionados*, and in 1920 a White Russian émigré in New York hit the jackpot. He sold a translation to Ernest Liebold, Ford's chief of anti-Jewish intelligence. Cameron then edited this crude translation, gave it a contemporary flavor, and serialized it in the *Independent*. For the next year and a half this incredible flow of paranoidal gibberish continued, and the resulting text was published as *The International Jew*. It became the "standard" version of the *Protocols* and was translated into dozens of foreign languages. In 1922 a *New York Times* reporter in Munich noted that a German translation of *The International Jew* and a picture of Henry Ford were notable features in Adolf Hitler's headquarters, and it was later alleged that sections of *Mein Kampf* were direct plagiarisms (if that is the appropriate word) from Ford's publication.[35]

The Dearborn Publishing Company published (largely at government expense; Ford deducted its large deficit as a business loss for tax purposes) [36] and distributed, through the inevitable Ford dealers, four volumes: *The World's Foremost Problem* (1920), *Jewish Activities in the United States* (1921), *Jewish Influences in American Life* (1921), and *Aspects of Jewish Power in the United States* (1922), all larded up with the "authentic" unveiling of the plans of the Jewish politburo. Had the whole episode not carried such heavy overtones of tragedy, there would have been something comic about the standards of evidence that were involved. How did Nilus get the document? Well, according to one version, "from a deceased friend, unnamed, who received them from a woman also unnamed, who stole them from one of the most influential and most highly initiated leaders of Freemasonry." [37] When in 1921 Philip Graves of the London *Times* revealed that the *Protocols* were in fact plagiarized from an 1858 French novel, *Dialogues of Hell*, by Maurice Joly, the defenders of the document had the answer ready. Joly was actually a radical Jew named Moses Joel, a Communard shot in 1871, who had uncovered the truth independently; it was hardly surprising that the versions should be similar—indeed, it was further proof of the validity of the *Protocols* that the two descriptions converged. (Joly in fact was a Catholic, monarchist anti-Semite!) [38]

Unfortunately, logicians were a small component of the American public in 1920, while the Ku Klux Klan boasted a membership approximating two million,[39] and there were millions of others who were less militantly in search of the Enemy, the forces that had silently invaded the American Garden of Eden and destroyed the bucolic euphoria of the Victorian era. The Jews were stunned by this unanticipated assault, its very irrationality made it impossible to comprehend. Ford, for example, had fought the "Wall Street" (and State Street) bankers and should have recognized the unmistakably "Anglo-Saxon Protestant" character of his opposition, but now he talked of "Wall Street Kikes." And what could one say when confronted with the charge that Benedict Arnold

betrayed the American cause at the instigation of Jewish bankers?
Or that Queen Isabella of Spain was a tool of the Jewish conspiracy when she sponsored Columbus? [40] To the American Jews,
Ford's motives, his "facts," his logic were simply unintelligible—
it was rather like being hit by a falling brick while peacefully
walking down the street.

Jewish defense organizations moved immediately to counter the
Ford campaign. On December 1, 1920, an *ad hoc* organization of
nine of the biggest Jewish groups in the country, acting under the
leadership of the American Jewish Committee, issued a devastating
analysis of the *Protocols* in a pamphlet *The "Protocols," Bolshevism and the Jews.* The Anti-Defamation League, which cooperated in the joint statement, also issued a refutation of its own,
The Poison Pen. In the months that followed, the Federal Council of Churches also issued a vigorous condemnation of Ford's
bigotry, and John Spargo, the former Socialist who was always
found in the front ranks of those fighting against prejudice, circulated a strong statement on "The Peril of Racial Prejudice"
which was signed by former Presidents Taft and Wilson, Cardi-
nals O'Connell of Boston and Hayes of New York, William
Jennings Bryan, and more than a hundred other outstanding
Americans of the Christian faith.[41] Leading newspapers similarly
denounced the *Independent*, and when Graves demolished the
Protocols in the London *Times*, *The New York Times* reprinted
his elaborate study in full.

Ford, however, was unmoved by what he took to be the latest
stratagem in the Jewish plot, and for seven years the *Independent*
and the Dearborn Publishing Company continued their steady out-
put of anti-Semitic literature. Then in 1927 two things occurred
which led Ford to do an abrupt about-face. First of all, the *Independent* had gotten a bit too specific. Benedict Arnold and Queen
Isabella were in no position to employ the law of libel, but Aaron
Sapiro, a Jewish attorney and organizer of cooperative marketing
groups, was not only alive in Detroit but also convinced that the
Independent had given him cause for action by listing him as
part of "a conspiracy of Jewish bankers who seek to control the

food markets of the world," and implying that he was a tool of the "Jewish Communist movement in America." [42] Sapiro sued for a millon dollars, and it was quite clear that he would use the trial as a vehicle for exposing the whole farrago of the "International Jewish Conspiracy." He planned, in particular, to get Henry Ford in the witness box and examine his credentials as a historian of the Jews.

Second, Henry Ford, who had refused to alter his Model T, was in financial trouble. The competition of General Motors and Chrysler, who had gone in for imaginative new auto designs, was cutting into his standing and profits. And part of his difficulty was a boycott of Fords both by Jews and by sympathetic Christians. [43] In May, 1927, Ford reluctantly abandoned the Model T and began retooling for a new design, the Model A. This change-over would take almost a year—during which Ford sales would be at a standstill—and it appears that when he decided to desert the Model T, Ford concluded that it would be wise to liquidate his other liability—the *Independent* and its anti-Semitism. [44]

Sapiro never got Ford in the witness box; a mistrial was declared for technical reasons before a summons could be enforced. But Ford had good reason to dread cross-examination (he had spent a memorable week under attack in his libel suit against the Chicago *Tribune* in 1919) and was maneuvering for a settlement of this and his other ailments.

Unexpectedly, two months before the Sapiro suit was scheduled for retrial, Ford sued for peace, sending two plenipotentiaries, Joseph A. Palma and Earl J. Davis, a one-time U.S. Attorney, to consult Louis Marshall of the American Jewish Committee on "terms." Marshall drafted a suggested statement of apology. [45] On June 30, 1927, Ford sent the signed statement to Davis with instructions to forward it to Marshall as an apology to Jews in general, after it had first been given to Arthur Brisbane for general publication.

Despite the clear fact that Cameron and Liebold had been long-time intimate associates of Ford, the fiction was elaborated that they had acted without Ford's knowledge and approval in

their anti-Semitic ventures. "Mr. Henry Ford," the formal statement announced, "did not participate personally in the publication
of the articles and has no personal knowledge of what was said
in them." [46] He apologized to Jews for the "gross forgeries" published in the *Independent* and added, "I deem it to be my duty
as an honorable man to make amends for the wrong done to Jews
as fellowmen and brothers by asking their forgiveness for the harm
that I have unintentionally committed . . . and by giving them
the unqualified assurances that henceforth they may look to me
for friendship and good will." [47] It was on paper a great triumph
over the forces of bigotry, but anti-Semites never took it seriously.
The removal of the principal source did not end the circulation
of the lies, or the foreign translations of *The International Jew.*
Ford quickly passed the matter over. In December, 1927, he put
$156,000 worth of Ford advertising in the Yiddish and Jewish
newspapers, and in 1933 he blandly remarked, "I have never contributed a cent, directly or indirectly or any other way, to anti-
Semitism anywhere." [48] American Jews, however, could well ob-
serve with Pyrrhus, "another such victory and we will be destroyed."

Fourteen years after the Sapiro suit, the pressures on Ford for a
repudiation of anti-Semitism were different; the United States was
at war and anti-Semitism was a tool of the enemy. Acting on
Ford's initiative, Harry H. Bennett, the motor company's personnel director, called Richard E. Gutstadt, the national director of
the Anti-Defamation League, for consultation, and on January 2,
1942, Ford wrote to Sigmund Livingston, A.D.L.'s national
chairman, recounting his retractions and his belief "that the hate
mongering prevalent for some time against the Jew is a distinct
disservice to our country, and to the peace and welfare of humanity."

"No one," wrote Myers, "could find grounds for impugning
this declaration as not being entirely voluntary; anti-Semitic publications which had twisted his repudiation of the *Protocols* as due
to 'Jewish pressure' might repeat the same charge in this case,
but it would be even more absurdly untenable."

The 1920's, it should be apparent by now, were indeed "lean years" from the viewpoint of the civil libertarian or, more broadly, of the individual concerned with the basic problems of intergroup relations. And this is not the whole story by any means—certain issues such as the rights of labor and freedom of radical opinion have been reserved for composite treatment in the next chapter, since there is very little that can be said about them here that would not be repetitive. (For all its emotional content, the Sacco-Vanzetti Case was a footnote to the Red Scare—it was important primarily as a focus for civil liberties sentiment.)

We have been examining the rights of minorities largely in the context of social history and have put little emphasis on legislative or judicial action. This emphasis reflects reality, but two legal developments should be mentioned in passing. First, there was a growing demand in the multi-ethnic and religiously pluralistic industrial states for civil rights legislation, a demand which successfully incorporated into the statutes of perhaps a dozen states various antidiscrimination provisions.[49] However, these laws in themselves accomplished little: the problem was enforcement, and the courts tended to give them very limited construction. Even in New York, a leading state in terms of legislative rhetoric, it was necessary constantly to amend the Civil Rights Act to repair judicial damage. (The courts held, for instance, that neither a saloon nor a golf course was "a place of public accommodation, resort, or amusement"!) [50] Of course, the national government took no hand in civil rights matters. The Anti-Lynching Bill which, as we saw, passed the House in 1922 was introduced without any Congressional action in 1923, 1925, 1927, 1929, 1933, and 1935. In 1937 it was passed by the House, but again filibustered to death in the Senate.[51]

Second, there were several Supreme Court decisions which indicated that the high tribunal was no longer willing to give the states plenary authority to define the scope and content of civil rights. The first set of cases arose in 1923 as a consequence of laws, passed by eleven states, banning the teaching of all foreign languages (aimed mainly at German) in public or private grammar schools (grades 1–8). Thirty-four states required that English be the language of instruction in all schools. The Court, through Justice McReynolds, ruled that the statutes barring the teaching of foreign languages violated the due process clause of the Fourteenth Amendment because they materially interfered with "the calling of modern language teachers, with the opportunities of pupils to acquire knowledge, and with the power of parents to control the education of their own." [52] A more clear-cut case occurred in 1925 when the Justices declared unconstitutional an Oregon law, originated by the Ku Klux Klan, which compelled all children between the ages of 8 and 16 to attend public school—thus driving private and parochial schools out of existence. The provision was held an unreasonable interference "with the liberty of parents and guardians to direct the upbringing and education of children" and an invasion of property rights. [53]

The demise of these statutory reflections of racial and religious chauvinism was a matter for rejoicing, but it hardly struck to the core of the civil rights problem. In 1925, however, the Court took a truly revolutionary step—one with enormous future consequences —when it reviewed the conviction of Benjamin Gitlow, then a leading Communist. Gitlow had been sentenced to 5–10 years' imprisonment under the New York criminal anarchy law for publishing in 1919 the "Left Wing Manifesto," the platform of the Communist Labor Party. Anyone who has read the "Manifesto" must concur in the late Zechariah Chafee's incisive summary of the impact of this document: "Any agitator who read these thirty-four pages to a mob would not stir them to violence, except possibly against himself. This Manifesto would disperse them faster than the Riot Act." [54] But New York had found Gitlow and his associates to be an imminent threat to the stability of the Empire State and locked them up in Sing Sing. (Had John Reed, the left-wing journalist and author of *Ten Days that Shook the World*, been in town, he would have shared their fate and, ironically, might have lived to share an American Legion platform with Gitlow as an expert anti-Communist—as it was, he died of typhus in Russia in 1920.)

The importance of the Court's decision in *Gitlow* v. *New York* was not its conclusion on the merits—the Justices held, with only Holmes and Brandeis dissenting, that New York was within its authority in determining that the cadres of the Communist Labor Party were in fact a menace to the security of the state.[55] Gitlow and his colleagues thus spent three years behind bars before they were pardoned by Governor Alfred E. Smith. What was vital in the holding was the basis on which the Court reviewed the conviction, the criteria of evaluation it employed. Without launching into a long background essay on constitutional technicalities, it is sufficient to note that as recently as 1922 the Justices had noted that the limitations of the Bill of Rights were not transferred to the states by the operation of the Fourteenth Amendment. That is, in specific terms, the civil rights guaranteed by the First Amendment against the encroachments of the national government (freedom of speech, religion, press, assembly) were *not* protected against state invasion by the first section of the Fourteenth Amendment. The effect of this was to give the states free rein—there was no constitutional reason why a state could not, for example, establish a church and, presumably, hang blasphemers and heretics. (A *state* bill of rights might bar this, but the federal Constitution was no obstacle.) [56]

But in the Gitlow Case, the Court reversed this tradition and held that the due process clause of the Fourteenth Amendment established the same restrictions on the states that the First Amendment did on the national government. As we shall see, this was a decision fraught with consequences: it opened up the whole area of state invasion of freedom of opinion, and later of state procedures in criminal actions, to *federal litigation*. The defenders of the American Dream were no longer to be confined to political agitation, to rhetoric and propaganda—now they could work by litigation to get the Constitution and the Bill of Rights—for so long lofty abstractions—implemented as instruments of liberation. Gitlow lost and returned to jail, but, as Chafee said, civil libertarians found victory in this defeat.

And one other point should be made in conclusion. The 1920's were grim years for American ideals, but if one watches carefully he will note the steady growth of the civil liberties constituency. No longer were minority rights the concern solely of minorities. The Catholics were not left to fight it out alone, the Jews were not deserted in their hour of need, the Socialist Assemblymen found defenders such as Charles E. Hughes and Al Smith. Indeed, the finest elements in the "old order," those of the "Anglo-Saxon Protestant" tradition who had truly been nourished in freedom, rose to the defense of their ancient principles, of the cherished banner which the Ku Klux Klan and the crossroads bigots were dragging through the muck. And their contribution was crucial —it provided a vital link, a bond of trust, between the old and the new.

Sustained in the face of brutal defeat and constant attrition— Sacco and Vanzetti were executed, Tom Mooney stayed in jail, the *Independent* published, the Klan rode, and the Negro remained in political limbo—the ideals of American freedom somehow survived the test of the twenties. The Catholics saw Smith vilified and defeated; they wept and cursed, but returned to fight again (this time for a Protestant) in the ranks of the Democratic Party. The American worker, deprived of his dignity and treated like a commodity, refused the lure of extremism and remained convinced that somewhere *in the system* lay the key to his future. In short, as the Great Depression settled over the United States, it did not, as in Germany, pull the last props from under a bitterly divided and disillusioned political community. Americans, despite the economic blows that rained thick and fast after October, 1929, held together. Faith in the ideal and hope for the future triumphed over alienation and despair, and this was a far greater victory than has been properly appreciated.

THE NEW DEAL:
THE YEARS
OF RECONCILIATION

Normally the 1920's are considered as a time of stagnation and the 1930's as an era of turmoil, with the implication that there was something dangerous about the New Deal years. From the viewpoint of this analysis, the opposite was in fact the case. The stagnation of the 1920's properly interpreted was what the Greeks called *stasis*, a choking up of the arteries of the body politic which both Plato and Aristotle considered the prime cause of revolution and social disintegration. And the turbulence of the 1930's, far from being a symptom of social malaise, was a function of the vital readjustments that were taking place as the disinherited were reconciled and admitted to the political community. It is noisy to break windows, but sometimes the noise is necessary to get some air into a stultifying or even noxious atmosphere.

It was also Aristotle, not Karl Marx, who first suggested that a ruling class—*politeuma*—determined the character of a state in terms of its interests, and that if its interests grew too narrow, *stasis* and revolution could result. Without unduly belaboring Aristotle's categories, it might be added that he saw selfishness as the key danger to a ruling class, as the source of degeneration: thus, an aristocracy, the rule of a few *in the interests* of all, was likely to succumb to self-interest and degenerate into an oligarchy, the rule of a few *in their own selfish interests*.

Judged by these standards of political metabolism, the United States was at the beginning of the Great Depression dominated by a political class—Schlesinger's "old order"—which had abandoned the far broader vision of McKinley and Mark Hanna and Theodore Roosevelt in favor of a narrow concentration on the interests of the white Anglo-Saxon Protestant *business* community. In the course of the 1920's, the agrarian component of the "old order" had found itself abandoned by its Eastern allies, and, while the Republican farmers voted for Hoover, tremendous discontent was seething under the surface. While the Republican magnates did throw the agrarians a bone in the form of tariff protection, this gift hurt more than it helped (the United States was an exporter of agricultural goods and the Smoot-Hawley Tariff led to foreign reprisals); and on the one big issue—federal support for agricultural credit—the G.O.P. business leadership was rigidly unsympathetic.[1]

In short, if we examine the political class in Hoover's time, we find that it represented a narrow segment of *even the Republican* constituency. This was not the outcome of a clever capitalist conspiracy, but rather a natural if shortsighted consequence of electing to the Presidency such incarnations of the business ideology as Calvin Coolidge and Herbert Hoover. The "business of the United States," Coolidge had observed, "is business," and leading figures of the Establishment such as Andrew Mellon, Ogden Mills, or Charles Dawes were frankly proud of their "businessman's government" run on "sound business principles." The business philosophy provided answers in every sphere, even international relations. When the French asked Coolidge for special consideration on war debts (because German reparations were not coming to them as anticipated), the President dismissed the whole complex tangle of European public finance in the phrase of the village banker condemning the defaulting innkeeper: "They hired the money, didn't they?"[2]

The Republican political class then stood firmly on an extremely small base, and, as long as prosperity continued, its stance was secure. As I have indicated, there were profound fissures in the political community and large, though often politically inert (or repressed: the Negroes) groups within the society questioned the legitimacy of the "old order" at one level or another of political consciousness. But these naysayers were doomed to remain on the margins of the political community so long as the Republican myth remained intact: the "Party of Prosperity," which had received 59 percent of the vote in 1928 and carried forty states, had reaped the profits of success. The men with the golden touch seemed invincible, but if nothing succeeds like success, nothing fails like failure.

Let me make it clear that these were frequently sincere, decent men who held a quite genuine conviction that their business values were the core of the national interest. If they deceived the people, they went to great effort first to deceive themselves, and they surely held no monopoly on self-deception. Their sin was not that they identified their values with the common good (what man of strong convictions has ever avoided this *hybris?*), but that they lost their grip on reality and failed to make any real adaptation to the fundamental changes that were transforming American life. They became, in sum, a rigid, frozen political elite which committed the gross political error of believing their own press releases, and, when the world ended, all they could do was mutter the old incantations and await the spirits, which never came. Without knowing it, they had become exhibits in the museum of historical antiquities; their fate was almost a model of Aristotle's description of the degeneration of a political class.

The election of 1932 marked the end of a remarkable period of Republican hegemony. In terms of *votes*, the Democrats had won the Presidency only once in the twentieth century (1916, and one can suspect that had T.R. been elected in 1912 he would have carried the day again in 1916). In the face of the Depression, the Republican coalition simply fell apart. In a dramatic reversal of 1928, Hoover carried only six states and received 41 percent of the vote. More significantly, he won only one big state, Pennsylvania, and lost the farmers lock, stock, and barrel (in 1932, 52 percent of farm mortgages were in default!).[3] The American people voted for a "New Deal," but had little notion of its content. It was sufficient that they closed the door on the "businessman's government" and looked forward to a new beginning. Father Coughlin called the New Deal "Christ's Deal"; the Communists called it Fascism; Franklin D. Roosevelt, glowing with vitality, but chary of ideology, threw himself into the tasks at hand and left fine questions of theory to the scribes.

It was F.D.R.'s destiny, whether he conceived of it in this fashion or not, to preside over the reconstruction of the American community in an epoch of fearful crises. Elsewhere in the world, the timeless values of the "old orders" had similarly collapsed in the face of depression, and a host of prophets of "new orders" —Communist, Fascist, corporative—had risen and turned political life into a shambles. It was Roosevelt's genius that, at a time when the sharpening of ideological conflict was disrupting society after society, he succeeded in muting the ideological thrusts in the United States and, indeed, encouraged a process of social reconciliation from which the United States emerged united as never before.

True, the President was aided in this by certain objective historical considerations. The isolation of the United States, and Roosevelt's isolationist foreign policy through at least 1938, made it possible for the American people to work out their problems without the distraction or interference of foreign commitments. Unlike the French, living in the memory and shadow of German aggression, we had no critical issues of national defense to divide opinion. Our Navy planners spent much of the thirties devising a battle plan to cope with a joint British-Japanese attack! [4] We took what was virtually a leave of absence from the international arena, and—though we were later to regret our indifference to the rise of Nazi power—this (unplanned) vacation eased the solution of many domestic issues. Second, despite the widespread poverty and unemployment that the Depression brought to the United States (gross national product dropped from 104.4 billion dollars in 1929 to 56 billion in 1933; in 1933, there were 12,830,000 unemployed, 25 percent of the labor force [5]), we had tremendous national assets awaiting solution of the *distribution* problem. Roosevelt was not confronted by any imperative need for belt-tightening (as the British were in the immediate post-World War II period) or any danger of national bankruptcy. In other words, Roosevelt did not have to take from the rich what he gave to the poor in some drastic program of wealth redistribution; there was plenty for everybody if the national economic potential could be unleashed.

Yet Germany too was a rich country which subsequently proved capable of incredible economic mobilization for aggression. Another man than Hitler could perhaps have channeled that immense creative energy into the democratic solution of Germany's domestic problems. And, as we sadly appreciated later, the Nazis were permitted to build their war state in an isolation which could hardly have been more secure had they been protected by two oceans. No, objective historical considerations, while worth recording, cannot provide the answer to the question *How did Roosevelt succeed?*

It would be profitless to linger with biography, particularly since James M. Burns has in his *Roosevelt: The Lion and the Fox* [6] made most further efforts mere exercises in space-wasting. But we must try to get to the heart of the Roosevelt dilemma. An understanding of his role is the key to any interpretation of the events of the 1930's and especially to the transformation of civil liberties and decent intergroup relations from the realm of the agitator to the content of public policy. Radical intellectuals both then and since have turned Roosevelt-baiting into a fine art, but when all is said and done, F.D.R. still has the final, genial chuckle. The inexorable fact cannot be avoided: under the Presidency of Franklin D. Roosevelt, the United States left the paths of tribalism for the high road of due process of law and substantive justice and equality. When he died in 1945, he left a nation far different from the one he inherited from the "old order" in the dark days of 1933, a nation which had fought the greatest war in history without chauvinism or xenophobia, and in which even the most downtrodden minority, the Negroes, were sensing the light that heralds the dawn. Perhaps the change was inevitable, but what change cannot be proved inevitable *a posteriori?* Perhaps his lieutenants were responsible, but were they not *his* lieutenants? Perhaps he did it for political reasons, but *he* did it while other politicians went into oblivion cherishing their rigid formulae. He may have been an unprincipled opportunist, an improviser without ideological moorings, an inefficient administrator—to list a few of the main accusations—but the hard reality is that to eliminate Roosevelt from the accomplishments of the years 1933–1945 is to play *Hamlet* without the Prince.

In a curious way, the characteristics of F.D.R. which most infuriated the intellectuals—and not just the radicals; Raymond Moley echoed the same complaints from his perspective [7]—were perhaps the key to his success as a catalyst of reconciliation. Justice Oliver Wendell Holmes, that shrewd campaigner with a mind like a coiled spring, put the essence in a brilliant *aperçu*. "A second-class intellect," observed the 92-year-old pirate after talking with the President-elect, "but a first-class temperament!" [8] Roosevelt, with the intuition of a wholly *political* man, detested ideological confrontation and automatically, as by a conditioned reflex, moved in any tense situation to blur the lines of conflict. He was convinced to the very foundation of his personality that only disaster could result if political conflict were transformed into ideological warfare. This penchant for avoiding sticky problems could lead to absurdity on occasion—Moley tells of Roosevelt's handing him two draft speeches, one high tariff and one low tariff, with instructions to "weave the two together"! [9]—but it provided the President with immense freedom of maneuver and the opportunity to deal indirectly and gradually with issues of great complexity. Moreover, it made matters extremely difficult for those trying to build an ideological constituency, i.e., for those trying to implement True Believer politics and launch a crusade. The Communists on one side and the Liberty League on the other had the same problem. They simply could not keep Roosevelt in their sights and ended up firing random shots into the air.

To put it differently, Franklin D. Roosevelt stands as a classic example of the virtues of *inefficiency*. One of the curses of our time, an inheritance from classical economics and utilitarianism which dogs both Marxist pundits and the sages of the National Association of Manufacturers, is the worship of the brazen idol of Efficiency. Avoiding the interesting question of how efficiency should be defined—in long-run terms or in short—the advocates of Efficient Politics have attempted to impose on the public the notion that men with the best technical proficiency should be allocated the power to govern. Politics is reduced to a branch of mechanics, and the role of the leader is to take that straight line which is the shortest distance between two points. Since the time of Plato's "philosopher kings," the original government by experts, eager earnest men have labored to denature politics, to eliminate the contingent factors and establish a "Science of Government." This quest for the Holy Grail had been exemplified in the 1920's by the widespread conviction that salvation would come from the application of business methods and principles, with the implicit premise that a good government would be a profit-making corporation. Oddly enough the same fundamental precept—"Get the Messy Human Factors Out of Politics"—nourished both Communist and Fascist ideologies: each offered Government by Experts.

Roosevelt—to the despair of his expert advisors—had not the slightest concern for efficiency in this sense, and all his instincts told him that a straight line was in politics usually the shortest route to trouble. Moreover, he seemed to realize that what passes as "expert" opinion is usually only the surface manifestation of basic ideological convictions. His first Budget Director, Lewis W. Douglas, could, for example, present him with interminable graphs and tables to demonstrate the indispensability of the gold standard, but the foundation of Douglas' opposition was not economic, but broadly ideological. The gold standard was part of a traditional way of life; as Douglas put it when he learned that F.D.R. had demonetized gold, "Well, this is the end of Western civilization." [10] This is not to say that F.D.R. did not respect expert judgment, but rather that his respect was tempered with skepticism and hard empiricism. He was prepared to try almost any plausible scheme, but he never confused instrument with purpose, nor put all his money on one horse.

This fondness for improvisation led to such wild statutory concatenations as the National Industrial Recovery Act which lurched in at least three directions at once. First of all, it embodied a concept of industrial efficiency which had been widely canvassed here and abroad (in Britain under the aegis of the Mond-Turner Plan) as rationalization and partnership. The inefficient producers were to be eliminated by industry-wide associations which would establish "Codes of Fair Competition" (Herbert Hoover as Secretary of Commerce had earlier encouraged trade associations to become self-regulating bodies, but the N.I.R.A.—at least on paper—put the workers into the picture as partners). If carried to its logical conclusion, this principle would have knocked the anti-trust laws over the head. Second, the N.I.R.A. paid tribute to John Maynard Keynes by instituting a large public works program which hopefully would pump purchasing power into the bottom of the economy. And, third, it established state supervision over the industrial associations and provided that the codes drawn up by these private bodies would, upon approval by the President, have the force of law. This brought the left out screaming "Fascism," and, if one worked at it a bit, he could find similarities between the N.I.R.A. and the Italian "corporate state." [11]

The point was that nothing was carried to its logical extreme; F.D.R. was incapable of logical extremes. Consequently, the N.I.R.A. resulted in an incredible amount of chaos, but also the beginnings of a substantial public works program, a recognition of the legitimacy of the trade-union movement, a certain encouragement of oligopoly in various industries, and a feeling on the part of the populace that something was being done. The shrieks of "dictatorship" from the right and "Fascism" from the left only contributed to the diminution of influence of these ideologues. How could any sane person believe that this dynamic, joyous leader (who ever thought of *him* as a cripple?), with the great booming laugh and obvious dedication to the welfare of *individual* Americans, could lead the nation into slavery? Unlike a number of reformers, who like people in the abstract but not on the beach, Roosevelt conveyed to the average citizen his personal warmth. He had in him nothing of the inquisitor. If he lacked the moral fervor of a Wilson, he also lacked the latter's greatest liability, his ruthless commitment to abstractions which made him quite capable of sacrificing liberty in the name of Liberty. What other crisis leader has ever called upon his constituents to "laugh, live and love"—and clearly meant it?

(An irrelevance, perhaps, but in midsummer 1936 a New York family was driving wearily up Route 9 in a coffin-like 1929 Buick which overheated every ten miles or so. The driver, my father, who had been semi-employed for three years, was taking his family to its first vacation since God knows when with a great-aunt near Albany, but at Hyde Park the car was ordered to the side of the road by police. The President and Mrs. Roosevelt were about to drive by en route to a wedding [Ruth Bryan Owen's, I now realize], and we sat in the heat and waited. Suddenly the caravan swept into sight, F.D.R. and Eleanor in the back of a huge open car with Secret Service men hanging on the running boards. My father, a dogged egalitarian, leaned on the horn as they passed, and, while the Secret Service guards looked unsettled, the President and his wife looked over, waved, and smiled *at us*. They didn't just smile in the perfunctory political manner—*they waved and smiled at us*. There was something exhilarating about it. And I remember my father's brutally unfair but nonetheless symbolic remark: "Hoover would arrest you for that.")

It is hard to find an appropriate category for F.D.R. Much that has been said here might suggest that he was merely a master of the politician's trade, a champion broker totally lacking in any fundamental theoretical purposes. It surely is the case that no coherent ideological position emerged as the core of the New Deal, and it is equally true that the President on many occasions acted like a man without a rudder. He was a superb manipulator— Harold Ickes wrote a huge diary which in its published form shows its author to have been unknowingly an almost perfect patsy,[12] and Raymond Moley's "sour grapes of wrath" (to use Clinton Rossiter's neat phrase) are a vivid description of a naïf in the hands of a master.[13] He could be sly, dishonest, disingenuous, disloyal, and ruthless—a very rough customer to deal with. And there is a library full of books criticizing his administrative and policy-making talents.

Yet at base there was something very important there, particularly in terms of the framework of this book. It is beside the point to say that Roosevelt "played by ear"—so did Vladimir I. Lenin, one of the world's greatest improvisers. The crucial question is *what* did he play by ear? Take, for example, nationalism. Throughout the centuries, hard-pressed leaders have attempted to divert public attention from domestic crisis by external adventures, and "making the eagle scream" was not an unknown technique in American politics. (Secretary of State Seward calmly suggested to President Lincoln in the spring of 1861 that a nice war with England would solve the crisis of secession.[14]) Elaborate military preparations were also a useful antidote for unemployment. But Roosevelt until the very eve of the war (some would say with undue caution) never beat the drum. Military expenditures under Hoover in 1932 amounted to $702,000,000 in a total expenditure of $4,266,000,000; they dropped to $541,000,000 in 1934; and by *1940* had only reached $1,567,000,000 in a total of $10,000,000,000.[15]

More important for our purposes, what about the quest for scapegoats, for the enemy within on whose shoulders could be placed all the blame for the horrendous events that had, almost overnight, knocked the United States from peaks of prosperity to the pit of depression and despair? As we have seen, there was no necessary shortage of candidates, and one hesitates to imagine what might have ensued had Roosevelt turned his magnificent speaking talent to the cause of demagoguery. The 1920's had demonstrated that there was plenty of dynamite lying around in the best of times, and the Depression hardly lengthened the fuse; but the President ignored what would have been to another the tempting recourse to "class warfare," or to singling out some religious or ethnic minority for damnation. Indeed, he resolutely moved in the other direction, calling for national unity in such comprehensive terms that faithful Democrats began to fear that their seniority in merit would be overlooked.

True (like his cousin Theodore), he was capable of fearsome rhetoric on occasion, notably against "economic royalists." But even then the enemy was abstract, and the leaders of the business community were in no way hindered in their ferocious campaign against F.D.R. by his generalized anathemas. Indeed, in retrospect it is hard to understand why the organized business community hated Roosevelt so. The New Deal was not in any *tangible* sense "anti-business," and it did not lead to a radical redistribution of national income. In 1932, the top 5 percent of the total population received 32.99 percent of national income; in 1936, this fell to 28.82 percent, a drop which hardly justified the howls of "Bolshevism." [16] The Socialists were in a sense correct when they claimed that Roosevelt had preserved the structure of capitalism, but what they failed to realize—and the President's great crime in the eyes of the Chamber of Commerce—was that he had destroyed the mythology of the business community, at least for a generation. You can do a great many things to a man if you leave his myths alone, but when you undermine his self-image—even if it costs him nothing in economic terms—the result is an implacable enemy. Roosevelt never took business myths seriously; when the magnates talked solemnly about "business principles in government," he simply chuckled like a biology teacher hearing from children that storks bring babies. For this desecration of the temple, he was never forgiven. I doubt if he could have been more despised had he actually put the members of the National Association of Manufacturers before firing squads.

What this amounts to is a different Roosevelt than the one usually depicted by his admirers or denigrated by his foes. The former acclaim his "boldness," and the latter denounce his "rashness"; but in fact Franklin D. Roosevelt was neither bold nor rash *in policy terms* (a bold/rash President would surely have nationalized the banks in 1933) but infuriatingly cautious, empirical, and circumspect. It was his rhetoric which conveyed the image of iconoclasm and daring; Roosevelt could make climbing a hill in Central Park seem like the conquest of Everest. He never considered himself to be a radical or innovator. The task before Americans, he said on June 8, 1934, "does not require the creation of new and strange values. It is rather the finding of the way once more to known, but to some degree forgotten, ideals and values." [17] To employ a more conceptual formula than he ever articulated, F.D.R. saw his role as that of the mediator between the best traditions of the "old order" and the aspirations of the new society. This, he sensed, called for plenty of slack, and a great deal of experimentation; above all, it required a low-pressure ideological atmosphere. It is a political commonplace that once ideological lines are clearly drawn, all policy questions, no matter how trivial, become a source of controversy. (For example, big planters in Louisiana refused to admit the 1860 census takers to their demesnes on the ground that if the federal government could *count* slaves, it might claim the power to *regulate* slavery!) Roosevelt kept the pressure down by refusing to define his program except in open-ended terms, by incorporating measures which seemed to fulfill the hopes of all significant groups in the community, and perhaps most importantly by repudiating "gallows politics." Even his most bitter opponents realized that Roosevelt was incapable of shooting his enemies, that he was committed to the ground rules of freedom.

"Second-class intellect," said Holmes, "but a first-class temperament!" The temperament, we might add, of a superb mediator and conciliator who, unhindered by intellectual commitments to precision and efficiency, untroubled by the "logical consequences" of his actions, rushed from one problem to another with an endless supply of *ad hoc* remedies. Some were excellent, some were passable, some were absurd. But underlying this whole random technique there was hidden away a vital and invigorating major premise: that he was as President responsible for the welfare of the whole community, not just one segment of it, and that the way out of the perils and hardships of the Depression could be discerned by the democratic process. This might be a thoroughly inefficient way of doing business, money might be wasted on abortive schemes, but the most precious possession of the American people, its freedom, would not be risked in the effort to find a historical shortcut. In sum, Roosevelt never pretended to supernal wisdom, never was deluded that he had been vouchsafed a Vision which would justify suppression of Evil opponents. When he was asked his philosophy, the President observed in somewhat puzzled fashion that he was just a "Christian" and a "democrat" and let it go at that.[18] This naïvete brought cackles of sardonic laughter from the cognoscenti, but in fact it was a pretty good combination. These were precisely the values which first nourished the American ideal, which provided the substance of the American Dream.

Under Roosevelt's auspices, the atmosphere in Washington changed radically. Politics, which had been considered a dull enterprise, the running of a political business, suddenly attained a new luster, assumed once again the high reputation it had held among the ancients, where the word "idiot" had been coined to describe a nonparticipant in the affairs of the community. Throughout the United States able young men, who a decade previous would have gone "into bonds," or humbly accepted an apprenticeship at the bottom of a great law firm, headed for the nation's capital to help build the new society. Felix Frankfurter was famous as the intermediary between Harvard Law School and government agencies, but he was not alone in his employment services. A new vitality permeated the rapidly increasing administration as the representatives of the "old order" found themselves inundated by the enthusiastic new arrivals. There was a good deal of resulting disorder: if the new civil servants shared the President's *joie de vivre*, they also tended to imitate his administrative pluralism. Moley relates that the President once assigned the same task to five separate individuals and was appalled when on the appointed day five different memoranda turned up. F.D.R.'s reaction was characteristic: he directed that the five be put in a room and told to emerge with one proposal![19] The Republicans denounced the wastefulness of New Deal administration and trembled as the nation went in for deficit financing. The national debt rose from almost twenty billion in 1932 to forty-three billion in 1940, giving Republicans and conservative Democrats a frightful feeling that we were going bankrupt, that creditors might appear at any time to evict us from the country. However, when it rose to *two hundred billion* dollars during the war, few complaints were heard. Fighting Germans and Japanese was in a different category from warring on hunger, disease, and unemployment. The G.O.P. also fired off salvos at the New Deal "radicals," suggesting that Washington was filling up with Socialists, statists, collectivists, and un-catalogued crackpots.

Eric F. Goldman has suggested, correctly I think, that the problem with the New Dealers was not an excess of ideology, but an insufficiency.[20] Reform became identified with experimentation; tinkering with the machine became a substitute for political theory. I have argued that Roosevelt's distaste for ideological clarity was objectively one of his strong advantages in his role as President, but it is something else again to institutionalize improvisation throughout a huge administrative structure. For one thing, it was in the narrow sense inefficient and sloppy, but far more significantly this absence of a coherent *telos*—a sense of direction—made the New Deal merely F.D.R.'s shadow. To put it differently, American liberalism became a by-product of Roosevelt's charisma rather than a solid package of ideas and programs. This provided enormous strength while he lived, but when he died the dynamic went out of liberalism, and Washington became a place populated by high policy makers who substituted pilgrimages to F.D.R.'s grave for independent thought.

Let me make clear the fact that I am not trying to have it both ways. In the descriptive sense, I have suggested, Roosevelt's existential liberalism was extremely important to his function as a catalyst of community, as a conciliator. However, at the same time, these mediative talents raised great barriers to the development of a coherent, modern liberal political theory (or, for that matter, a conservative political theory: conservatives too find F.D.R. firmly planted across their route to the past, strangely resembling Edmund Burke's ideal of the statesman). We have, in short, had to pay for Roosevelt's protean capacities, and there are many liberals who think the bill came too high. Weighing all the factors involved, and observing the alternative political forms that elsewhere have emerged from the vortex of industrialization, I do not think the bill excessive.

Moreover, while the New Deal did not incorporate any set of substantive principles (some agencies were run by bucolic Progressives of 1912 vintage, others by Dewey-eyed pragmatists, still others by quasi-Socialist collectivists), it did carry into office what might be described as a *procedural* syndrome. All groups in the community had the right to be full participants in the process of experimentation, and relations among these groups and between these groups and the sovereign were to be conducted decently, i.e., in a gentlemanly fashion. In the jargon of the law schools, this notion of decency and fair play is designated as procedural due process.

The concept of procedural due process is central to the development of civil liberties in modern America, and broadly construed it also supplies the lubrication for decent intergroup relationships. Although procedural due process begins as the institutionalization of certain techniques, it rapidly moves beyond mere procedures into the realm of atmosphere. Starting as an emphasis on procedural regularity, it soon intrudes into fundamental substantive matters which the British call the principles of "natural justice." Leo Frank, for example, had all the procedural lineaments of a fair trial—judge, jury, appeals—but, as Justice Holmes suggested, he was in fact lynched under color of law. Consequently, a necessary precondition for the proper utilization of procedures is a climate of opinion which takes these procedures seriously. (It is probably a truism to say that decent social relations depend on an atmosphere of decency, but an outstanding aspect of truisms is their truth.) Both the federal government and the states had plenty of procedural safeguards against injustice incorporated in bills of rights and criminal codes, and in the great bulk of "nonsensitive" cases these undoubtedly gave considerable security to the defendant. Unfortunately, cases dealing with the rights of unpopular minorities usually fell in the "sensitive" sector of litigation where the general rule was "no holds barred." (There is the perhaps apocryphal story of a Wobbly who in 1918 deliberately committed a burglary and got caught so he "would be sure to get a fair trial.")

Under the New Deal, there occurred a basic shift in the climate of opinion (the actions of government obviously play a vital, if not a decisive part in shaping the juridical atmosphere) toward universalizing due process, i.e., toward expanding the sector of "decency" to include matters previously in the "sensitive" areas. This took place on two levels: legal and institutional. On the first, the Supreme Court, followed by other tribunals, expanded the protection of the Constitution to individuals and groups theretofore left to the tender mercies of their neighbors. On the second, the President and Congress welcomed into the community as equal participants segments of the population which had previously worn the bar sinister, or if not treated as illegitimate, were at best considered marginal elements in American life. Space limitations make it impossible here to deal extensively with this twofold expansion, but we can look in some detail at examples of each.

The broadening of the constitutional guarantee of due process of law began, as was indicated in the last chapter, about 1925, but it was not until 1931 that the Supreme Court *overruled* a state conviction as violative of fundamental liberty. This it did in two important cases: *Stromberg* v. *California* and *Near* v. *Minnesota*, involving respectively a Communist and an anti-Semite who had fallen afoul of the law. Yetta Stromberg ran a summer camp for young Communists where the day began with a flag salute and pledge of allegiance—to the emblem of Soviet Russia—and the environment was resplendent with liturgical trappings: oleographs of the saints (Marx, Lenin, Stalin) and canonical writings (*Capital, State and Revolution, Problems of Leninism*). California convicted Miss Stromberg under a statute which punished as felonious displaying a red flag "as a sign, symbol or emblem of opposition to organized government," "an invitation or stimulus to anarchistic action," or to aid "propaganda that is of a seditious character."

There was a certain amount of confusion as to what role the flag was supposed to play at Stromberg's camp: surely no one running a camp for children between ten and fifteen encourages "anarchistic action," and the Soviet flag, as Chief Justice Hughes later pointed out, was hardly a symbol of opposition to "organized government." But California did not trouble itself with specifics: the jury said "guilty" and let it go at that.

The Supreme Court, seven Justices concurring, held the California law void for vagueness. "A statute," said Chief Justice Hughes, "which upon its face, and as authoritatively construed, is so vague and indefinite as to permit the punishment of the fair use of [free political discussion] is repugnant to the guaranty of liberty contained in the Fourteenth Amendment." This was, as Justice Butler noted in dissent, a curious approach to the problem since it equated flying a flag with giving a speech: the red flag was treated by the Chief Justice as a symbol of radical opinion which, in the absence of evidence to the contrary, must be construed as peaceful and lawful in its thrust. Red flags had in many states been treated as the outward and visible manifestations of subversion and sedition; while Hughes did not block off the prosecution of subversion and sedition, he made it clear that the sign could no longer be employed as conclusive evidence of criminal intent.[21]

Near v. *Minnesota,* ironically, coped with the civil rights of a notorious anti-Semite who had been publishing a vicious smear sheet in Minneapolis. Minnesota had on its books a form of censorship of obscene and defamatory publications employing an injunctive remedy: Near was enjoined by a state court to cease publishing the *Saturday Press* on the ground that it was a malicious, scandalous, and defamatory public nuisance. Thus the "Minnesota Gag Law" put a permanent padlock on the *Saturday Press,* and, if Near persisted in publishing, he could be summarily punished for contempt of court. Again the Chief Justice invoked the Fourteenth Amendment, ruling that this provision deprived Near of freedom of the press, of liberty to publish even malicious and defamatory opinion *without prior restraint.* He could, of course, be sued for libel *after* publication. The decision was close, 5–4, but it broke a new path: freedom of the press was withdrawn to some considerable degree from the restraints of local authorities.[22]

In 1936, this principle was reaffirmed in a clearer context: Huey Long devised a singularly ingenious penalty for newspaper opponents of his regime. A 2-percent gross receipts tax was levied on all commercial publications in the state of Louisiana with weekly circulations over 20,000—a figure which was chosen carefully as the line of demarcation between the small papers which supported Long and the big ones in New Orleans which opposed him. Long's attorneys maintained with straight faces that this was merely a nondiscriminatory tax which hit alike all those similarly situated (a state can tax big cars more heavily than small cars, but all big cars must be treated on the same basis; there cannot be discrimination *within* a category). The Supreme Court was, however, in no mood for sophistry of this sort. The Justices recognized dirty pool when they saw it and unanimously threw out the Louisiana tax on the ground that it was not really a tax but a restraint in the "guise of a tax to limit the circulation of information to which the public is entitled" by the Constitutional guarantee of freedom of the press. "A free press," declared Justice Sutherland, "stands as one of the great interpreters between the government and the people. To allow it to be fettered is to fetter ourselves." [23] A fourth important case in this genre found Hughes declaring void on its face a municipal ordinance forbidding the distribution of literature without permission which had been enforced against the Jehovah's Witnesses. Pamphlets and leaflets, said Hughes, "have been historic weapons in the defense of liberty." [24]

Two further decisions should suffice to indicate the new direction of the High Court; the first concerned a Negro Communist caught in the toils of a Georgia law originally drawn to penalize slave revolts. From the time of the Sixth Comintern Congress in 1928, the American Communist Party had been imprisoned in a program which removed its advocates from the political universe as effectively as if they had taken monastic vows.[25] F.D.R. was a "Fascist," Norman Thomas and the leaders of the labor movement were "social Fascists," and the American Negro was a "national minority" in the specifically Stalinist sense; i.e., like the Armenian, the Khazak, or the Ukrainian of the U.S.S.R., the Negro was visualized as a member of an authentic "national" culture. The solution to the Negro problem which Stalin imposed on the American Communists was the creation of a "Black Republic" where the Negroes would enjoy their own culture and exercise political sovereignty. This was madness, but by 1928 Stalin was boss. The American Communists obediently set to work, and shortly pamphlets appeared with a map of the South showing exactly where the "Black Republic" would lie.[26] (The contemporary Black Muslims seem to espouse the same notion, but have not yet provided a map.)

Now the key proposition about the American Negro so far as the relevance of this program was concerned was that slavery stripped him of his authentic culture. Perhaps a few African chants, some words of patois, a style of dress lingered on here and there in isolated areas of Negro settlement, but there was no foundation for a "national culture" in the sense of the Soviet nationalities policy. Moreover, the Communist policy of "red crow" ran head on into the major demands of the Negro intelligentsia: integration and equality. Thus the Stalinists were forced to denounce as "racial traitors," "bourgeois reformists," and "lackeys of Yankee imperialism" the leading Negro spokesmen of the era. The net result was an almost total indifference to Communism among the Negroes, but this did not prevent the state of Georgia from arresting Angelo Herndon, one of the Communist Party's few Negro cadres, for incitement to insurrection when in 1934 he appeared in Atlanta with literature advocating the "Black Republic."

Herndon could have been sentenced to death, but the jury—perhaps in view of the fact that no evidence was presented to indicate that he had distributed the subversive documents—recommended mercy: he was only sentenced to 18–20 years at hard labor. After much legal maneuvering, Herndon got his case before the Supreme Court, and by a vote of 5–4 the Justices threw out the Georgia conviction. Justice Roberts, obviously outraged by the litigation, declared that the statute "as construed and applied [to Herndon] does not furnish a sufficiently ascertainable standard of guilt," but amounted "merely to a dragnet which may enmesh any-one who agitates for a change of government if a jury can be persuaded that" he constituted a potential threat. It was a narrow holding, but wide enough to get Herndon off and to warn the states that the days of shotgun indictments under broad, vague statutes were numbered.[27]

The final decisions for consideration here dealt with a different type of civil right, but the same fundamental issue: the "fairness" of state criminal procedures. They provide a vivid contrast to the Frank case. The "Scottsboro Boys" were once as well known as Sacco and Vanzetti had been a decade earlier. In both cases the Communists and their civil rights front organization, the International Labor Defense, turned obscure criminal trials into world-wide *causes célèbres*—angry crowds marched on American embassies, distinguished intellectuals signed petitions, and considerable sums of money were raised for Communist purposes. In 1931, nine young Negroes were convicted of rape in Scottsboro, Alabama, on the evidence of two white girls of questionable reputations with whom they had shared a gondola car on a slow freight train. After one-day trials in a lynch atmosphere, eight were sentenced to death. National guardsmen were employed to protect them from summary execution by an inflamed mob.

Then began a course of litigation which before it concluded involved two Supreme Court decisions, *four* trials for some of the defendants, a savage struggle inside the defense movement between the NAACP (which labored to get the "boys" acquitted) and the I.L.D. (which utilized their convictions to pillory American justice, raise money, and build a Communist constituency among the Negroes), and finally an extradition proceeding in Michigan in 1950—Patterson, who at his fourth trial had been sentenced to 75 years on the chain gang, escaped and was arrested by the FBI in Detroit, but the Governor of Michigan refused to grant extradition. The case, again like Sacco-Vanzetti, triggered a series of books by various participants and an enormous amount of controversy and recrimination.[28]

Our concern, however, is with the two trips that the Scottsboro litigation took to the Supreme Court. In the first, *Powell* v. *Ala-*

bama, the Justices determined, 7–2, that the defendants had been denied a fair trial because they had not really had the aid of counsel. True, the trial judge had appointed lawyers to assist them, but said Justice Sutherland, this was a meaningless gesture: "the defendants, young, ignorant, illiterate, surrounded by hostile sentiment, haled back and forth under guard of soldiers, charged with an atrocious crime . . . were thus put in peril of their lives within a few moments after counsel for the first time . . . began to represent them." The Court, in other words, insisted on looking behind the externals to the basic conditions under which the trial occurred.[29] This was 1932. Three years later, the "Scottsboro Boys" were back before the Court in *Norris* v. *Alabama* claiming they had been again denied a fair trial because Negroes had been excluded from the jury panels in Alabama. The Court unanimously reversed the conviction, holding that the complete absence of Negroes from jury panels in Morgan County, in the memory of living man, established a *prima facie* case for discrimination. Both decisions became landmarks in the development of criminal due process.[30]

It is worth emphasizing that all these Supreme Court decisions took place *before* F.D.R. had the opportunity to appoint a single Justice. These notable cases were decided by "nine old men" under the leadership of that singular spokesman of the "old order," Charles Evans Hughes. We have already seen Hughes dissenting with Holmes in the Frank case and defending the rights of the New York Socialist Assemblymen. Austere, conservative in the best sense of that much abused word, a superb administrator and a consummate politician (he masterminded Roosevelt's worst New Deal defeat, the "Court Packing Bill" of 1937),[31] Hughes as Chief Justice of the United States succeeded in building a Court majority behind vital, and theretofore ignored, principles of civil liberty. (I have often suspected that his defeat by Wilson in 1916 deprived the nation of a President who could have played a powerful role in bridging the old and the new, in assimilating the emerging realities with the enlightened inheritance of urban Progressivism and urbane Republicanism.) At any rate, the Court, with

Hughes playing the key role, demonstrated an increasing sensitivity to those issues of civil liberty which were part of the New Deal temper: due process of law in the area of *human* rights became an active ingredient of American constitutionalism.

We will return to the judicial forum in a later chapter to examine the amplification of the civil liberties tradition by the "Roosevelt Court." Now, however, we must leave the legal environs and turn to a different level of development—to the role of the New Deal in broadening the political community to include groups which had been denied their rightful place by the obsessively business-oriented, and eventually self-destructive, convictions of the "old order." In the next chapter, we will look in some detail at the changes that took place in the status of ethnic and religious minority groups during the "Age of Roosevelt"; let us conclude this section with an examination of the legitimation of the trade-union movement.

Organized trade unionism just about made it through the 1920's and was confronted by the Great Depression at a time when the unions were pretty thoroughly shell-shocked by the mauling they had taken during Prosperity. The American Federation of Labor was clearly lacking in dynamism, but only an uncompassionate critic can justifiably sneer at the record of the AFL. Too often those who excoriate the "unimaginative leadership" and lack of "militance" of the labor movement in this period overlook the character of the conflict the unions had been engaged in. A battalion which has been desperately holding a defensive perimeter against a division with heavy artillery is unlikely to launch a militant bayonet charge. Indeed, after undergoing prolonged siege, it is likely to forget the techniques of offensive warfare entirely; the minute an enemy is sighted, it digs in. By the end of the 1920's, the solid old proletarians of the AFL Executive Council were in no mood for adventures. They had witnessed the total defeat of the well-organized and powerful British unions in the 1926 General Strike, and had reason to congratulate themselves for surviving the crushing offensive that American employers had launched in the name of the "open shop." They were, in short, suffering from what might be described as an armadillo complex.

The Communists, Socialists, and other radicals bitterly criticized the AFL for its inertia, particularly for its reluctance to stimulate organizing drives in the heavy industrial sector, and accused the leadership of being wedded to the conservative principles of craft unionism, of building unions only among the skilled "labor aristocracy." Now several of the largest unions in the Federation were established on industrial principles—the United Mine Workers, the Brewery Workers, the Machinists, the International Ladies Garment Workers Union, for instance, took in all workers in their trades irrespective of speciality—but in strategic terms an industrial union is the most difficult to organize. The unskilled and semiskilled workers of the great industries are for one thing the least capable economically of staying off the job; for another, because they are easily replaceable, they are obviously the most vulnerable to strikebreaking. (In contrast, it is very difficult to find qualified men to replace striking plumbers.) Thus, to launch an effective organizing campaign in, say, the steel industry is a logistic undertaking of the first order—and it had been tried in 1919 when, despite superb leadership from John Fitzpatrick and William Z. Foster and the loyalty of over three hundred thousand strikers, the victory went to the steel masters and their "scabs."

In hard, antiunion times then, craft unionism became the Main Line of Resistance, and the AFL leadership was undoubtedly both battle-weary and pessimistic: whenever a dynamic leader would call for a vigorous new offensive, they rubbed their scars and dragged their heels. They were particularly suspicious of the radicals. The Communists and Socialists had the habit, from time to time, of establishing dual unions which were ideologically pure, but, in the view of the AFL magnates, split the workers and aided the bosses. Part of the Comintern line from 1928–34 was the creation of dual unions, and the American Communists organized, under Foster's leadership, the Trade Union Unity League which set up splinter unions in half a dozen areas.[32] When it is recalled that typically trade unions waxed in times of prosperity and waned in times of economic distress, the AFL Executive Council had little reason for optimism in 1932 when there were at least 12,000-000 (and perhaps as many as 15,000,000) unemployed workers. United States Steel, for example, had, in 1929, 224,980 full-time employees, but this figure had dropped to 18,938 by the end of 1932, and by April 1, 1933, all of Big Steel's employees were on part-time, and the total of part-time workers was half the full-time work force in 1929.[33] A worker was glad to have any job at all, and he realized that there were plenty of candidates for his spot if he should get on the wrong side of the foreman.

It seems quite obvious now that the transformation in the status of the American worker could not have been accomplished by the unions alone—that state intervention on behalf of the labor movement was an essential prerequisite for success—but the AFL was extremely reluctant to call for help. Samuel Gompers had left a rigid dogma of "voluntarism" as his bequest to the AFL; i.e., he maintained that the political objective of the labor movement was to obtain a neutral state which would permit labor to fight it out with management and win its own way. Although this had an individualistic ring about it, the doctrine seems to have been a reflection of Gompers' residual Marxism, an inheritance from Marx's fierce polemic with the Lassallean "state Socialists." Gompers similarly opposed antitrust legislation as a futile effort to halt the concentration of capital, a reactionary attempt to frustrate historical imperatives.[34] After Gompers' death, the AFL began to modify the voluntaristic philosophy somewhat, but, until the Cincinnati convention in late 1932, the organization was on record *against* state programs of unemployment compensation! [35] Voluntarism probably reached its high point with the passage of the Norris-LaGuardia Act in 1932, which effectively outlawed the labor injunction but in no positive way aided the unions to reach their goal.[36] However, the AFL got little solace from this belated gift: unemployment was hindering organization more fundamentally than injunctions.

When Roosevelt assumed office in 1933, it is fair to say the American worker was excluded from the public interest. Roosevelt and his supporters did not change this by inventing the "welfare state"—every state is by definition a "welfare state"; i.e., its decisions and actions contribute to the welfare of *some* of its citizens —but by enlarging the public interest to include the welfare of the worker. Perhaps it is worth remembering that in 1929, before the bust, over 50 percent of the American industrial work force put in more than 48 hours a week.[37] There was no minimum wage law. There was no public system of social security, and few private corporations had established retirement systems for their workers. There was no unemployment compensation; when the unemployed had run through their savings, they could go on the "dole," on public relief which was in most areas of the nation still patterned on the Elizabethan Poor Laws (there was a degrading means test, loss of voting rights, and similar punishments for sinful behavior). Essentially the unemployed or aged worker was dealt with by precapitalistic standards designed to cope with marginal vagabondage in a rural society; the steelworker idled by impersonal economic forces far beyond his understanding, let alone control, was punished in Tudor terms as a "sturdy beggar." This was hard enough to take, but in fact the machinery of public relief simply collapsed under the burdens of the Depression. The city of Detroit, for example, "was the focal point of 70 percent of the unemployment that gripped the state. In 1933 one-third of the wage earners of Michigan had been partly or totally unemployed for four years in succession. When the depression was only two years old, the army of 211,000 dependents on Detroit's relief rolls was equal in size to the entire population of Grand Rapids. An additional 150,000 persons had fled Detroit, trekking to the homes of relatives, . . . to the South, or back to the farm."[38] Only the federal government could mobilize the resources necessary to meet this crisis.

What the New Deal did is, of course, now ancient history. The National Labor Relations Act, the Social Security Act, the Fair Labor Standards Act (which in passing eliminated child labor) were the keystones in the structure, but perhaps as important as the statutes themselves was the type of person who was assigned to enforce and implement them. While a certain number of jobs in these agencies were passed out as political plums, the administrative backbone was provided by civil servants who were firmly committed to the policy objectives of the legislation. The staff of the National Labor Relations Board was prolabor. They saw the statute as a historical redressing of the rightful grievances of the American worker and acted accordingly. The result of this government intervention in favor of organized labor, which began with Section 7a of the National Industrial Recovery Act of 1933 and the slogan "Mr. Roosevelt wants you to join the Union," was a profound alteration in the character of the American labor movement. Voluntarism went by the boards, and when the armadillos on the AFL Executive Council refused to seize the opportunity presented by the change in government attitude, the CIO rushed to fill the vacuum, and soon penetrated the inner fortresses of heavy industry.[39]

The turmoil of organization, the great strikes on the West Coast in 1934, in steel, rubber, automobiles in the mid-thirties, frightened the business community to the brink of despair: the revolution was underway. In the name of the free enterprise system, they called for state action to suppress these trespassers on the labor market, these subversives who were transforming labor from a commodity to a vocation. But the injunctions no longer materialized, the Coal and Iron Police were demobilized in disgrace, the La Follette Committee exposed to the nation the techniques of repression which management had utilized to forestall unionization, and the National Guard could no longer be depended upon. Ironically, the power of the "rugged individualists" had rested at base on the much despised state—*their* welfare state which had protected their interests in the name of the commonweal. So, with a good deal of old-fashioned random American violence but with no revolutionary impetus, the shift in power continued. What the frightened reactionaries had taken for revolution was—in Mr. Dooley's famous phrase—merely the American people "beatin' the rug."

From the long view, what had taken place under F.D.R.'s (curiously reluctant) [40] auspices was the reconciliation of the industrial work force, the admission of the American worker to full membership in the society. While the trade unions played an important part in this process, the decisive consideration was the enlargement of the welfare state to incorporate the interests of the workers. (Similar action was taken with regard to the farmers in the first and second Agricultural Adjustment Acts.) While it has now become fashionable to carp at the trade unions and to expatiate on the worker's lack of interest in his union, it should be kept in mind that this very lack of militance, of "working-class consciousness," is a function of the success of the New Deal. The American worker, whatever may be his legitimate (or illegitimate) claims on the community, recognizes that he is involved in the decision-making process. He may win today, and perhaps lose tomorrow, but he realizes that win, lose, or draw, the dispute will continue within the framework of American ideals. The dice are not loaded against him.

Perhaps a contrast will help convey this difficult but vital proposition. If one visits among French industrial workers, he soon gets the feeling that he is moving in a strange world: an alienated working-class enclave which occupies certain sections of France and looks with hatred, disgust, and contempt upon the ruling elite, the bourgeois parties, and the whole political process. It votes Communist as a symbol of this alienation, though in fact there are few ideological Communists—not enough to support a daily paper. The French worker justifiably feels that he is a stranger, an outsider, whose interests play only a remote role in the formulation of public policy. His militance has been numbed by perpetual defeat, but he waits, glowers, and nurses his historical grievances.

The attitude of the American worker, despite his inability fully to attain many of his legitimate objectives, is radically different: he no longer feels excluded from the councils of the community. (Perhaps the title of a union song, popular in CIO organizing drives in the late thirties, put the matter most succinctly: "I Ain't

No Stranger Now.") To state it in more sophisticated fashion, the American worker became in the course of the Roosevelt years a fully accredited citizen, a conscious participant in the movement toward the implementation of the American Dream.

VII

THE DECLINE
AND FALL OF
THE YAHOOS (*1933-1941*)

The Roosevelt who emerges from these pages differs a good deal from the President as usually portrayed by New Deal epigones. F.D.R. was not, I submit, a "liberal" in the usual ideological sense of the term. He was not the militant exponent of a coherent liberal program, and, indeed, his instinctive distaste for theory put him far closer to the traditional conservative ideal of a statesman. Yet, if his intellectual commitments were traditional, his temperament was vigorously experimental. (In a curious way, he was the obverse of President Kennedy who is intellectually liberal but temperamentally conservative.) And everything he touched quivered with osmotic vitality, frightening to death those who confuse movement with revolution. In the early years of the New Deal, there were actually "Roosevelt Refugees," wealthy businessmen who fled from "Bolshevism" and the impending terror to Cap d'Antibes, Majorca, and other insulated climes.

Thus F.D.R. was perhaps loved as much for the enemies he made as for the policies he implemented. In the early 1960's, when businessmen have returned to a state of political grace, it is almost impossible to convey—except to those who experienced it—the virulent skepticism of business which dominated the mood of the American people during the Great Depression. It would, for example, have been impossible for a Nelson *Rockefeller*—however great his talents—to run for Governor of New York, much less win election. A candidate who boasted of his business experience as a qualification for office would have been hooted off the hustings. This was an understandable swing of the pendulum: businessmen had capitalized on their popularity during the era of prosperity and had to take the consequences when their formulae brought, or seemed to bring, national disaster.

Throughout the Western world, this widespread disillusionment with capitalism led to the growth of extremist movements. Some were left wing in orientation, others adhered to the classic pattern of right-wing military dictatorship, while the most potent utilized the historic appeals of the "left" to attain a new variety of state: totalitarian Fascism. What set Fascism apart from traditional authoritarianism was its mass base; the military junta built its power on a narrow elite, but the Fascists brought "the masses" into politics with a vengeance, and by demagoguery and police techniques channeled political alienation into an advantage for the ruling party. All three types of political extremism shared one fundamental concept: they denied the legitimacy and the utility of democratic methods of social and political change. In the tragic fall of the German Republic, all three segments—Communists, old-line authoritarians, and Nazis—played a role, and the unstable democratic center was unable to resist such a potent united assault.[1] In February, 1934, France narrowly escaped a similar fate when Premier Daladier turned machine guns on a composite Communist-Fascist mob attempting to storm the Chamber of Deputies.[2]

In these same years, the United States was undergoing its first great economic crisis, and it is hardly necessary to indicate that political extremism was an active American heritage. There were millions of ex-Klansmen around, awaiting the burning cross; civil war had been averted in the farm states only by effectively destroying the right of creditors to foreclose mortgages; anti-Semites longed to revive the faked *Protocols* (which, in their hatred, they just *knew* the Jews had blackmailed Ford into repudiating); and millions more nursed their memories of the holy war of 1928. In November, 1932, the American people turned out Hoover and the Republicans and put Roosevelt in office, but this could have been a finale rather than a beginning. The extremists were waiting in the wings as the new President assumed the responsibilities of coping with the virtual collapse of the national economy. Elsewhere the collapse of the economic order had all too often led to the destruction of the political system which was its concomitant; it remained to be seen whether Franklin D. Roosevelt, who had been described in January, 1932, by Walter Lippmann as a "pleasant man, who, without any important qualifications for the office, would very much like to be President," [3] could master the crisis, and adapt traditional American institutions to the imperatives of a new epoch.

To do this successfully, the President had to conduct a two-front war. On the one hand, he had to deal effectively on the political level with the rampant extremists; on the other, he had to establish the infrastructure of the modern state, the administrative apparatus which could at least begin to deal with the problems arising from a complex industrial economy and an increasing pattern of urbanization. (Between 1920 and 1930, the population of the continental United States increased seventeen million, the urban sector as a whole increased by *fifteen* million, and the increase in cities of over a hundred thousand was nine million.) [4] In the last chapter, we examined the New Deal and Franklin D. Roosevelt from the viewpoint of a historical astronaut. Here we are concerned with developments at ground level, and developments which were extraordinarily important in the growth of a healthy community and in the implementation of civil liberty.

Let us turn first to the containment and eventual defeat of the Yahoos, the extremist movements of a quasi-Fascist character which seemed to many observers to be sweeping the nation in the early Roosevelt years. Then we can examine the *character* of the state which gradually emerged under Roosevelt's ministrations to discover the extent to which this new Leviathan, rather than enslaving the people, contributed positively to the growth of a tradition of due process of law and of substantive freedom.

Since this is not a history of political extremism in the 1930's—a book which has yet to be written—we can for convenience concentrate on the Yahoos major and consign the Yahoos minor to the oblivion which they merit. (There are always uncounted one-man movements flooding the mails with eccentric tracts, but they can safely be left to the attention of psychiatrists and postal inspectors.) Moreover, it should be noted that there were curious amalgams sprouting in various parts of the nation, organizations which defy categorization. A movement like "New America" which called for the application of the technocratic principle to politics had distinctly elitist tendencies despite its formulation of traditional radical goals—the achievement of "Socialism" was a job for trained "social engineers." [5] Upton Sinclair's famed crusade to End Poverty in California (EPIC) in 1934 had strong overtones of elitism, and how does one evaluate Sinclair's suggestion that "farmer-Fascists" and "vigilantes" be prosecuted under California's antisyndicalism statute? [6] But however idiosyncratic, both "New America" and "EPIC" fall outside the extremist rubric because of their fundamental recognition of the legitimacy of the democratic process.

Among the Yahoos major, two were clearly outstanding: Huey Long and Father Charles Coughlin. Interestingly enough, they represented two distinct types of extremist appeal. Long, "a moral idiot of genius," [7] was an ideological gangster who in his own homegrown fashion converted Louisiana politics into something which approximated Latin Fascism. Father Coughlin, on the other hand, concocted a strange nostrum, but from traditional components: the "funny-money" dreams of the old Populists and Greenbackers, the anticapitalist encyclicals of Popes Leo XIII and Pius XI, isolationism, and militant anti-Communism. And like many others who began with these premises, he ended up in vicious Jew-baiting on the triple ground that the Jews controlled American foreign policy, invented capitalism, and gave birth to "Jew-Bolshevism."

Huey P. Long, the "Kingfish," was—as he once put it—"sui generis"; nothing like him has appeared on the political stage in the history of the United States. Winning the governorship of Louisiana in 1928 on the basis of a violently radical, anticorporate campaign, Long had by 1934 literally destroyed traditional politics in that state. He accomplished this by a spectacular combination of cunning, ruthlessness, popular appeal, and genuine benefactions to the people of Louisiana. A masterful demagogue, he was equipped with that most dangerous rhetorical weapon: a trenchant sense of humor. Secretary of Agriculture Henry Wallace was, for example, rendered speechless by the Kingfish's designation of "Lord Corn Wallace," and even the acerbic Hugh Johnson met his match: the nation roared when Long christened him "Sitting Bull." [8] The South had spawned a regular succession of talented demagogues like Tom Watson and "Pitchfork Ben" Tillman—to say nothing of the untalented, such as Long's contemporaries "Tom-Tom" Heflin, whom we met vilifying the Catholics in the Senate, and Theodore "the Man" Bilbo, who specialized in Negro-baiting—but none of them was in a class with Long. The others were local exhibits, men who tailored their appeals to the prejudices of their constituencies; Long was a regional phenomenon with a rising national constituency when the assassin's bullet cut him down. He did not just play to the prejudices of the people: he shaped them. In Louisiana, historically divided between "red-neck" Protestant North and "Cajun" Catholic South, the Kingfish developed a political formula which transcended ancestral hates: he got Protestant majorities in the north to vote for Catholic candidates, and became the ideal of the south to such a degree that at death he achieved local sainthood, the first Baptist since John to attain this elevated, if noncanonical status.

But above all, Long was an organizational genius. Effortlessly he watched all the cash registers, checked all appointments, knew everything about everybody. His intelligence system was unnerving, and no one appreciated better than he that the mechanical basis of effective politics is good combat intelligence, that the most painless way of destroying the cohesion of the enemy is to convince them that everything they do or plan is known. He never forgot, seldom forgave, and though he loved to clown there was always a hint of menace in his laugh. Behind the joviality lay a substratum of egocentric ruthlessness. And behind that? No one really knew—Huey was incapable to real intimacy—maybe real, but twisted idealism; maybe only a core of megalomania. Biographies tell us little. Indeed, no formal study has delineated this baffling personality half so well as Robert Penn Warren's fictionalized but dazzlingly perceptive *All the King's Men*.

The Kingfish came from Winn Parish, old Populist territory where the IWW once fought bloody battles with the lumber barons, and where the Socialists rather than the Republicans filled out the two-party system,[9] and throughout his life he paid lip service to the old radical slogans. He rarely attacked the Negroes (though he did not aid them either), eschewed religious issues (for obvious political reasons), and while he made friendly references to Mussolini (the Italian Ambassador received an honorary degree from Huey's kept academicians at booming Louisiana State University), he was cold toward Nazism. Some of his best friends *were* Jews, and besides, the Jews in Louisiana outnumbered the Germans by at least 20 to 1; the German Ambassador received no honors from his hands.[10] When he rang the gong, the old aristocrats and new capitalists were panicked into terror-stricken opposition. He was a bloodcurdling master of class-war strictures.

From William Jennings Bryan's "Cross of Gold" speech, Long borrowed the line "Every Man a King" and set out to build a nationwide clientele on the basis of his "Share Our Wealth" program. Though he continued to run Louisiana, in 1932 he promoted himself to the United States Senate and shortly achieved a reputation as the most obstreperous freshman Senator in the recollection of living man. He insulted everybody but did it in such a way as to achieve an enormous amount of free national publicity. An early Roosevelt supporter—he noted to his constituents who had their doubts about F.D.R. that "When I'm satisfied with a man, you know he's got something" [11]—he soon began to jam

Jim Farley's extremely sensitive political radar. Farley tried to keep Long in the boondocks during the 1932 campaign, recognizing that the irrepressible and dangerous Senator was trying to "steal the national spotlight" with a view to advancing his own presidential ambitions. But Long did get loose in some of the big cities with, in Farley's foresighted intuition, appallingly effective results. Farley privately marked the Kingfish for the knife, particularly after the latter, in the summer of 1932, conducted a brilliant commando raid into Arkansas which elected his private candidate, Mrs. Hattie Caraway, to the Senate over the choice of the Democratic organization. The Postmaster General initiated a long campaign of attrition against Long which involved, *inter alia*, denial of federal patronage and persistent efforts to indict the Senator and his close associates for income tax evasion.[12]

In 1933 and 1934, as Roosevelt tried one *ad hoc* remedy after another (and simultaneously) to master the Depression, Long went into full-scale opposition and turned the Senate chamber into his private forum. In one tirade after another, he denounced the inertia and conservatism of Roosevelt and the New Deal and called for a radical program of wealth redistribution. He puzzled the liberals who distrusted him but yet were intrigued. Here is Raymond Gram Swing writing in 1934:

One does not understand the problem of Huey Long or measure the menace he represents to American democracy until one admits that he has done a vast amount of good for Louisiana. He has this to justify all that is corrupt and peremptory in his methods. . . . Taken all in all, I do not know any man who has accomplished so much that I approve of in one state in four years, at the same time that he has done so much that I dislike. It is a thoroughly perplexing, paradoxical record.[13]

And Carleton Beals in 1935:

He has been perhaps called a demagogue too freely, or at least without proper examination of the word. Is the man who has the power to rouse the multitude necessarily a demagogue? Is one who promises what he cannot fulfill more of a demagogue than the one who deceives the public without such promises? Certainly no President in the history of the republic has so departed

from his original campaign promises as has President Roosevelt. Is there
any worse demagogue in America than Herbert Hoover . . . ? Is not a
demagogue a thousand times more desirable in public life than a gross machine politician like Mr. Farley . . . ? Whatever the folly of his proposals,
[Long] will stand as a remarkable social and political critic of the evils and
misfortunes of our day.[14]

It was a "perplexing, paradoxical record" only if one believed,
as many liberals unfortunately did in the period before the true
nature of totalitarianism became obvious, that hard-surfaced roads,
new bridges, and an elaborate state university were a fair trade
for basic human rights. Whatever may have been the deficiencies
in character of Herbert Hoover, Franklin D. Roosevelt, and
James A. Farley, no one has ever seriously suspected them of kid-
napping and murdering their political opponents, of using troops
to guarantee proper election results, or of turning the Federal
Bureau of Investigation into an instrument of political terror
comparable to Long's "Cossacks" of the Louisiana Bureau of Investigation.

By the middle of 1935, Long had built up a formidable following and had brought in a Shreveport minister as national organizer of "Share Our Wealth." This "kindly, eloquent and sincere Long enthusiast" [15]—in Swing's description—was Gerald L.
K. Smith who was to travel a long way after the death of his
master and add xenophobia and anti-Semitism to the weapons he
inherited from Huey. Long was now printing millions of copies
of his speeches for distribution, and "Share Our Wealth" claimed
a membership of nine million. This was undoubtedly exaggerated
—there were no dues—but Farley and Roosevelt were genuinely
worried. The Democratic National Committee in 1935 conducted
a secret poll which indicated that if Long ran in 1936 on a third-
party ticket, he would get between three and four million votes,
and not at the expense of the Republicans. Even worse, the poll
suggested that his appeal was nationwide: about as strong in
Maine as in the South, in California as in New York; the infection
could not be localized.[16] What really gave the Democratic strate-
gists nightmares was the possibility of a coalition between Long,

the Townsendites (who were particularly strong in the West where their $200-a-month pension scheme had wide support among retired oldsters whose investments the crash had wiped out), and the followers of Father Coughlin.

Indeed, Roosevelt and Farley got sufficiently distressed to commit what was probably a major blunder. In March, 1935, they sent blustering Hugh Johnson forth on a nationwide radio hookup to launch the counterattack against Long and Coughlin. "Sitting Bull" poured it on: crudely and directly he accused the two "Catalines" of dishonesty, power-hunger, and "rash and murderous" tactics—they were "enticing bums" who hoped to ride into Washington on horseback as the American Hitlers. But, he observed, Huey Long was better qualified as the rear end of a horse than as a rider! It was surely one of the most remarkable political speeches in recent history.[17] Coughlin rose to the bait and began a series of sententious, self-justifying radio speeches which continued for more than a month. Long, however, completely turned the tables on the administration: before what was estimated to be one of the largest radio audiences in history, the Kingfish sidestepped "Sitting Bull's" dull tomahawk, sliced Johnson's throat from ear to ear with a quick knife thrust of sardonic humor, and proceeded to an "earnest, deeply passionate exposition of his share-the-wealth" done with "consummate artistry." The flavor can be sensed from his condemnation of the N.R.A. and the A.A.A.:

While millions have starved and gone naked; while babies have cried and died for milk; while people have begged for meat and bread; Mr. Roosevelt's administration sails merrily along, plowing under and destroying the things to eat and wear, with tear-dimmed eyes and hungry souls made to chant for this New Deal, so that even their starvation dole is not taken away, and meanwhile the food and clothes craved by their bodies and souls goes for destruction and ruin.

"Is this government?" he asked, and replied, "It looks more like St. Vitus's dance." [18]

No one can really guess how far Long would have gone had he not made the mistake of attributing Negro ancestry to an opponent whose son-in-law combined ownership of a pistol with a militant sense of family honor. Long's assassination on September 8, 1935 (he lingered, fighting for life until the 10th), however, put an end to speculation—and to danger. "St. Huey" may have become a spiritual essence to superstitious Cajuns, but without his genius the Long machine became just another collection of warring bandits destined for eventual federal retribution. Despite the efforts of Gerald L. K. Smith, "Share Our Wealth" vanished as a political force almost overnight. To F.D.R.—who was, of course, without a scintilla of evidence accused of complicity in the murder—it may have seemed as though the hand of Providence had delivered him from a fearful burden. According to Tugwell, the President considered Long "one of the two most dangerous men in the country"; he felt that if the New Deal failed, Long would lead the offensive from the left and General Douglas MacArthur the forces of the right.[19]

Long's death left Father Coughlin as the chief Yahoo (the followers of Dr. Townsend, while they were glad to take support for their pension theories from any source, were never given demagogic leadership by their retiring leader), and the career of Coughlin is an interesting case study in the rise and fall of extremism in the 1930's. In the transformation of the National Union for Social Justice from a catch basin for essentially radical complaints into the Christian Front, a body of explicit or implicit supporters of Nazi Germany, we find a model instance of the failure and degeneration of American extremism. Essentially "Coughlinism" (to use a word as shorthand for a syndrome which included many not in the immediate following of the Radio Priest) fell into two periods: the first, before the election of 1936 when it appeared to many—Republicans, Socialists, Communists, and right-wing extremists—that the New Deal had failed utterly to meet the crisis; the second, after that astounding vote of confidence in Roosevelt and the Democrats, when it became apparent that the American people were not ripe for an alternative. In the first period, Coughlin exuded confidence; he had that inner serenity which comes from the knowledge that the people are listening and responding. To him was attributed the defeat of the effort in early 1935 to bring the United States into the World Court, and an audience estimated between ten and twenty million tuned in to his rich, mellifluous brogue on Sunday afternoons.[20]

Initially a supporter of the New Deal, Coughlin began to veer away almost before Roosevelt was firmly established in the White House. F.D.R. began to demonstrate, in his view, unfortunate procapitalist proclivities. Taking off from his proposals for "nationalizing the currency," Coughlin launched one attack after another on the "menace" of "capitalistic credit." On February 18, 1934, for instance, he announced:

The capitalistic credit system was a system wherein the entire viewpoint of wealth and of money was perverted. . . . Since modern capitalism has neither the ability nor the heart to extend credit to the idle laborer and to the distressed farmer but persists in extending it to [industrialists only], it is the high tide of time for us, as a people, to inaugurate a crusade for profitable leisure at the expense of the manufacturer and of the capitalist, and of the wealth of the nation. . . . The day has arrived when we who have amalgamated our lives together as one people in this nation shall cease to be governed, exploited and impoverished by a corporate group of banker-controlled industrialists.[21]

The following week, he summarized his position by categorically stating that "modern capitalism as we know it is not worth saving. In fact it is a detriment to civilization." [22]

Throughout this 1934 series, Coughlin banged away at the evils of capitalism in the name of a bowdlerized version of the Christian corporate state. His only remark about civil liberties had a curiously Marxist cast: "Liberty as we have experienced it— save the god-given [*sic*] liberty of conscience—is a cheap coin to trade even for the exactitudes of Communism or the fetters of Fascism if these systems of economics supply heat and shelter and a chance to live. Without economic liberty . . . little else matters." [23] However, he was—as Swing aptly put it—undergoing the "wonder of self-discovery" and becoming more and more convinced of his messianic role in American politics.[24] His role in early 1935 in defeating the World Court proposal seems to have tipped the scales of his inner psyche, and he stepped forward as the man to save the country from Roosevelt.

Throughout 1935 and 1936, he grew increasingly savage and raucous. On November 17, 1935, he declaimed:

. . . like a grotesque colossus this Administration stands astride the two extremities of social error. While its golden head enunciates the splendid program of Christian justice, its feet of sordid clay are mired, one in the red mud of Soviet communism, and the other, in the stinking cesspool of pagan plutocracy.[25]

In the course of 1936 he referred to F.D.R. as a "liar," a "betrayer," and a "scab" and heaped abuse on the second and third echelon New Dealers. American Catholics found him an increasing embarrassment, but, ironically, the apparently monolithic structure of Church organization in fact makes disciplining a priest extremely difficult if his ordinary (bishop or archbishop) is unwilling. The liberal Cardinal Mundelein of Chicago, a vigorous supporter of F.D.R., Cardinal O'Connell of Boston, the Archbishop of Cincinnati, and other prelates all disowned Coughlin's views at one time or another, but his ecclesiastical superior, Michael Gallagher, Bishop of Detroit, stood firmly behind the stormy priest. Later even *l'Osservatore Romano*, the "unofficial" organ of Vatican opinion, took up the cudgels against Coughlin's extremism, but the most that Gallagher would do was exact apologies to Roosevelt for the most outrageous of Coughlin's *ad hominem* accusations. (Gallagher had himself been a problem in his day: at a time when the Irish Sinn Féin was under Church ban, he had sponsored a rally for Eamon de Valera in Detroit! [26])

Finally, in 1936, Coughlin, intoxicated by his own self-esteem, cut the cord which, however tenuously, held him to the New Deal. Abandoning the role of the internal critic, one who fights within a movement to establish his views, he openly called for the organization of a third party and the defeat of Roosevelt. In coalition with a strange congeries of rural radicals and urban reactionaries, he sponsored the Union Party which ran Congressman William Lemke of North Dakota and Thomas C. O'Brien of Massachusetts for President and Vice-President. At the Union Party Convention, held in Cleveland in August, 1936, Coughlin appeared without his clerical garb and poured billingsgate on Roosevelt; shortly thereafter he stated that if the Lemke-O'Brien ticket did not receive nine million votes, he would go into retirement, disband his National Union for Social Justice, and cease broadcasting.[27]

With Coughlin breathing fire on behalf of the inconspicuous Lemke and O'Brien ticket (the ticket became less and less visible as election day approached; in the states where it got on the ballot, Union Party spokesmen were heard in sullen silence as they presented their program and with enraged booing, hissing, and heckling when they attacked F.D.R.), we can shift back to the main context of American politics to see what factors were vitiating the appeal of the extremists. Essentially Coughlin (and earlier Long) were committed to the proposition that the American people would vote their stomachs—they were vulgar economic determinists. If this analysis of popular motivation were correct, Coughlin's estimate of nine million votes was rational and possibly minimal. In economic terms, the New Deal had in no sense mastered the Depression: in 1936 seventeen percent of the labor force (nine million!) was still unemployed.[28] The country was well-populated with calamity-mongers, the Republican leadership amongst them, who knew that destruction was in the offing.

Yet, while its fondness for improvisation and lack of a coherent program laid the New Deal open to assault from every quarter, something important had taken place in the years 1933–36. Franklin D. Roosevelt had convinced the great majority of the American people that—however difficult the times might be in economic terms—the government was an instrument of succor which was concerned with the well-being of all strata in society. Extremism thrives on alienation—the conviction that one is not a participant in the effective political process—and, curiously, alienation is usually founded mainly on noneconomic considerations. As Alexis de Tocqueville pointed out in his perceptive study of the *ancien régime* in France, the group which led the revolutionary movement was economically better off, by and large, than its aristocratic opponents. And Morris Watnick and others have noted that Communist leadership in the emerging nations is generally composed of lawyers and intellectuals—men who in objective economic and social terms are well situated, but who resent bitterly their exclusion from the leadership circle in society.[29]

Thus it appears in retrospect that the more the Liberty League denounced Roosevelt's "statism," the more Coughlin attacked his "Bolshevik-plutocratic" tendencies, the more the Communists and Socialists assaulted his lack of planning, the more the G.O.P. inveighed against his drive for "dictatorship," the more the American people decided that F.D.R. was "their man." Moreover, while Roosevelt's platoon system had its drawbacks—particularly when two platoons began fighting each other—fundamental pieces of social legislation somehow emerged from the vortex of New Deal decision-making. Maybe Long and Coughlin pushed the President to the "left"—as Moley and others have maintained [30]—but however motivated, the passage of the Social Security Act, the National Labor Relations Act, the Civilian Conservation Corps statute, the WPA and other "give-away" legislation (in the Republican phrase) altered the basic structure of American politics. The people may have been strangely silent throughout the 1936 campaign; with 80 percent of the press castigating F.D.R., they may have felt there was no particular point in arguing with pollsters, the *Literary Digest*, or newspapermen. But the electorate had the last word, and it knew precisely where it stood: only Maine and Vermont held out for "freedom."

It is probably unfair to go back from the results of the 1936 election and review the political events of the campaign year. But everybody was not misled (Jim Farley called the results right on the nose), and the 1936 confrontation was vital in the transformation we have been examining in this book. All the stops were pulled out in the effort to get Roosevelt: the CCC, according to Communists, Socialists, *and* Republicans, had been a training program for storm troops; the N.L.R.A. had been tagged a phony by the left (the Communist line changed shortly before the election) and "Bolshevism" by the G.O.P.; the Social Security Act in the hands of Republican prophets was the beginning of totalitarianism—all Americans would shortly be required to wear dog tags, and be known by their numbers! (Many of the men would, but for an entirely different reason.) In short, what occurred was an almost unbelievable loss of contact between the spokesmen for both extremist organizations and respectable oppositions such as the Republican and Socialist and the temper of the American people. Roosevelt won on an electoral tidal wave: he received 27,753,000 votes, Landon got 16,675,000, Lemke, despite all of Coughlin's frenzied rhetoric, 882,000, and Norman Thomas a little less than 200,000.[31]

This was the end of the political road for the Yahoos—their army defeated on the battlefield, they took to the hills and mounted guerrilla campaigns of an increasingly desperate and psychotic sort. The Republicans, on the other hand, read the omens correctly: never again would the G.O.P. go to battle nationally in defense of the "old order." Whatever their inner reservations, the men who controlled the Republican Party set to work to establish a new image, one of rational, constructive criticism of the "excesses" of the New Deal. Candidates like Wendell Willkie, Thomas E. Dewey, and in recent years Dwight Eisenhower and Richard Nixon have never challenged the welfare foundations of the New Deal era—the Wagner Act, the Social Security Act, or the Fair Labor Standards Act, to mention the most significant—but have asserted that the Republicans are the men who can most effectively implement such measures in the true national interest.

The reaction of other groups was variegated: the Socialists wandered off into isolated futility, the Communists, following the new Comintern line, rushed to embrace the "masses" and soon were offering themselves as the only authentic New Dealers. (This so-called "Popular Front" tactic led to an increase in Stalinist influence in various liberal organizations and in the trade unions, but it is often overlooked in discussions of Communist subversion that it was the party which was "fellow-traveling" with the New Deal, not the converse.) These were in broad political terms relatively harmless responses, but the Yahoos took a different and malevolent tack: they turned to Nazi Germany for spiritual guidance against the "insanities" of the American people.

Coughlin went off the air and temporarily dedicated himself to the care of souls in Royal Oak, Michigan. But pastoral duties in suburban Detroit could hardly fulfill his apocalyptic drives, and, within a year after the Union Party's debacle, he returned to an enlarged network and founded his journal *Social Justice*. A careful reading of his talks in the period before 1937 turns up little material of an anti-Semitic character, but now a new note and a new emphasis appeared. Communism and New Deal "plutocracy" suddenly developed a common source: the Jewish conspiracy. The major aim of the Jewish conspiracy was to involve the United States in war against Nazi Germany, and to thwart this sinister plot Coughlin called for the formation of a "Christian Front."

In the fall of 1938, Coughlin suddenly revived the *Protocols of the Learned Elders of Zion* and began quoting them as proof of the evil designs of the Jews. Immediately Jewish defense organizations, who by now had a considerable file on the *Protocols,* challenged the authenticity of the documents and brought forth the historical data we have already examined. Coughlin, however, was not inhibited by this material: "I emphasize once more," he said, "that I am not interested in the authenticity of the *Protocols.* I am interested in their factuality." Later *Social Justice* ran an article by an apparently nonexistent Jewish author, invented for the occasion, which put it even more neatly: "No one," observed "Ben Marcin," "is interested in the identity of the author, whereas everyone is interested in the contents of the book written by the unknown author." [32]

Fortunately the counterattack against Coughlin was vigorous and broadly launched. A coalition was formed called the General Jewish Council, comprising the American Jewish Committee, the Anti-Defamation League of B'nai B'rith, the American Jewish Congress, and the Jewish Labor Committee, which brought out a devastating analysis under the title *Father Coughlin: His "Facts" and Arguments.*[33] The Institute for Propaganda Analysis published an incisive volume, *The Fine Art of Propaganda,* devoted to exposing the speciousness of Coughlin's arguments and the paranoid character of his logic. George N. Shuster and Monsignor John A. Ryan excoriated him in the liberal Catholic journal *Commonweal,* and the spokesmen for liberal Protestantism were equally outspoken. Moreover, the American people will put up with a great deal of pretty vicious rhetoric when it is homemade, but Coughlin crossed the invisible boundary between public tolerance and contempt when he began to echo the Nazi line. It is interesting to note from public opinion polls of that time (which, if not exact in their measurements, presumably had a common margin of error and thus accurately delineated general trends) that although the American people did not want to fight the Nazis, they despised them and feared the consequences of Hitlerite expansion.[34]

Thus one of the most devastating documents in the General Jewish Council's book was the printing, in parallel columns, of a speech by Goebbels and an article by Coughlin. This article, "Background of Persecution," set forth in summary fashion the evils of "Jewish Bolshevism," with the conclusion that Nazi persecution was richly deserved. (Coughlin never *precisely* condoned persecution; his position in essence was that no Christian could justify it—but it was quite understandable.) In their reply to the Council indictment, which is a clinical document in its own right, "Father Coughlin's Friends" again employed the evasion he used with regard to the *Protocols:* "The important question is: Are the *facts* narrated by Dr. Goebbels and Father Coughlin true? They are."[35] (This flat statement still left a problem. Goebbels had accused Béla Kun, "a Jew, whose real name was Aaron Cohn," of murdering twenty hostages in Budapest in the 1919 Hungarian Revolution, while Coughlin announced that the "notorious atheist, Béla Kun, a Jew whose real name was Aaron Cohn, murdered 20,000." Which "fact" was "factual"?)

Nazi propagandists had been industriously cultivating various Yahoo organizations since 1933. In 1935 a Special Committee of the House of Representatives chaired by Congressman (now Speaker) John McCormack of Massachusetts completed an in-

vestigation into German propaganda activities and delivered a
blistering report on Nazi efforts to capture various cultural groups
in the German-American community and convert them into
branches of Goebbel's international network.[36] The German-
American community, which was one generation further away
from the Fatherland than in 1914 and also presumably recalled
the chauvinism of World War I, was not particularly responsive
to Goebbel's efforts; only a handful of the twenty million first-
and second-generation Americans of German descent ever supported the "Friends of New Germany" or the German American
Bund. The American Nazis, however, made a major effort to win
over isolationist groups and to use such Yahoo configurations as
the "Christian Front," William Dudley Pelley's "Silver Shirts,"
George E. Deatherage's "American Nationalist Confederation,"
the "National Gentile League," and the "Militant Christian Patriots" of Los Angeles as a spearhead in opposing American intervention in European affairs.

Isolationism was an issue with tremendous appeal, and as the
drums of the *Wehrmacht* echoed first through the streets of the
Rhineland, then Vienna, Prague, and Danzig, various organizations sprang to life in the United States to keep the nation out of
the inevitable war. After the war broke out in August, 1939, these
efforts were redoubled. Antiwar sentiment was channeled into
three movements: a small percentage of Socialist-pacifist per-
suasion formed the Keep America Out of War Congress; the great
bulk joined or associated with the America First Committee; and
another small segment worked with the Yahoos in overtly anti-
Semitic, anti-British, essentially pro-Nazi efforts.[37]

Some contemporary critics joined the two latter categories
into one, claiming that the America First Committee was a Nazi
front. This had considerable polemical value, but was a nasty
twisting of truth: the Yahoos did support the work of the committee, extremists did penetrate the ranks of the committee, and
occasionally committee spokesmen—notably Charles Lindbergh at
Des Moines in September, 1941—went onto the thin ice of quasi-
anti-Semitism. (It was hardly anti-Semitic *per se* to assert that the

Jews were militantly opposed to Hitler; much depended on the context, and the tone of voice.) But, however one may evaluate their wisdom, the leaders of the America First Committee were not pro-Nazi in their basic orientation; they drew their support and inspiration from traditional American convictions about foreign entanglements and from the bitter anti-British, anti-European backwash of the First World War. Indeed, the top figures in the America First Committee, realizing the danger of being tarred with the Coughlinite, Christian Front brush, went to considerable efforts to disassociate themselves from the extremists.[38] (I personally attended an America First rally—passing out Socialist antiwar literature—in Madison Square Garden where the first thing the Chairman, John T. Flynn, did was order Joe Mc-Williams, the Nazi apologist and Christian Fronter, ejected from the hall. Although several commentaries on this meeting assert that Flynn was booed by the crowd, in fact it applauded the chairman and booed McWilliams.)

The great mass of opponents of American intervention were puzzled, unhappy, and frustrated by the course of events, but they were loyal, decent citizens, and they wanted nothing to do with the Christian Front or the other pro-Fascist groups. Indeed, the opinion polls reveal a strangely schizophrenic public: in 1940–41, the overwhelming majority of the populace as reported in various studies 1) hoped for a British-French victory, 2) considered Nazism a vicious, menacing system, 3) wanted to stay out of war, and 4) believed that the United States *would* become involved! In short, the American people were anti-Nazi *and* antiwar.[39]

This strange configuration was the background for Roosevelt's esoteric (to use a kind word) maneuvering throughout 1940–41, notably in the election of 1940. He knew, like most Americans, that war was inevitable; he wanted the British to win, and after Dunkirk they desperately needed help. The American people favored helping them, but were antiwar, so aid was justified, and voted by Congress, on the ground that it would help keep us out of war! (Ironically, nobody paid much attention to the Japanese—

it was assumed, in the best racist tradition, that if they made trouble, the Boy Scouts could handle it.) And, of course, the American people were militantly in favor of self-defense against Nazi aggression. It was a politician's nightmare: if a decision could be explained as "self-defense" or as "aid short of war" (e.g., the draft and lend-lease), the people would support it. If it appeared to be a step on the road to war, the President might find himself repudiated—in October, 1941, the draft was extended for an additional year by a *one-vote* margin in the House of Representatives. At bottom, there was probably some justice in Charles A. Beard's taunt that Roosevelt was trying to force the Germans to force us to defend ourselves. Paradoxically, in the end, Hitler did take the initiative in declaring war on the United States; an egregiously stupid decision on his part, since, in the immediate aftermath of the disaster at Pearl Harbor, the United States might well have made a full-force commitment to the Pacific.

We cannot linger with the political intricacies of 1939–41, but this discussion is important in clarifying an important point. If the supporters of nonintervention had been undifferentiated, if the America First Committee and the Christian Front had been two sides of the same coin, the Jews would have been in a very bad way indeed. The fact of the matter was that most noninterventionists were anti-Nazi and repudiated the anti-Semitism of Coughlin, Pelley, and the *Lake Geneva Herald*. The same citizens who cheered Senator Wheeler at an antiwar rally wholeheartedly endorsed the government's actions against the German-American Bund and ignored Father Coughlin. In the fundamental sense, the destruction of the power of the Yahoos in the United States was a consequence of their becoming identified in the public mind with Nazism and anti-Semitism. As never before, the Jews felt the meaning of the bonds of brotherhood: President Roosevelt, commenting on the Christian Front genealogy which "proved" his real name was "Rosenfeld," simply said he would be proud to be a Jew; Wendell Willkie condemned "anti-Semitism in America as a possible criminal movement, and every anti-Semite as a possible traitor to America"; [40] the American League to Combat

Anti-Semitism was established among leading Christians to "Stop Coughlin"; [41] and perhaps best of all, Detroit got a new bishop—Coughlin took the veil as a radio commentator in September, 1940. In sum, anti-Semitism had become "un-American"; though it lives on to poison social relations and has flared up from time to time as a covert issue in an election, Jew-baiting had lost its punch and, indeed, become a liability in American politics.

This change in the climate of opinion affected the whole sphere of minority relations. Because of the virulence of Nazi anti-Semitism, the standing of the Jews in the American community became the spearhead, but it was the *point d'appui* for a broad attack on prejudice. In practical terms, despite the best efforts of Gerald B. Winrod—who combined in his *Defender Magazine* the standard anti-Semitic themes and a scatological brand of anti-Catholicism [42]—American Catholics emerged in the 1930's from the status of *Untermenschen*. In his curious, posthumous book, *My First Days in the White House*, Huey Long appointed Governor Frank Murphy of Michigan as Attorney General.[43] When Roosevelt followed his example in 1939, this liberal Catholic found his liberalism a far greater source of opposition than his faith. And a new generation of liberals began to do something which those of Wilsonian vintage seldom did—question the color line and the established patterns of Negro-white relationships. While F.D.R. was not himself a crusader for civil rights (he made remarkably few statements on the subject and never tampered with the racial status quo in the South), the President appointed to high office a number of men and women who were deeply committed to the expansion and fulfillment of American ideals.

To put it differently, there was a crucial transformation in the climate of government which meshed with the changes in American attitudes we have been examining. To search for causal significance would be futile: the climate of opinion both stimulated and reflected the mood of the administration. It should be recalled that until 1933—with the exception of wartime periods—the national government seldom dominated the policy picture. State and local governments carried the great burden of responsibility for whatever functions the sovereign exercised. However, the Great Depression and the inauguration of Roosevelt brought a new era in both quantitative and qualitative terms. State and local administrations were patently incapable of coping with the consequences of economic collapse. Many were literally bankrupt: the electric companies turned off the streetlights in some cities because their bills went unpaid! In the hour of crisis, states' rights were forgotten as governors and mayors rushed to Washington with demands that the federal government "do something." With this objective condition of incompetence was combined the eager centralist thrust of the New Dealers who, whatever their internal differences on the right policies to be followed, agreed that it was the responsibility of the national government to meet the challenge of the times.

Finally, on top of this, was the charismatic energy of a President who clearly saw himself as the incarnation of national purpose and—as his competitors learned over thirteen years—was constitutionally incapable of *not* dominating the stage. As late as 1948 this magic held sway: a poll in that year indicated that F.D.R. would have left even Dwight Eisenhower at the post.[44] We have already discussed Roosevelt's philosophy (or nonphilosophy) and temperament, but what is important to emphasize here is the extent to which he named to key posts in the administration officials who implemented the principles of due process and decency. The outside observer tends to judge the work of an administration by the big issues, the legislative programs and policy statements of a chief executive. These are, of course, important, but perhaps even more important are the invisible decisions, those which are made within the bureaucracy to deal with the day-to-day minutiae of public business.

When Congress passes a law, it essentially sets forth a framework for later decision. It is undesirable and indeed impossible for the legislature to attempt to deal in a statute with all the possible problems of administration. Thus every important statute passes the buck to some administrator—usually under presidential supervision—and necessarily leaves an area of discretion within which the latter can operate. The attitude, the political character, of the administrator therefore becomes crucial: he can construe his authority narrowly or broadly; he can give the benefit of the doubt to the individual or to the state; he can favor one set of interests and hurt another. All this he can do without dishonesty or violation of rules.

This is so important that perhaps an example or two should be introduced for clarification. Take the Immigration and Naturalization Service as a first case in point. Until the 1940 codification, American nationality laws were a shambles, and they are still extraordinarily complicated. One of the most Delphic Congressional pronouncements insisted that a candidate for naturalization be "of good moral character." This is not on its face unreasonable, but it leaves open an immense area of administrative and judicial discretion. And the judicial precedents on the subject provide little guidance—they go in every direction. One judge would admit a convicted bootlegger to citizenship on the ground that American views of Prohibition hardly made violation of the Volstead Act a crime "involving moral turpitude." Another judge would take the opposite course. However, most federal judges simply accept the recommendations of the Immigration and Naturalization Service on these matters, i.e., the advice of the service's legal officers is usually decisive.

One might think that bootlegging would be an open-and-shut case, and in fact criminal conviction generally was and is. But what about an applicant for citizenship accused of bigamy who introduces as his defense a rabbinical divorce from his first wife, a Polish document which has no legal standing in the United States? What about the Spanish refugee accused of robbery by the Franco regime who insists that the charge is trumped up, that his real crime was anti-Fascism? What, to take a classic case, of the Chinese who claimed citizenship by birth in San Francisco, but whose documentary evidence was destroyed in the 1905 earthquake? In cases such as these, the attitude of the legal officer makes an enormous difference in the outcome; particularly important is his unarticulated self-image. If he sees himself protecting the

United States from evil foreigners, he goes one way. If he looks with sympathy on the plight of the helpless and hopes to assist them where he can, he goes the other.

Another good example of this process is the work of the National Labor Relations Board. The Wagner Act established a substantial category of "unfair labor practices." To discriminate against a worker because of his union affiliation or to intimidate the workers in a bargaining election was declared illegal, but rhetoric is one thing, enforcement another. Take the case of a union organizer who has been fired: his employer asserts correctly that the law does not forbid dismissing union organizers —it only forbids dismissing a man *because* he is an organizer— and that the worker in question was fired for insubordination and, say, smoking in the men's room. The union maintains the man has been framed, that he was not insubordinate but only objected to the foreman's manner, that from time immemorial everyone has smoked in the men's room despite "No Smoking" signs. This dilemma cannot be solved from a distance. An examiner from the NLRB must personally investigate the situation and choose between the two versions. Similarly, intimidation may be easy to detect in its crude forms, but in sophisticated hands an antiunion campaign can be formulated in nuances and contingent implications which make it difficult to pin down. In both instances, the attitude toward unions of the examiner and of his supervisors all the way up to the members of the board will obviously play a decisive role in the ultimate decision.

Without suggesting for a moment that the New Deal was staffed exclusively, or even predominantly, by liberals—the Southern Democrats were always close to the patronage table—it is, I think, fair to say that the Roosevelt Administration saw a tremendous infusion of liberal sentiment into government and particularly into the new or expanded regulatory agencies. There was some truth in the reactionary jibe that the way to a Washington job was to go to Harvard Law School and "turn left" —so long as it is understood that "left" in this context did not imply becoming a Comintern agent but merely accepting the legitimacy of the New Deal! Certainly never in American history had such a mass of youthful talent been attracted to government service. There was a contagious enthusiasm about "working for Roosevelt" which can still be sensed in the veterans of that era—Washington was *alive*. Traditional topics of conversation at cocktail parties (who was marrying whom, the scandalous behavior of an ambassador's wife, the price of Georgetown brownstones) were replaced by vehement arguments about policy. Old Washington hands deplored the state of the world; the President's wife had *Negroes* to lunch![45]

It is my contention that this bureaucratic revolution made a major contribution to attitudes on civil and minority rights. The New Deal Leviathan which was greeted by wails of "dictatorship" from the right became in fact a significant force for the attainment of increased individual liberty and a buttress for minority rights. Never before had minority groups—Negroes included—had such access to government and to official positions. Moreover, as always occurs in any bureaucracy, public or private, whole sectors of government were colonized by the new men. It would have been absurd, for example, to staff the NLRB with antilabor personnel. The statute had been drafted to redress the imbalance of capital and labor, and the men who implemented it were vigorous supporters of this goal; i.e., in the context of the 1930's they were prolabor. Anyone who was satisfied with the status quo in industrial relations *was* antilabor; there was no third position.

When the Japanese bombs fell on Pearl Harbor, and the Nazis declared war, the United States massed to withstand and then defeat the greatest threat to survival it had yet faced. This time, as we shall see in the next chapter, there was little frenzied chauvinism. In May, 1942, the American Institute of Public Opinion asked a representative sample of Americans, "Do you think it would help us to win the war if our people were taught to have greater hatred for the Japanese and German people?" Twenty-three percent said "Yes," but 68 percent said "No." [46] The American people had traveled a long distance from the xenophobic excesses of World War I, as they had from the anti-Catholicism and anti-Semitism of the "old order." The New Deal years left much undone—the Negro with incredible patience still waited on the margin of the political community—but they were a vital beginning. Not only was Yahoo power discredited and demolished, but the government itself recognized and slowly began to fulfill the task of stewardship.

Perhaps no man better symbolized this change than Frank Murphy, who as a Detroit judge enforced the rights of Negroes, as Mayor fought for the unemployed, as Governor of Michigan stood stoutly for the rights of trade unionists, as Governor General of the Philippines supported self-determination for the people, and as Attorney General of the United States established the Civil Rights Section of the Department of Justice. When in 1940 Frank Murphy went on the Supreme Court, the doyens of the legal profession tore their hair at such a "political" appointment (that is, they did not like his politics). But whatever Murphy's technical competence as a lawyer—a topic which is still debated—his accession to the High Court signified the coming of age of civil liberties.[47] The Yahoos were still in the hills, capable of occasional fierce raids, but institutionally speaking their back was broken; civil liberties and minority rights had become part of American public policy.

VIII

THE "GOOD WAR"

In Great Britain, despite the terrors of saturation bombing, World War II was dubbed the "Good War." By comparison with World War I, and the organized butchery of Flanders' fields, British losses of life in the Second War were small. Although American casualties in World War II were greater than those of 1917–18, from the civil liberties viewpoint we too can consider it a "good war." It is in one sense odd that in the First War, when in fact we ran few significant risks, the American people were carried away by fears and hates, while in the second, when we were confronted by great peril, an entirely different attitude prevailed. However, if one considers the transformations that had occurred in the social, economic, and political character of the United States, this absence of chauvinism becomes explicable.

First of all, the era of the immigrant was over. In every nationality group, the second, even third, generation was in command, and, with the exception of lurid groups such as the German-American Bund, most ethnic associations had long since lost their real ties with the "old country." A meeting of the Ancient Order of Hibernians might still be regaled in full brogue by a catalogue of British sins, but the number of young Americans of Irish ancestry who brooded on the status of the "Six Enslaved Counties" of Ulster was trifling. (It was to decrease even further as Irish-American soldiers, packed like sardines into Army transports, brooded on German intelligence agents operating in neutral Ireland as spotters for U-boats.) Moreover, the nativist "pressure cooker" had a decade earlier broken the back of the foreign language press and discouraged the continuation of old ties. Even among the Japanese-Americans, who were to bear the brunt of World War II xenophobia, only a small percentage were literate in Japanese: typically the second generation reacted against the first by rejecting "alien habits," and the Nisei were no exception.[1] This was to give a particularly Kafkaesque character to their stay in purgatory in 1942–44.

Second, as we have seen, conflict with Nazi Germany necessarily involved a rejection of Nazi ideology, a repudiation in particular of the racial theories of the Third Reich. In earlier periods, racists could pose as advocates of "100-percent Americanism," but now the advocacy of anti-Semitism incurred suspicion of treason. This put a terrific crimp in racist rhetoric, particularly since the inclusion of the Soviet Union in the anti-Nazi coalition had put a damper on the frenetic anti-Communism that often camouflaged anti-Semitism. The authorities moved immediately against the leaders of the German-American Bund, and also subsequently launched an abortive, and ill-advised, sedition prosecution against the rag, tag, and bobtail of American "Fascism."

There were inconsistencies. Some government agencies utilized tasteless and vicious anti-Japanese propaganda, referring to the "Japs" as "yellow monkeys" and the like, and the army in the Pacific Theater of Operations issued a few manuals which rank among the vulgar classics of "yellow peril" literature. Moreover, sad to say (and this refrain is probably getting tedious), there was little change in the status of the Negro. The military services were run on Jim Crow principles, with Negro servicemen in separate units; and military posts adopted the law and customs of local areas: at all Southern installations, segregation was rigidly enforced on duty and off. There was much objection to this from liberal and Negro spokesmen, but the military authorities, backed by the President and, of all people, the Communists, insisted that wartime was hardly the appropriate backdrop for racial pioneering. President Roosevelt did, by executive order, establish a federal Fair Employment Practices Commission which, while it could not employ any formal sanctions against violators, attempted by various noncoercive techniques to improve the economic position of the Negro worker.

But in general ideological terms, racism was in bad odor. Public opinion polls taken during the war consistently showed a much greater public prejudice against "trade-union leaders" than against Jews or members of any other minority. This time there was none of the Wilson Administration's benevolent neutrality toward local acts of prejudice. Attorney General Francis Biddle, who had taken over Frank Murphy's old position, replacing Robert Jackson, and shared many of their concerns, undertook an active nationally sponsored campaign against state and local government excesses. All United States Attorneys, the men who represent the national government at the level of local prosecution, were instructed to clear with Washington before they went into the sedition-hunting business; and the Department of Justice took a dim view of most recommendations. Biddle (following a procedure initiated by Jackson in 1940) called regular meetings of state and local officials, briefing them on their responsibilities.[2] He also conducted a campaign of attrition against local military commanders, like General Hugh Drum in New York, who initiated action against alleged subversives; when Drum lost his actions in the United States District Court, the Department of Justice never got around to filing the papers for appeal! [3]

The fact that the national government took this praiseworthy position was highly significant. First, the national government in modern America tends to set the pattern for other governments. Just as in the late forties state and local governments began to forecast McCarthy by investigating "Communist subversion" and set up "security programs" roughly patterned on that established by the Truman Administration, so the air of calm and the emphasis on due process which Biddle and his colleagues supplied proved contagious. Second, Biddle's actions (which were, of course, backed by the President who must receive credit for the good deeds of his subordinates as he gets pilloried for the bad) had the effect of taking subversion out of politics. If the quest for subversion becomes part of political competition, the race for sensational exposures usually continues, at fearful cost to those implicated, until the limits of boredom are reached; i.e., until the public tires of the wretched business.

Few people appreciate the institutional aspects of competition; given the decentralized state of American political organization, local federal officeholders (such as United States Attorneys) are always potential candidates for state and local office. This is *a fortiori* the case when the state or local government is held by the opposition party, but it is also a standard technique of strengthening the President's wing of his own party. Thus if the Attorney General or a local United States Attorney initiates a spectacular offensive against vice, gambling, subversion, or drug addiction, the local law-enforcement officials rarely cheer him on in the interests of public virtue. They view his vigorous rectitude as the preliminary phase of a campaign for the governorship, the Senate, or some other high office, and hastily organize a task force of their own to cut into his monopoly, and hopefully neutralize his political impact. Mitchell Palmer hoped to get into the White House on his feats as a red-hunter in 1919–20; and certainly some of the frenzy of that era arose from the conviction on the part of his political competitors that if he could become famous for deporting a thousand "Reds," they could attain superior fame by demanding the execution of two thousand. We shall see the same sort of perverse rivalry churning up American politics in the McCarthy period. But during World War II, when Biddle took the search for subversives out of politics, the impetus for this sort of competition largely disappeared.

The fact that the United States had been attacked by the Japanese and that the Germans and Italians had declared war on us undoubtedly contributed to the tremendous sense of national unity which gripped the nation as the Pearl Harbor wreckage was cleared. The overwhelming percentage of isolationists had never been pro-German; indeed, the gravamen of isolationist policy was self-defense in a continental sense—the Western hemisphere should become a "Gibraltar" immune to enemy assault. They were not so much antimilitarists as they were anti-*foreign* wars, and, once the war was forced upon us, former isolationist organs such as the Chicago *Tribune* roared with patriotic enthusiasm.

Their former views did, however, lead to an interesting set of wartime priorities: they were far more concerned with vengeance in the Pacific than embroilment in Europe.[4] (This ex-isolationist syndrome lingered on in the post-World War II period as an emphasis on China and a disinterest in Western European recovery. It came to a head in 1950–51 over the question of risking full-scale war in Asia by attacking beyond the Yalu.) This was partly due to the feeling that the "Japs" deserved the full treatment, and probably also a consequence of the fact that General Douglas MacArthur, long a right-wing hero, was Supreme Commander in the Pacific. But at base it was unquestionably subsumed in a rejection of Europe and all it stood for in isolationist mythology. The fact that Soviet Russia was involved in the European war may have provided a nuance—a number of isolationists had previously felt that the Nazis and the Communists should be permitted to bleed each other to death—but once the United States was embroiled in hostilities, anti-Russian sentiment virtually disappeared. Ironically in the light of subsequent events—and the history of this era has been obfuscated by much covering of tracks —the Luce publications, New Dealers, leading Republicans such as Robert A. Taft and Alexander Wiley, and right-wingers such as Captain Eddie Rickenbacker *all* participated vehemently in the Russian celebration. What few serious voices were heard in dissent from the general glorification of "Uncle Joe" Stalin came from the democratic left: from Norman Thomas and trade unionists scarred in the battles with American Stalinism, such as David Dubinsky of the International Ladies Garment Workers Union.[5]

The American military planners had long since agreed with their British counterparts that Nazi Germany was the priority target, that once the Germans were defeated, the Japanese could be dealt with by involving the U.S.S.R. on the Asian continent and invading from the sea. But the ex-isolationists never let up the pressure for altering the priorities and indeed were successful to the extent that the military part of the Pacific War was converted from a holding operation into a brilliantly executed (whatever the character of his politics, MacArthur ranks as one of the world's great masters of amphibious warfare) counteroffensive which had victory within its grasp when the Nazis collapsed.

It is interesting to speculate whether this anti-Japanese emphasis played any part in American attitudes toward Japanese-Americans as distinguished from German- and Italian-Americans. Probably not, although it is significant that the Chicago *Tribune* and other ex-isolationist journals played up the threat to American security posed by Americans of Japanese birth or ancestry and devoted no space to any threat from Americans whose antecedents were in the Axis powers. It was, of course, impossible to take the Italian danger seriously. Italians in Italy were obviously opposed to riding the Nazi tiger and sympathetic toward a United Nations' victory, and, except for a few of Mussolini's hired propagandists, there were no currents of disloyalty in the Italian-American community. Moreover, with the exception of a few areas of intensive settlement, such as Yorkville, on the Upper East Side of New York City, or farm regions in the Middle West, the German-Americans had largely vanished as a discrete ethnic group. Intermarriage and dispersion had taken its toll and virtually eliminated the flourishing German-American bloc which had been so visible in World War I. In addition to this, Hitler had effectively destroyed the Germany to which those with articulate cultural loyalties looked with affection—and the FBI and military intelligence looked after those with Nazi attachments.

So Wagnerian opera was sung, children learned German in school, sauerkraut defied transformation into "liberty cabbage," and dachshunds walked the streets with impunity. A general named Eisenhower was sent out to lead the assault on the Continent, and no one raised a question (except a mad anti-Semite who claimed Eisenhower was a Swedish Jew). Elderly Italian-Americans talked their native tongue and on Sunday found the sermon at Mass still echoing the sibilant language of their childhood. The usual col-

lection of nuts turned up the standard indictments of treason—
"He keeps the lights on late and talks German over the phone!"
—but the lynch mobs stayed in their beds and left the policing to
the police. With one heartrending exception, there was no insanity
—the American people behaved with dignity and self-confidence
and exemplified the ideals they were defending.

The exception to this self-restraint and absence of hysterical
chauvinism was the treatment given to the Japanese-American
community on the West Coast, which was, in the words of Professor Eugene Rostow (now Dean) of Yale Law School, "our worst
wartime mistake." [6] Because to this day so little is understood of
the travail of this minority group, the episode deserves extended
treatment. Moreover, it provides an opportunity to examine the
position of our Asian minority groups in American society. They
have hardly been mentioned heretofore because they provided
such a small segment of the immigrant population.

While the Chinese had been imported into the United States
virtually as commodities in the 1870's—under rigorous labor con-
tracts approximating serfdom—and had been the hapless source
of virulent campaigns of anti-Orientalism, the Japanese arrived
later: the big years of their immigration were 1900–1908. The
number of human beings involved was statistically trivial: the
1880 census showed a total of 104,468 persons of Chinese birth
in the United States, and in 1910, when the Japanese peak had
similarly passed, there were 67,744 of Japanese origin.[7] A dispassionate observer viewing these statistics might wonder what all
the fuss was about. True, under the ruling of the Supreme Court
in *United States* v. *Wong Kim Ark* (1898) [8] the American-born
children of these Asian immigrants were automatically birthright
citizens of the United States, but the increment provided in this
fashion was still minute.

However, the Chinese and Japanese suffered like the Negro
from their high visibility and also from the fact that they were
not scattered at large throughout the nation but grouped in ghettos in the Pacific Coast states. As was noted in the first chapter,
the "yellow peril" had been invoked to choke off Chinese im-

migration in 1882 and Japanese, in 1907. After World War I, there was increasing agitation on the West Coast, led by the American Legion and the Native Sons of the Golden West, to restrict further the rights of the Asian minority. The American Legion, which could always be found in the front rank of nativism, carried the demand to the national level and was probably instrumental in attaining an absolute ban on "Oriental" immigration in the statute of 1924. (As "nonwhites," the Asians had been ineligible for citizenship except under special conditions established, e.g., for war veterans.) The American-born generation could not be discriminated against except in traditional "separate but equal" terms—San Francisco and other Western communities had segregated schools in which they could learn the principles of "Americanism"—but all sorts of ingenious harassments were devised to penalize the foreign-born.[9]

While the Chinese found themselves confronted by laws designed to hamper their work in the service trades, the Japanese found themselves, to their surprise, threatening the agricultural hegemony of the master race. Those who followed the history of Arab-Jewish relations in Palestine will recognize the situation as it developed in California, Oregon, and Washington. Like the Jews in Palestine under the Mandate, the Japanese were permitted to purchase land which was by American standards marginal. They thus bought swampy plots, dry acreage, or hilly land which no white farmer was interested in cultivating. Then, by the use of backbreaking labor, terracing, irrigation, ditching, and by utilizing age-old Asian techniques of intensive farming, they built up the value of their holdings. At this point the white farmers—who had been chuckling at their acumen in disposing of worthless land —suddenly decided they had been tricked, robbed of valuable holdings by these "sly little yellow men." Like the Palestinian Arabs, who similarly claimed deception when the land they had sold the Jewish *kibbutzim* was developed by its new owners, the Native Sons of the Golden West never took into consideration the crucial fact that Japanese work and ingenuity had provided the increment in value.

These swindled innocents demanded action, and the state legislatures were obliging: they passed so-called alien land laws very cleverly devised to penalize only "aliens ineligible for citizenship," i.e., Asians, or other colored peoples. These laws forbade such aliens to own or lease agricultural land and, despite their apparent conflict with treaties between the United States and Japan, were sustained by the United States Supreme Court as a legitimate exercise of state power.[10] Moreover, the legislatures devised "presumptions" which were designed to prevent alien Japanese from transferring their holdings to or employing as their intermediaries American citizens who would be their dummy entrymen. (The California proviso to this effect was not declared unconstitutional until 1948.)[11] It appears that these laws were "paper dragons"—in California there were only twenty attempts at enforcement by escheat between 1913 and 1941[12]—but they always hung over the heads of the immigrants and were symptomatic of the atmosphere on the West Coast.

The Asians were also subjected to the standard minority indictments. They were kept in the ghetto by the refusal of the whites to sell them homes elsewhere—the restrictive covenant was standard form in housing sales—and then accused of being clannish and secretive. Their children were segregated in schools and were later arraigned for their refusal to "mix." In short, the society at large denounced the Asian minorities as "unassimilable," and then did everything in its power to bring this prophecy to fruition.

The humiliation of China and the rise of Japanese power in East Asia led to some differentiation in prejudice. American sympathy, for historical reasons, was overwhelmingly on the side of the Chinese. Since the nineteenth century, there had been close missionary ties between various Protestant churches and the Chinese, and Secretary of State John Hay's "Open Door" policy was considered as a quasi-guarantee of Chinese sovereignty on which the Japanese were trampling. Chinese-Americans benefited from this attitude in the 1930's, as the Japanese-Americans suffered from their identification with the "Co-Prosperity Sphere" and the militarism of the Japanese government. (It is interesting to note that sinister Japanese became standard movie fare, and in the late 1930's "Mr. Moto," John P. Marquand's omniscient and benevolent Japanese detective, vanished from the screen.)

December 7, 1941, left the United States in an advanced state of shock from which the American people emerged in cold fury. There was little wild hysteria, and even on the West Coast there were few anti-Japanese incidents—and those were largely instigated by angry Filipinos. The FBI and military intelligence officers rounded up known Japanese agents (mostly from among the Kibei—young Japanese-Americans who had been sent back to Japan for their education) and the authorities called for calm. The Japanese and Nisei population, expecting the worst in December, began to breathe more freely as the new year began. But just as it seemed that the danger was over, there began, slowly at first, a campaign spearheaded by newspaper editorials, columnists, and radio commentators to "relocate" the Japanese community. It was rapidly picked up and boomed by traditionally anti-Asian politicians both on the Pacific Coast and in Washington —where Southern advocates of white supremacy supported their Western colleagues. By February, 1942, the Japanese were in dire peril. The campaign against them had a self-fulfilling character, and, as the citizens of California heard of the alleged treasonable behavior of their neighbors, the ominous growl of the lynch mob was mounting in the countryside.[13]

Words are inadequate to describe the vicious and irresponsible character of the attack on the 112,000-member Japanese community on the West Coast (of whom 75,000 were birthright Americans—Nisei). Never in modern times has the American press behaved in such an unprincipled and meretricious fashion, and with such disgraceful unanimity. The basis of the assault on the loyalty and integrity of the West Coast Japanese minority was a series of sensational newspaper articles describing in painstaking detail the "treasonous behavior" of the Hawaiian Japanese. They had allegedly spied for the Japanese, signaled to enemy planes by cutting arrows in the sugar cane, blocked the roads, sabotaged antiaircraft installations, even machine-gunned American pilots as they rushed to their fighter planes. The conclusion was clear: the Japanese, citizens or not, were sunk in treason and had cruelly betrayed the United States in its moment of peril.[14]

Soon the "treason" infected the mainland. Mysterious lights were supposed to blink at night, curious codes filled the short-wave bands, and saboteurs lurked around defense plants, oil refineries, harbor defenses. The press was in an uproar as reporters competed for sensationalistic exposés; like medieval witchfinders, newsmen prowled about Japanese areas in search of sinister portents. Not unsurprisingly, they found them. When Japanese were ordered to turn in short-wave radios, cameras, and firearms to the authorities, the newsmen rushed to photograph the ominous piles—few bothered to point out that most of the weapons in the collection were shotguns and .22's, or that the cameras and radios were hardly distinctive from those owned by non-Japanese. What the public saw was a front-page picture of a room full of menacing equipment, firearms (confiscated from a sporting-goods store) heaped front and center.

Confronted by this daily frenzy in their papers, accompanied by stories chronicling unpunished treason, the citizens of the West Coast became understandably unsettled. Who can blame them? When the *Sacramento Bee* observed that "experience with the fifth column in Hawaii" provided overwhelming evidence of disloyalty,[15] the citizenry began to grumble; when Westbrook Pegler declared that the "Japanese in California [citizens and noncitizens alike] should be under guard to the last man and woman right now and to hell with *habeas corpus*," [16] the populace began to roar. When Walter Lippmann added his authoritative *imprimatur* to the demand for action,[17] even the most sober elements in the community began to panic. By this time, the middle of February, 1942, the mood of the West Coast was so bellicose that even those sympathetic to the Japanese began to feel that evacuation might be necessary to protect the minority from vengeful mob action.

Only a reader of Franz Kafka's *The Castle* or *The Trial* can fully appreciate the savage, irrational universe into which the hapless Japanese were flung. If the latter protested their loyalty, they were told either 1) that naturally spies and saboteurs would defend their patriotism as an artifice to trick simple-minded Americans; or 2) that the way to demonstrate loyalty was to accept evacuation and "relocation" (the euphemism for the concentration camps) in a good spirit. When defenders of the Japanese argued that there had been no sabotage, it was Earl Warren, then Attorney General of California, who sprung the classic mousetrap. Warren pointed out to a Congressional committee that the *absence* of disloyal acts was itself highly significant since it indicated that the disciplined Japanese were awaiting a signal for concerted action.[18]

But the most appalling aspect of the whole affair was that no authoritative voice proclaimed the innocence of the Hawaiian Japanese. How then was the public to know that every "factual" account of the Japanese "fifth column" in Hawaii was a mendacious fabrication? The public, to be blunt, had been swept along on a torrent of lies. There was not one single documented instance of sabotage by Hawaiian Japanese, and the West Coast stories were equally unfounded.[19] The newspaper accounts had been made up from whole cloth by reporters who were either hysterical or dishonest, though one may suspect that the military authorities encouraged these wild tales to deflect public anger from their own sins. It is worth noting in the light of later events that although Hawaii was placed under martial law after Pearl Harbor, there was no serious discrimination against the sizable Japanese minority (over a third of the population), while on the West Coast "military necessity" was employed to justify the removal and incarceration of the tiny Japanese segment of the populace.[20]

This is the external background of the evacuation and "relocation"—the combination of public hysteria, a mendacious press, economic self-interest, and historical prejudice which provided the rationale for the action. The internal background is perhaps even more significant, both for its contribution to the formation of public opinion and for the insight it provides into a thrombosis of the democratic political system. The key inside figure was Lt. Gen. John L. DeWitt, Commander of the Western Defense Command, who was charged by the President with the defense of the West Coast. Whatever may have been his military accomplishments, the crucial consideration for the Japanese and for this study was his outspoken racism. "In the war in which we are now engaged," he informed the Secretary of War, "racial affinities are not severed by migration. The Japanese race is an enemy race and while many second and third generation Japanese born on United States soil, possessed of United States citizenship, have become 'Americanized,' the racial strains are undiluted." [21] Elsewhere he stated it more concisely: "A Jap's a Jap, and that's all there is to it." [22]

Beginning shortly after Pearl Harbor, General DeWitt bombarded Washington with demands for summary action against the Japanese in his jurisdiction, and with complaints against the work of the Department of Justice. Attorney General Biddle, who had moved against individual Japanese and had taken restrictive measures against alien Japanese in general (forbidding them to live or work in sensitive areas, requiring them to turn in arms, and the like) was extremely distressed by DeWitt's exhortations and did his best to contain the general's extravagant ultimata. However, Biddle was at a great disadvantage in coping with DeWitt since the latter constantly invoked "military necessity" as the basis of his requests and kept suggesting that, unless his "military" needs were complied with, he could not be responsible for the outcome. Under any circumstances it is difficult for a civilian to question a general's expertise, and in the three months after the outbreak of war it was virtually impossible. Biddle later explained his predicament in these terms: "I never thought evacuation was necessary and I still don't think it was. Nevertheless, there was no way that I could stop it. The Army authorities were insistent, they talked in terms of military necessity and, in time of war, there is no way you can stop the Army on such a thing." [23]

With a fearful clamor from the West Coast ringing in their ears—a clamor that reverberated in the Washington echo cham-

ber as politicians climbed on the anti-Japanese bandwagon—the
Attorney General and two of his top aides met with DeWitt's
spokesmen on the evening of February 17. Although the meeting
was ostensibly called to discuss the evacuation of enemy aliens
from Los Angeles and other large cities, the representatives of
the Department of Justice were handed the draft of an executive
order (already cleared by the top civilian and military officials of
the defense establishment) authorizing the Army to evacuate "any
and all persons" from "military areas" to be designated by the
Secretary of War or his delegates. Biddle, apparently convinced
that fighting was useless, and perhaps glad to get rid of the politically explosive problem, capitulated.[24] Two days later, without any further exploration or Cabinet discussion, President Roosevelt signed Executive Order 9066.[25] Congress shortly thereafter
passed Public Law 503 which made it a federal offense to violate
the executive order. There was no dissent, and the President signed
the measure on March 21.[26]

Between March and November, with DeWitt firmly in the
saddle, anti-Japanese actions came thick and fast. It would be
pointless to detail the process; suffice it to say that by November
110,000 Japanese—aliens and citizens alike—were in concentration camps scattered through the Western states. These people
were ringed with barbed wire and guarded by troops under arms
—70,000 merely for possessing enemy chromosomes. And it happened virtually without public objection. Only Norman Thomas,
a few dogged civil libertarians such as A. L. Wirin of the Northern California Branch of the A.C.L.U. (the national A.C.L.U.
refused to condemn the action!), and a sprinkling of educators
and Protestant ministers spoke out. The Communists, committed
fully to the "People's War," endorsed the evacuation and even implied that it would not be a bad idea if Norman Thomas were
sent to join the Japanese.[27] In addition, the evacuees were, of
course, subjected to economic disaster; it was estimated that their
losses exceeded $400,000,000 as they were forced to abandon
businesses, agricultural leases, and most of their household fur-
nishings. In 1948 a miserly Congress appropriated $38,000,000

as compensation for personal property, but the destruction of "intangible" interests—e.g., the projected worth of a leasehold had a Japanese not been forced to abandon it—went unremunerated.[28]

All this was founded on the myth of "military necessity"; it was a military decision based on the maxim *inter arma leges silent:* the law cannot adjudicate questions of military necessity. General De Witt, General George Marshall, Secretary of War Henry Stimson, and Commander-in-Chief Franklin D. Roosevelt had all concurred in the proposition that military imperatives required the evacuation, and then imprisonment, of the Japanese West Coast population. In December, 1944, the Supreme Court also agreed: Justice Hugo Black lamely announced in *Korematsu* v. *United States* that war was tough on everybody and that the courts were not equipped to evaluate the plea of military necessity in a time of national emergency. In other words, Black, speaking for the six-judge majority, accepted the government's contention that evacuation and "relocation" were based on a military decision.[29] Justice Owen Roberts dissented on narrow grounds,[30] and Justice Robert Jackson penned what Dean Rostow called "an essay in judicial nihilism," suggesting that the Court should have ducked the case rather than hand down what the majority knew to be an appalling decision.[31]

Frank Murphy neither quibbled nor ducked. In one of the most powerfully reasoned polemics that has ever entered the Court *Reporter,* Justice Murphy excoriated the whole concept of "military necessity" as it had been applied in the case at bar. His flaming, passionate dissent tore the government's case to shreds. A military decision, he insisted, was not just any decision by a military official—it had to be a decision *founded on military considerations.* Drawing on the record in the case, Murphy went on to demonstrate in crushing fashion that DeWitt's decision was not based on military imperatives, but on his personal, racist convictions. Its standing as a "military decision" had emerged *only* from the fact that DeWitt was a general.[32]

In *Korematsu,* the Court had carefully distinguished between the process of evacuation from the West Coast and the subsequent imprisonment in "relocation centers"—although for those involved the movement had been continuous, and there had been no means of evading the destination. The reason for this labored exegesis became apparent on the same day when, after sustaining evacuation, the Court in *Ex parte Endo* ruled that Nisei could not be held in the camps unless they were individually charged with criminal behavior. That is, the continued imprisonment of the Nisei (and Sansei, the second generation of American birth) was unconstitutional and presumably had been unconstitutional since it was initiated in July, 1942.[33] Actually about 17,000 had been released by the War Relocation Authority by the end of 1943 and another 18,000 left the camps in the first six months of 1944. The worst problems were created for Nisei who felt obliged to remain with aged parents who simply had no place to go.[34]

Under the circumstances what was remarkable was the dogged loyalty of the Japanese-Americans. About one-sixth of the evacuees (a figure which included family members) had been screened out as "disloyal" and segregated under maximum security at the Tule Lake Center in California. Of these, 2,524 were aliens who asked for repatriation, while 4,698 were Nisei who renounced their American nationality.[35] On the other hand, about 14,000 mainland Nisei—there were another 12,000 from Hawaii—served in the Army, mostly in Italy where the 442d Combat Team inscribed its allegiance in blood and became one of the Fifth Army's most decorated units.[36] And quietly, as the American people learned that they had been deceived, public attitudes changed. As the war ended, the Japanese-Americans began to sense that their tribulations were largely over, that while no responsible political figure was willing to offer them an overt apology for their Golgotha, the door was open to a brighter future. Covertly, in an atmosphere of guilt and shame, they were inducted as full members of the American community. With them came the Chinese-Americans, who had earned their own way (fortunately without the misfortunes of the Japanese), and it should be emphasized that with all the hue and cry about Red China there has in recent years been no resurgence of the "yellow peril." While individual Chinese- and Japanese-Americans may still find themselves the victims of prejudice, anti-Asian demagoguery has vanished from American politics.

The fate of the Japanese-Americans has been discussed at length for two reasons. First, because there has been such a conspiracy of silence about it and such a failure to appreciate its potential impact on American constitutional law. The *Korematsu* decision will always remain, in Justice Jackson's phrase, "a gun behind the door" for use in crisis situations; and it is ironic that analyses of Justice Hugo Black's standing as a civil libertarian invariably skirt around or ignore his shameful opinion in this case where the chips were *really* down. The second reason is that the handling of the Japanese-Americans was qualitatively different from all previous instances of racial prejudice. They were not tarred and feathered, or mobbed by irate neighbors in a flush of hate; rather they were coldly, efficiently, impersonally shipped into concentration camps as victims of *bureaucratized prejudice.* They were, in short, a case study of what the modern, centralized American government can do when the democratic decision-making process goes off the rails. Only a moral idiot could compare their fate with that of the Jews under Nazism or the kulaks under Stalinism, but the lesson is there to be pondered and remembered.

Passing from this morbid episode to more cheerful topics, it is, I think, fair to say that the growth of the civil liberties tradition was accelerated rather than impaired during the war. The Roosevelt Court continued to expand the meaning of due process of law to prevent restrictions on freedom of speech, press, religion and assembly. Probably the most interesting litigation in this connection arose from the objection of Jehovah's Witnesses to the flag salute in the schools. Asserting that the compulsory salute in the schools was a violation of the Second Commandment, a symbol of the supremacy of the state over God's majesty, the Witnesses told their children to refuse to participate in the traditional ritual of patriotism. Irate school boards retaliated: in Minersville, Pennsylvania, for example, Superintendent of Schools Charles E. Roudabush expelled William and Lillian Gobitis. He had attempted to convince their father of the legitimacy of the flag salute, but had been brought up short by that stalwart's curt observation that the Gobitis family were citizens "not of the United States but of Heaven"! Gobitis' further observation that his children were obviously victims of a Catholic plot hardly improved the situation. With the encouragement of the American Civil Liberties Union, Gobitis initiated action in federal court to enjoin the enforcement of the salute, claiming that the latter deprived his children of freedom of religion, freedom of speech, and equal protection of the laws.[37]

To make a long and confused legal story short, Gobitis won his case and won his appeal; the essence of the unanimous decision of the Court of Appeals, Third Circuit, was that "We do not find the essential relationship between infant patriotism and the martial spirit." In March, 1940, the Supreme Court agreed to review the holding below, and on June 3 it reversed the Court of Appeals and sustained the Minersville school district. Although two weeks earlier the Justices had unanimously reversed the Connecticut convictions of several Witnesses who had been arrested for breach of the peace when their violent anti-Catholic diatribes had infuriated members of that faith,[38] the Court divided 8–1 against Gobitis. In essence Justice Frankfurter held for the Court that freedom of religion was constitutionally inviolable, but that saluting the flag had nothing to do with religious conviction—it was a secular ceremony designed for the "promotion of national cohesion." He also expatiated at length on the deference the Court should pay to the elected representatives of the people in matters such as this: the Supreme Court should not, indeed was incompetent to become the "school board for the country." [39] Justice Stone alone dissented, asserting that "by this law the state seeks to coerce these children to express a sentiment which, as they interpret it, they do not entertain, and which violates their deepest religious convictions." [40] David Manwaring, in a recent careful study of the Jehovah's Witness litigation, has suggested that Stone's experiences in World

War I, when he was appointed by Wilson to a board of inquiry on the status of conscientious objectors, made him permanently sympathetic toward this notoriously mistreated minority.[41] Justice Frankfurter, less charitably, has implied that he was under the influence of a Quaker law clerk.[42]

Following the Gobitis decision, the Jehovah's Witnesses found themselves subjected to nationwide abuse. From Maine, where persecuted Witnesses fired shotguns into a visiting mob, to Nebraska, where a Witness was kidnapped and castrated, to Wyoming, where the ancient American remedy, tar and feathers, emerged from the pharmacopoeia, to Oregon, where a group of Witnesses were beseiged and stormed by a thousand vigilantes, the violence spread. In a fascinating statistical table, Manwaring has analyzed the demographic environment of the mobbings. His conclusion, which should come as no surprise here, was that the persecutions were largely confined to Yahoo country. According to his "Persecution Index" (which correlated the number of incidents with the size of population units), in urban areas of 100,000 or more the Witnesses were virtually undisturbed (index=1.56), while in small towns and villages of 2,500 to 10,000 population they ran the greatest risks (index=34.83).[43]

These small communities were the stronghold of the American Legion, the organization which spearheaded the attack on the Witnesses. They were also the bailiwick of those units of government in which law enforcement was least bureaucratized; i.e., the sheriff, an elected official, would turn to his comrades of the American Legion for his posse in times of crisis so that it often became difficult to distinguish between the mob and the officers of the law. In 1940, New York's Mayor La Guardia sent distinctively Jewish policemen to the Yorkville neighborhood to prevent Joseph McWilliams, the Christian Fronter and anti-Semite, from being mobbed. The policemen stood like statues, impassively protecting the noxious agitator from enraged Jews. In small-town America, such impersonal law enforcement was almost impossible to establish because of the intimate political, social, and economic ties between the police and the power structure of the community. In the 1962 battle of "Ole Miss," the sheriff with jurisdiction over Oxford, Mississippi, was also chairman of the White Citizens' Council! [44]

Justices Black, Douglas, and Murphy were deeply distressed by the wave of anti-Witness violence which they feared the Court's decision in the Gobitis Case had spurred. This led them to take the extraordinary step, in a dissenting opinion in 1942, of doing public penance for their concurrence in Gobitis.[45] The Witnesses' dogged constitutional lawyer, Hayden Covington, who for years almost single-handedly kept the Court enmeshed in the fine points of religious freedom, waited and counted. When in October, 1942, Justice James F. Byrnes resigned and was replaced by Judge Wiley Rutledge of the United States Court of Appeals, District of Columbia, Covington reached the mystical number: *five*. (Rutledge, at the Circuit level, already had indicated his support of the Witnesses' position.) Back came the flag-salute issue, this time on an appeal from West Virginia.[46]

As it turned out, Covington had a Justice to spare, as the recently appointed Robert Jackson joined Stone, Black, Douglas, Murphy, and Rutledge in overruling the Gobitis decision. Ironically enough, the Court's decision was handed down on Flag Day, June 14, 1943; Jackson wrote an Opinion for the Court which was as eccentric as it was quotable. In effect, he dismissed the religious question from consideration and announced that nobody, whether he held religious scruples or not, could be compelled to salute the flag. Jackson was shrewd enough to realize that if special exemptions are established for the religious in these matters, a problem is created in the realm of the separation of church and state—e.g., if Quakers are permitted not to fight, and Witnesses not to salute, *on religious grounds*, why should Orthodox Jews not be entitled to do business on Sunday and Catholics not be constitutionally exempted from public school taxation? [47]

The significance of the decision in *West Virginia State Board of Education* v. *Barnette* for our purposes here is not the character of the constitutional arguments, but the broad cultural impact of such a striking Court opinion. In the middle of a war which in

1943 seemed touch and go, what with the Germans in the Caucasus and in the suburbs of Moscow and the Japanese bombing Australia, the United States Supreme Court held that the compulsory flag salute was a violation of individual freedom. As Jackson put it in a ringing peroration, "If there is any fixed star in our constitutional constellation, it is that no official, high or petty, can prescribe what shall be orthodox in politics, nationalism, religion, or other matters of opinion, or force citizens to confess by word or act their faith therein." [48] What made this remarkable holding even more significant was the general chorus of approval with which it was greeted in the press, in news magazines, and in law reviews. When one compares the mood of the nation in 1943 with that in the First World War, he gets a sudden sense of the degree to which American democracy had come of age in barely more than a generation.

When the war ended in 1945, it was possible to draw up a balance sheet of civil rights and intergroup relations which suggested that the concern for American ideals which was naturally basic in a conflict with Nazi barbarism had permeated the home front. Few conscientious objectors (except "absolutists" who refused to register or cooperate in any way with selective service) were treated as criminals. Those who were certified by their draft boards as pacifists, the government turned over to the historic peace churches (Mennonites, Brethren, Quakers) which administered camps and put the men to work on nonmilitary projects. As was mentioned earlier, a wild group of 28 pro-Nazis and domestic Fascists was brought to trial for sedition—the *Daily Worker* vigorously applauded *this* enforcement of the Smith Act— [49] but, after seven weary months, the trial judge died and a mistrial resulted. Biddle had never been enthusiastic about the prosecution; civil liberties issues aside, the game was clearly not worth the candle, and the defendants were never brought again to trial. [50] In the one case coming to the Supreme Court under the Espionage Act of 1917, the conviction of a pro-Nazi for circulating a defeatist newsletter was reversed. [51] And the Court in two decisions— one relating to a Communist and the other to a Nazi—severely circumscribed the government's power to denaturalize, to deprive a person of his naturalized citizenship, on political grounds.[52] During World War I, a German named Wursterbarth who had become a naturalized American in *1882* was denaturalized for disloyalty! The charge was that by his opposition to the war in 1917 he demonstrated that he had taken the oath of allegiance in bad faith 35 years before.[53]

Moreover, in the quest for national unity, the federal authorities and the Office of War Information laid a heavy emphasis on the "un-American" character of racial, ethnic, or religious prejudice. The contributions of all groups to the war effort were lauded, distinguished figures in the various subcultures were given official advisory positions, and posters of the "Four Freedoms" were found hanging on the walls of schools, post offices, and all public buildings. There was no anti-Semitism such as we saw in World War I; indeed, the death of the four chaplains on the *Dorchester*, the only American troop transport sunk throughout the war, became a symbol of the united contributions of Protestants, Catholics, and Jews. Troop education programs were launched to bring home to the men in the Armed Forces "Why We Fight," and I can state from personal experience in the Information and Education branch that the material was generally excellent—though seldom compelling enough to keep tired soldiers awake.[54]

Excepting the Japanese-Americans, of whom enough has been said, the Negroes were the great body of the disinherited, the one major group in American society which was excluded from the celebrations of unity and common purpose. Large numbers of Negroes migrated to industrial areas to get jobs in booming war industries, creating fearful housing problems and employment tension. There was a nasty race riot in Detroit in 1943; Los Angeles (where the Negro population doubled between 1940 and 1945!) suffered from endemic racial violence; and there was a close call in New York's Harlem. The Negroes were bitter, and they found articulate leadership as never before—one Negro leader put it neatly. Chastised for his militance at a time of national danger, he was asked reproachfully, "What will they think of your attitude in Berlin?" He replied, "I don't know what they will think of my attitude, but they invented yours." [55] Morale was bad, and it was worsened by the fact that the Negro soldiers were clearly the pack mules of the Army, the construction battalions, the aviation engineer units, the dock laborers, and truck drivers. Under the command of white officers who generally hated him, treated like a slave and discriminated against even in combat zones, the colored enlisted man had little to remind him that he was fighting for democracy against racism. (One twenty-year-old white sergeant watched an aviation engineer battalion [N] clear through a port of embarkation on its way to build air strips in New Guinea, noted the malevolence of the white officers, who seemed to be wholly from the South, the sullen, hopeless despair of the troops, and got sick.[56])

High government and military officials were profoundly concerned about the status of the Negroes in both civilian and military contexts, and efforts were made to help them and to appease the righteous anger of the Negro press and leadership. The National Fair Employment Practices Commission, alluded to earlier, was one such attempt, and, although the body had no real punitive powers, it made some headway in the North and West.[57] With much fanfare and publicity, Colonel Benjamin O. Davis, Jr., took his 332d Fighter Group, an all-Negro unit, into action in Italy, but the Air Force ran a segregated officer candidate school for colored flyers. There were two all-Negro infantry divisions—the 92d in Italy and the 93rd in the Southwest Pacific—but only after the American advance crossed the Rhine into Germany was any effort made to integrate white and Negro soldiers in the same combat units, and then on a "checkerboard" rather than an individual basis—Negro units at platoon strength were mixed into white regiments and retained their racial identity.[58] Throughout the war, the Red Cross stored "Negro plasma" in segregated blood banks and shipped it in distinctively marked containers—even though it is impossible to make any scientific differentiation on a racial basis.

In other words, enlightened officials chewed away at the edges of racial discrimination (a 1944 War Department General Order, for example, forbade racial segregation in recreational facilities, buses, and other off-duty enterprises on all Army posts),[59] but were impotent and perhaps somewhat unwilling to confront the crux of the matter: the surrender of the American military system to Southern prejudices. The Southern Congressional magnates always loomed ominously in the background. Thus, whatever the high purpose, there was no effective enforcement of equality. Army posts in the South simply disregarded the General Order mentioned above; [60] the commanding officers assumed that General George C. Marshall, the pride of Virginia Military Academy, had been the victim of political blackmail; and the Chief of Staff did nothing to disabuse them of that notion. But as Negro leaders and their liberal white allies insisted on fighting a two-front war—symbolized by the "Double V": victory over the Axis, *and* victory over racial discrimination—it became apparent that the war had brought the issue of equality squarely to the center of the American stage. The inevitable confrontation between American precepts and American practice, which had been avoided for almost a century, could no longer be put off. The Negro was about to challenge his status as the "invisible man" and demand his rightful inheritance.

World War II can therefore be seen in double perspective. On the one hand, it seemed to write finis to the fearful story of chauvinism and mutual suspicion among minority groups which had made World War I such a graveyard of freedom. On the other, it was clearly a prelude to a militant struggle for full equality, for the realization of the full logical implications of a victory over Nazi racism. But before we turn to the details of this battle for full equality, we must take time out to examine the postwar revival of the Yahoos, the crusade, often referred to as "McCarthyism," to turn the clock back to the 1920's and destroy the power of liberalism in America.

IX

COMMUNISM
AND INTERNAL
INSECURITY

The death of Franklin D. Roosevelt, followed shortly by the end of the war, created a new mood in American life, a mood which had as its main features a nostalgia for quiet times and a sense of dislocation and anticlimax. Harry S. Truman was a political cipher, the man who just happened to be Vice-President when the clock ran out. A whole generation of young Americans had never known a national spokesman other than F.D.R.; he had dominated the political stage so completely, and effortlessly, that it somehow seemed impossible that the Age of Roosevelt was over.

When the President died, it was not surprising that the liberals were thrown into disarray. Roosevelt had never concerned himself with the creation of a viable liberal tradition, one which could exist without his dominating magic. He had no ideological compulsions, but rather permitted and encouraged *ad hoc* efforts by his liberal subordinates as one manifestation of his essentially personal pattern of political leadership. Truman, whose great virtues were as yet unrevealed, found himself in 1945, '46, and '47 engaged in an arduous program of on-the-job training. As we now know, his education was strikingly successful, but in the crucial postwar years he was incapable of re-establishing Roosevelt's role as a liberal catalyst. And the liberals, suddenly on their own, wandered around like lost sheep trying to invoke the authority of their dead shepherd.

With Democratic vitality seemingly a thing of the past, the Republicans rallied for a comeback and in 1946 captured both houses of Congress on what amounted to a "return to normalcy" program. However, the G.O.P. had learned its lesson in the 1930's: the "normalcy" it had in mind, despite some militantly reactionary rhetoric, was not pre-1932, but pre-1940. Even the much abused Taft-Hartley Act, foolishly denounced by organized labor as a "slave labor bill," did not endanger the fundamental accomplishments of the National Labor Relations Act; and no effort was ever made by the Republican majorities to repeal the Social Security Act or the Fair Labor Standards Act. Indeed, had Thomas E. Dewey been elected President in 1948, and turned to work with a Republican legislature, one can confidently say that the great liberal gains of the New Deal era would have been sustained. While the Yahoos held real power in certain sectors of the G.O.P., notably among senior Senators and Representatives, the leadership of the party was not animated by a death wish and had no intention of permitting them to dictate its course. (The Democrats, of course, have a comparable problem with the Southern racists who are powerful in Congress but impotent as a national Democratic force except as they can block proposed liberal legislation.)

At this point, with the Democratic Party a shambles and the Truman Administration apparently conducting a holding operation until it could gracefully retire in January, 1949, the Yahoos found an issue, and in the hills the drums began to sound. The Communists were taking over the country! The Roosevelt Administration had been riddled with Soviet agents! The Democrats were the "party of treason"! The New Deal, in fact, was nothing but the first stage of a Communist take-over in the United States! Back into active service came the old veterans of the crusade against "Jewish Bolshevism"—the American Fascists whose views had been under wraps during the war. And for reasons we must now examine, their extremist tirades received a wide hearing.

Once again we have to take time off from the narrative to fill in some strokes on the background canvas. In my opinion, three major propositions have to be elucidated before we can properly understand the phenomenon known as "McCarthyism": first, the nature of the American Communist operation; second, the fear and perplexity which the beginning of the Cold War and Korea created in the American people; and, third, the extent to which Yahoo slogans were used for expediential political purposes by men who knew them to be false but were prepared to use any stick to beat the Democratic dog.

We have hardly touched here on the American Communist Party for the simple reason that it played no significant role in the development of American ideals of civil rights and civil liberties. Indeed, until the new "Popular Front" program emerged in the wake of the Seventh Congress of the Communist International in 1935, the American Communists might just as well have been in Central Asia insofar as their impact on American life was concerned. As supporters of dual unionism, they were considered little better than scabs by American trade unionists; as backers of a Negro Republic in the Black Belt, they were considered mad by Negro radicals; as patrons of the Arabs in Palestine who denounced Zionism as a form of British imperialism, they were despised by even non-Zionist Jewish leaders. In the early 1930's, Communist insistence that Roosevelt was the "American Hitler" had hardly endeared them to the "masses." [1]

The American Communist movement was from the days of its schizophrenic foundation—two parties were founded simultaneously in 1919—nothing more nor less than the American branch of the Communist International.[2] As the old Socialist joke put it, the Communist Party, like the Brooklyn Bridge, was suspended on cables—from Moscow. The party's hatchet men denounced those who asserted its dependence on Moscow, but the plain fact of subservience was written down in the famous "21 Conditions" for membership in the Comintern, imposed by the Soviet leaders in 1920. By these club rules, the authority of national parties was strictly subordinated to the Executive Committee of the Comintern, which the Russians dominated, and in the American case the International had intervened several times to straighten out the locals.[3] The most famous episode of this sort was the deposition in 1929 of the elected leadership of the American Communist Party and its replacement by the previously defeated minority.

The French Communists used to boast that they were "not a party like the others," and this generalization was valid for all sections of the movement. The model for their tactics was laid down by V. I. Lenin, notably in his *Left-Wing Communism: An Infantile Disorder,* and amounted to an endorsement of total flexibility, providing that organizational discipline was maintained. Thus the Communists were in one manifestation a political party running candidates for office; in another, a Soviet intelligence *apparat* operating underground for revolutionary ends; in still another, a civil rights organization, or an insurance company, or a trade union, or a promoter of summer camps, or a publishing house, or a nature club . . . The list could be extended for pages. In other words, the Communists were not just another organization of radicals located, say, ten degrees to the left of the Socialists. On the contrary, they constituted a protean apparatus controlled from Moscow. Their policy decisions were not made in terms of American imperatives, or the membership's view of American needs, but on the basis of a worldwide strategy determined by the Soviet leaders on the basis of their expediential requirements.

In 1927, assuming that world capitalism was entering its final death throes, the Comintern laid down a "hard line" of no compromise with any bourgeois organizations; and it included in this category the social democrats (smeared as "social Fascists") and all liberal groups and trade unions. Indeed, the Stalinists reserved their special venom for the "social Fascists" who in their view stood between the proletariat and the revolution as a front and buffer of capitalism, misleading the workers and obscuring the real dimensions of the class struggle. It was in Germany that this policy received its maximum application. Ruthlessly purging the German Communist Party of those who felt that the Communists should unite with the Socialists to confront the rising menace of Nazism, the Comintern proclaimed *"Durch Hitler kommen wir!"* —Hitler will bring us to power in his wake. The world Communist movement, in short, was monolithically geared to a politics of catastrophe: the worse the situation got, the better for the Communists.[4]

Stalin, however, had seriously miscalculated the situation. As it became apparent that Nazism was not the death rattle of the German bourgeoisie, but a system which was developing massive power and posing a threat to Soviet security in Eastern Europe, the Comintern line began to shift. The first indication was in France where, as was noted earlier, the Communists had joined the Fascists in marching on the Chamber of Deputies in February, 1934, and had found themselves isolated from the other parties of "republican defense" and repudiated even by their own trade unions. Within a few days, after much consultation between Paris and Moscow, the *Parti Communiste Français* shifted gears and announced its participation in the defense of the Republic. Characteristically, it congratulated the other parties for at last realizing the dangers of Fascism and affiliating with the Communists, a standard rhetorical device which has created much confusion among those who look to the Communist press for authoritative information. If one, for example, turned to a recent issue of the *Freiheit*, a New York Communist paper, one could read that John P. Roche had announced his endorsement of the Communist position on the Internal Security Act of 1954, when in fact I have publicly condemned this measure since the day it was introduced in Congress for reasons that have nothing whatever to do with the Communist Party *per se*. But someday some vigilant defender of the American Way of Life will turn up with a citation: "John P. Roche, cited by Communist paper *Freiheit* as supporter of Communist position on Internal Security Act of 1954."

This so-called "united front" technique became Comintern doctrine at the Congress in July–August, 1935. Technically speaking, it involved a shift from the "united front from below," i.e., attempting to get Socialist and liberal ranks and files to repudiate their "reactionary leaders," to the "united front from above," i.e., forming coalitions with Socialist and liberal organizations by what amounted to treaties. The underlying premise of this transformation (which was tactical rather than strategic—it involved no abandonment of long-range Communist goals) was that the immediate enemy was Fascism and that all possible force must be mobilized for the defense of the Soviet Union from this rising threat. Overnight the Communists changed from bitter opponents of the capitalist order to militant defenders of democracy against the menace of Fascism. The American Communists, for example, put away their poison pens as far as F.D.R. was concerned and virtually converted him into a "Hero of Socialism." Earl Browder, who through some inadvertence turned up as the Communist candidate for President in 1936 (the American Communists were always slow on the draw), practically apologized for running and suggested that Roosevelt was the proper recipient of Communist votes.[5]

Between 1935 and August, 1939, the Communists moved with their characteristic energy and discipline to build the "Popular Front" in the United States. Uninhibited by the normal restraints of American politics in that era, nostalgic isolationism and confusion about foreign policy objectives, they rapidly assumed the leadership of the movement which demanded vigorous action against Hitler. For this purpose, with typical cynicism, they employed an organization formed in the previous "hard" period to fight *against* rearmament, the American League Against War and Fascism. This organization, which was in 1937 rebaptized with the more sonorous title American League for Peace and Democracy, seemed to many non-Communists to be the only focus for militant anti-Nazism, and thus drew a considerable body of supporters who were totally unconcerned about the *nature* of the group but gave their endorsement to its *program*. They gained many adherents, for example, as the outstanding defenders of the cause of the Spanish Republic when the Civil War there brought open Nazi and Fascist intervention and the West stood by "nonintervention." [6]

It is hard to know how many real members the League had because of the standard party technique of parlaying group totals.
For instance, the International Workers Order, which specialized
in inexpensive insurance, affiliated with the League and brought
perhaps a million "members," i.e., those holding policies! The individual who took out low-cost insurance with the I.W.O. had no
realization that he was also a member of the League, but he was;
and his vote was cast for him at League congresses by some party
stalwart.[7] The handful of Communist-controlled unions also affiliated, bringing into the League another half a million unsuspecting
participants in its councils.[8] On the other hand, if a Communist
joined the League individually, he could find himself being sepa-
rately represented by a delegate from the International Labor Defense, the Jewish Peoples Fraternal Order, the Furriers'
Union, the International Workers Order, and the Flatbush Committee Against Nazi Aggression—organizations to which he also
belonged. And no reliable estimate can be made of the number of
"paper" organizations with essentially fictitious memberships that
the party created. A "Harlem Committee Against Slum Land-
lords" could mysteriously materialize, its membership consisting
of those who, when stopped in the street, had signed a petition
against evictions.

Thus all quantitative evaluations of Communist strength in
the late 1930's have an insubstantial quality about them. But it is
still clear that as the party remade its image by strongly supporting the League of Nations and collective security on the international front, and vigorously backing the New Deal domes-
tically, its stock rose, and a number of people with no sympathy
for Communist objectives were prepared to work in its ambience
for what they conceived to be sound national policy. The number
of distinguished Americans who permitted their names to be used
on Communist-front letterheads has in the last fifteen years become a matter of public notoriety—indeed, collating these names
has almost become an industry. A small percentage of these men
and women were conscious, disciplined fellow travelers. There
were some cynics who enjoyed the party's "valet service"—a co-

operative author could get warm reviews and a guaranteed claque if he played along with the American Writers' Congress and turned up to speak at party and Communist-front functions.[9] There were others who held their noses and cooperated because only the Communists seemed to evaluate the dangers of Nazism and to be capable of bringing the issue dramatically before the public. And finally there were the "innocents" who awoke with chagrin and shock in the fall of 1939, discovering that they had been used in a "transmission belt" run by Moscow. The collapse of the fronts after the Stalin-Hitler Pact was probative evidence that the great bulk of the active members (as distinct from those who were simply joined by virtue of belonging to affiliating organizations) were in the last category.

This point needs to be emphasized in the light of subsequent revelations about the "Red Decade." There was a great deal of stupidity and purposeful blindness; e.g., a number of liberals who were not Communists simply refused to believe the Moscow Trials were frame-ups, and, indeed, perhaps because their blindness was purposeful, got extremely annoyed at those who tried to force them to confront the Purges realistically. The Communists, in effect, were given a sort of special dispensation. They were young, crude, and bad-mannered but *vital*. Yet few of the liberals who worked with them ever made the existential leap from a sloppy and often intellectually dishonest brand of fellow-traveling to disciplined subordination within the party framework. The party's popularity, in other words, was a function of *its* fellow-traveling with New Deal liberalism and *its* formulation of what many liberals thought was the appropriate *liberal* foreign policy— one of vigorous anti-Fascism. Thus when the line changed, and the *Daily Worker* began to denounce Britain and France as the instigators of the "Second Imperialist War," the liberals vanished; and the party leaders discovered when they counted the house in one front after another that they had succeeded in capturing themselves.[10]

Separate from the Communist Party's political activities and the opinion-shaping endeavors of its fronts was an underground espionage apparatus. The Soviet leaders always took a dim view of the American Communist movement, and apparently trusted only a handful of party cadres to do the essential underground work. Usually the key threads were held by some trusted Comintern functionary who was sent to the United States and instructed to build his *apparat* independently of the party, though drawing upon it for agents. From the viewpoint of an intelligence organization, this was eminently sensible. Spies are valued for their invisibility, and, even in the naïve United States, a man in the State Department handling secret cables who came to work with the *Daily Worker* in his overcoat pocket would have been suspect. When Whittaker Chambers was chosen as the espionage "drop" in Washington, he had long since been instructed to cut all ties with the American Communist Party.[11]

Thus, the notion that all Communists were spies has a certain logical validity (like the proposition that all Christians should be willing to accept martyrdom), but in fact it appears that few members of the party were ever aware of the existence of the dual apparatus. The Russians simply did not trust them—and given the large number of strange characters who took a pilgrimage in the party as background for a tortured autobiographical confession, they were wise. Moreover, the effort to link a distinguished liberal to espionage by cataloguing his front affiliations is the sheerest sort of absurdity. But in the postwar world, this was precisely the formula the Yahoos developed: liberal = front sponsor = Communist = spy and traitor. The autohypnosis of some distinguished liberals in their relationship to the Communists almost defies rational belief, but, except in the insane world of the Moscow Trials, self-deception and stupidity are no evidence of treason.

Once Russia was an ally in the war against Nazism, there was a resurgence of the Popular Front mentality, particularly in California where it sometimes seemed as though the news of the Stalin-Hitler Pact had not penetrated. But this time, dominated by the overriding desire to win the war, virtually all sectors of the political spectrum joined in the celebration of Soviet virtues. (The League for Peace and Democracy, which had in December,

COMMUNISM AND INTERNAL INSECURITY   217

1939, become the American Peace Mobilization, got little support in its last transmutation: the American Peoples' Mobilization for War.) As was indicated in the last chapter, the Communists during World War II made the American Legion look like defeatists: they opposed and broke strikes, denounced efforts to aid the Negro as the work of "Nazi-Trotskyist wreckers," endorsed the use of the Smith Act against first a group of Minneapolis Trotskyites and then the twenty-eight Americans indicted as pro-Nazi, and generally attempted to document Earl Browder's thesis that "Communism is Twentieth-Century Americanism." The background music supplied by the party's ubiquitous folk singers shifted from "Plow Under Every Fourth American Boy" to "Keep Your Hand on the Gun, Hold On!" and Roosevelt—who had been an "imperialist warmonger" in 1940—resumed his status as a folk hero.[12]

In May, 1944, in an excess of zeal for national unity and the "two-party system," the Communist Party actually abolished itself and became the Communist Political Association. As distinguished Americans gave their blessing to the Soviet system ("The family is higher in Russia than in the United States," noted Monsignor [now Bishop] Fulton J. Sheen, "and God, looking from heaven, may be more pleased with Russia than with us." [13] The dreaded NKVD, *Life* informed its readers, was just "a national police similar to the FBI." [14] Even racist Congressman John Rankin found a place to put his lever: "Stalin is a gentile and Trotsky was a Jew." [15]), the American Communists reciprocated by joining the American celebration: "We frankly declare," said Browder, "that we are ready to cooperate in making Capitalism work effectively in the post-war period with the least possible burden upon the people." [16] Alas for Browder, this euphoric period was all too brief. Less than a year later, both he and his policies were dumped by Moscow in one of the weirdest sequences in Communist history.

It began in April, 1945, when the French Communist leader Jacques Duclos, who had recently met with Stalin, excoriated Browder and Browderism in the theoretical organ of the French party *Cahiers du Communisme*. The indictment first appeared in English when an enterprising writer on the New York *World Telegram* published a translation in that paper! No one in Moscow seems to have bothered to alert the Americans to their destiny, and for some time the *Daily Worker* officially ignored the Duclos pronouncement. Then the denunciations began, and in July, 1945, the same people who had unanimously endorsed Browderism shortly before denounced him with equal unanimity and reestablished the Communist Party. Six months later he was expelled for the esoteric crime of "social imperialism." [17]

This episode has not been included here for its anecdotal value or for the perspective it casts on the Byzantine aspects of Stalinism. Although its symbolic meaning was not appreciated at the time by many commentators, it pointed up two important considerations. First, that the American Communist Party, despite its wartime love affair with "Americanism," was still a total dependent of Moscow; and, second, in the realm of policy, that Stalin was moving toward the "hard" line that was soon to precipitate the Cold War. Browder, as Duclos pointed out, took the wartime coalition and its common goals to be an *end*, whereas they could properly be understood only as a temporary truce in the struggle between Communism and capitalism. This, said Duclos, was a "dangerous opportunistic illusion." [18]

Unfortunately, at the top level only Winston Churchill seemed to appreciate that the war had as its objectives matters of a political character—that military decisions had to be made in terms of broad power problems. Churchill, for example, labored furiously to move the Anglo-American armies eastward as Germany collapsed, and in particular urged the Americans to secure a land corridor to Berlin as insurance against Soviet postwar ambitions. General Dwight Eisenhower, backed by General Marshall and President Roosevelt, refused on the ground that to do so would arouse Soviet suspicions. Churchill's argument that Russian behavior during the war indicated that they were incorrigibly suspicious, and that under the circumstances the West would be advised to negotiate from strength was taken by the Americans as evidence of *his* incorrigible anti-Bolshevism.[19] In this connection, it is worth noting—particularly in the light of later mythology—that Roosevelt's East European concessions to Stalin at Yalta were founded on a military judgment that the U.S.S.R. had to be involved in the war against Japan, a judgment which was in turn based on the advice of General Douglas MacArthur.[20] Roosevelt must, of course, take the blame for these policies, but it is important to keep in mind that his decisions were not a by-product of Communist or pro-Communist advisors, but of his excessive reliance (already noted in the case of the Japanese-Americans and General DeWitt) on his military staff for advice in areas that were not, properly defined, the jurisdiction of military expertise.[21]

If we can summarize, at the point in 1946 when it slowly began to dawn on the politically conscious American that trouble was brewing with the Soviet Union, the Communist Party was utterly insignificant in American politics; Russian espionage *apparats* were engaged in all-out efforts to gather atomic secrets and other less vital data; there was a good deal of sympathy for the Soviet Union among the American people based on their respect for the heroic Russian efforts and great losses (perhaps 20,000,-000) in the war; and a number of American liberal organizations and trade unions had been infiltrated to some degree by the Stalinists, who were still talking more about George Washington and Abraham Lincoln than Karl Marx or V. I. Lenin. Allied foreign policy, over Churchill's dogged objections, was grounded on the view that the U.S.S.R. had learned from experience in World War II that the Western powers were not its mortal enemies, and that this recognition of the decency of the "capitalist" powers would lead in the postwar world to cooperation rather than rivalry and conflict between the leading states of the United Nations.

It is hardly necessary to recapitulate here the gloomy story of Stalin's betrayal of the Grand Alliance. Suffice it to say that the American people, basking in the sunshine of permanent peace in 1946, found themselves confronted by an accelerating program of Soviet expansion in Europe, the capture of mainland China by

220

the Chinese Communists, and in June, 1950, the invasion of South Korea. The national budget, which had gone to a wartime peak of ninety-eight billion dollars in 1945, had dropped to thirty-three billion by 1948. The Army budget alone (including the Air Force) declined from fifty billion to eight, while the Navy dropped from thirty billion to four.[22] The huge warmaking machine mobilized in World War II was scrapped almost overnight. The United States, still holding monopoly control of atomic weapons, proposed the establishment of an international agency to oversee the development for peaceful uses of nuclear power. In sum, the United States was prepared to live in peace with Communism and far from making any preparations for the Cold War, was caught utterly flat-footed by the Czechoslovak *coup* and the Soviet take-over (in violation of the Yalta Agreement) in Eastern Europe. The Chinese debacle came as a complete surprise—even to Stalin, who had written off his Asian supporters by recognizing Chiang Kai-shek's regime as one of the "Big Five" in the Security Council of the United Nations.[23]

Something was obviously wrong. What had happened to Peace? How could it be that within five years of winning the greatest war in history, the American people could find themselves confronted by a new crisis? their young men once again fighting an enemy on some filthy Asian peninsula? their atomic secrets apparently conveyed to the Russians by highly placed spies? The situation was ripe for an irrational answer, and shortly from the Yahoos came the inevitable reply: "You have been betrayed!"

But not just from the Yahoos could this diagnosis be heard. The Republican Party had fallen on bad times, having snatched defeat from the jaws of victory in the presidential election of 1948, and was in desperate search of a formula which could invigorate its trailing and depressed constituents and provide it with mass appeal. Thus, while it was quite clear that such an intelligent Republican leader as Robert A. Taft never believed for a minute that the Democrats were the "Party of Treason," he and men like him simply stood aside as the Yahoo bulls gored the Democratic matador—and occasionally encouraged the bulls a bit. In their view, the first priority was to get the Democrats out of power in 1952, and, if some of the country boys played a little rough, well, these irregular commandos could be domesticated and taught some manners after the fighting was over. And while the Democrats had won the '48 election, President Truman's clear-cut affiliation with the liberal wing of the party had led to deep divisions in its ranks, divisions which made it incapable of fighting back as an effective unit. The Chairman of the Senate Judiciary Committee, Pat McCarran, for example, clearly hated Truman more than he did the Republicans, and the Southern barons in Congress were quite willing to participate in stamping out the "Communist-liberal" heresy of racial equality.[24]

From the viewpoint of intelligent liberals, the situation in the late forties and early fifties had a nightmarish quality about it. The Truman Administration found itself being simultaneously denounced as the "war party" because of its commitment to the lingering Korean War and as "appeasers of Communism" because it had *not* saved China from the Communists or Eastern Europe from the Soviets, which could certainly not have been accomplished without a major conflict. Moreover, the liberals who had organized in 1947 behind President Truman's policy of "containment" (for example, in Americans for Democratic Action) were quite aware of the existence of a Communist threat to American freedom. Indeed, they had fought this issue out with the so-called Progressives or Wallaceites, who called the whole anti-Communist mobilization a "witch hunt," by insisting that Communists, unlike witches, did exist.[25] Yet, from the Yahoo perspective, all liberals were guilty: in the classic phrase of a policeman who told a sidewalk orator he wanted no "Commies" on his beat and was informed by the speaker that he was an *anti*-Communist"—"I don't care what kind of a Communist you are—off you go."

To put the matter bluntly, from 1947 to 1952 the Democratic administration and its liberal allies were brutally whipsawed on the Communist issue. When in November, 1946, President Truman established the Temporary Commission on Employee Loyalty, his action was immediately interpreted as a confession of guilt and an effort to cover up previous malfeasance. When in March, 1947, he set up in Executive Order 9835 the Federal Loyalty and Security Program, liberals denounced what they correctly believed to be an extraordinary erosion of due process of law, while reactionaries claimed the measure was utterly inadequate to cope with the vast underground network of Soviet espionage which they envisaged.[26] (The fact that few spies were turned up was utterly irrelevant to this argument; indeed, it only testified to the superhuman cunning of the underground apparatus that so *few* of their number were apprehended.) To supplement what they took to be the halfhearted efforts of the administration to deal with subversion, Congress decided to set up a large-scale antisubversion operation of its own, first by expanding the scope and resources of the House Committee on Un-American Activities, and then in the Senate with the notorious McCarthy and Jenner Committees.

As Professor Robert K. Carr (now President of Oberlin College) has pointed out in his careful study of the House Committee,[27] the body lurked in legislative limbo from its founding, on a temporary basis, in 1938 until the Republicans took over Congress in 1947. As the "Dies Committee," it had raised a certain amount of turmoil from time to time and had captured the headlines with extravagant claims of subversion, but the Congress had never taken the investigators seriously. However, from 1947 on, the committee really went to work ferreting out activities which fitted into its broad definition of "subversion": its first big splash was probably a natural—it investigated Communist activities in Hollywood. It had long been common knowledge among anti-Communist liberals that the Stalinists had some close sympathizers in the movie colony, but few had ever gone so far as to suggest that the movies they produced were instruments of Communist propaganda. Rather it was their fund-raising potential in Communist causes that caused distress; they could fill the Hollywood Bowl for the League for Peace and Freedom or the Progressive Party. But the committee, chaired by J. Parnell Thomas, set out to demonstrate substantive indoctrination.

It did rather badly. The problem in a nutshell was that pro-Communist screenwriters were specialists in *kitsch*—otherwise they would not have been successful in Hollywood—and were thus almost incapable of presenting any thesis sharply except boy-meets-girl. John Howard Lawson, for example, was closely identified for years with Communist organizations and was later pilloried for his movie about the Spanish Civil War, *Blockade*. But anyone who has seen *Blockade* will recall that nowhere in the film were the political positions of the protagonists defined. The result was a total ideological blur! During World War II several pro-Russian films were made, but this was hardly startling. Hollywood always jumps on current popular themes and not surprisingly in this case converted the Soviet war effort into boy-meets-girl (see *Song of Russia* or *North Star*). The one wartime film that did have some ideological content was *Mission to Moscow*, a cinematic version of Ambassador Joseph E. Davies' best-selling book. The book was suffused with naïvete, and the movie did improve a bit on the original by showing Russian generals plotting with Nazis (at a cocktail party, of all places) and suggesting that the Moscow Purges were justified.

Thomas and his colleagues may not have turned up much in the way of movie indoctrination, but they did hit the headlines just the same, thanks to the cooperation of the "Hollywood Ten," a group of screenwriters and other movie technicians who turned the hearings into a two-ring circus by refusing to answer any questions about their political affiliations and delivering speeches denouncing its investigation as Hitlerite scare techniques. This encounter was one of those unhappy situations in which the extremes feed each other: the Communists and their allies arguing that it demonstrated that the United States was on the "abyss of Fascism," while the Yahoos claimed that it proved that Hollywood *was* infiltrated, that subversive propaganda *was* slipping into the movies, that the Communist enemy was everywhere. A number of anti-Communists felt that the conduct of the hearings violated the basic principles of due process and later unsuccessfully urged that the convictions of the "Hollywood Ten" for contempt of

Congress be reversed, but it was perfectly clear that the party tactic had been designed to get the maximum publicity for its slogans. And thanks to the House Committee it was eminently successful.[28]

It was, however, the case of Alger Hiss which brought the Great Fear, and he was clearly the prize of the House Committee, specifically of committee member Richard M. Nixon. No other single event contributed more to what James Wechsler called the "Age of Suspicion" [29] than the disclosure that this handsome, urbane graduate of Harvard Law School had been a Soviet agent. Certainly there has been no more dramatic scene in the history of Congressional investigations than the confrontation of the arrogant, self-assured Hiss and the convoluted, tortured Chambers. Once the details of the Hiss case were out, the problem of Communist espionage became dramatized for Americans in a new framework. Hiss wore no beard, spoke with no accent, moved casually in the best circles. Even anti-Semitic fanatics could not make a Jew of him; they settled for identifying him as a lackey of Felix Frankfurter. As Walter Lippmann pointed out forty years ago,[30] men find security and solace in stereotypes, but now the stereotype of the Communist agent was irremediably shattered. Hiss looked like the man down the block in Scarsdale or Evanston, the man in the office across the hall on Wall Street or State Street. If this man could be a spy, anybody could.

Moreover, to the public, the Chambers saga indicated that Hiss had high-level protection in the State Department.[32] How could a man whom Chambers had denounced to Assistant Secretary of State Adolf Berle almost a decade before have continued on in authority, attending the Yalta Conference (ah, *that* was significant!), and acting as Secretary-General of the United Nations Conference in San Francisco in 1945? Few realized that Chambers had never produced his documents, had merely in generalized terms without documentation announced to Berle his *opinion* that Hiss was an agent. When this strange man told Berle his views, the latter was sufficiently impressed to send a memorandum on the subject to the men for whom Hiss worked, but without evidence of any sort to back the charge it was almost inevitable in a rational bureaucracy that Chambers would be written off as an anti-Communist crackpot. And Chambers did *not* go to the dumbwaiter in Brooklyn where he had secreted them and bring in the microfilms —those damning items which later achieved fame as the "Pumpkin Papers."

With new confidence, gained by its success in the apprehension of Hiss, the House Committee set to work to "expose" the Communist conspiracy. Its task forces ranged far and wide, and everywhere they went the publicity mounted. The standard operating procedure involved discovering a "friendly witness" who would testify at great length about the Communist organization in, say, Portland, Oregon, and in the course of testifying name all those whom he or she had known as Communists. These would then be subpoenaed and the "friendly" ones encouraged to amplify the story of the original witness and add more "names." Then the "unfriendly" witnesses would be brought in, confronted by the accusation (though not permitted to cross-examine the accuser), and asked *the question:* "Are you now, or have you ever been a member of the Communist Party of the United States?" Since the "friendly" witnesses had already been screened out in executive sessions, the "unfriendly" ones uniformly replied by taking recourse to the privilege against self-incrimination of the Fifth Amendment, often after attempting to denounce the Committee for its "Fascistic invasions of freedom of association." [33]

This led to the technique, later perfected by Senator Joseph McCarthy, of labeling the recalcitrants "Fifth Amendment Communists," though in federal court the invocation of the privilege establishes no presumption of guilt. (HUAC Chairman J. Parnell Thomas was to utilize it when accused of payroll padding, and in the early case of *Marbury* v. *Madison* [1803] the Attorney General of the United States took refuge behind its provisions when questioned by Chief Justice Marshall!) Leaving the legal problem aside, the use of this amalgam (Fifth Amendment = Communist) was a very effective device for propagating the notion that the nation was full of people who were "hiding behind the Constitution" to prevent exposure of their sinister activities. Thus it cloaked the fact, which, however, the "friendly" witnesses demonstrated in their testimony, that the fundamental "crimes" involved were trivial: not espionage or sabotage, but organizing Negroes or infiltrating unions and other organizations in behalf of the party "line." In essence, the committee suggested that anyone who took "the Fifth" was a potential Alger Hiss—and the people wondered, worried, and demanded action.

They got it. As the administration brought action under the Smith Act against the leaders of the American Communist Party for "conspiring to teach and advocate" the overthrow of the government by force and violence and as it spread the nets of a loyalty program designed to eliminate subversives from government employment (and later from the employ of government contractors), everybody seemed to be joining in the great chase. State legislatures, notably in Washington, Maryland, and California—where the vicious irresponsibility of the "Tenney Committee" made the House Committee on Un-American Activities look like a British Royal Commission—established investigating bodies.[34] State officials launched hunts of their own; city councils and school districts took up the search; and on it went, accomplishing little of an effectively anti-Communist nature but leaving a wake of suspicion, hatred, and distrust. Books were purged from libraries, loyalty oaths became almost a fixation, and many innocent people suffered grievous damage to their reputations as flimsy charges filled the air. Private businesses were established devoted to advising businessmen on how to avoid hiring subversives, and on Madison Avenue it became standard practice to check out ("clear") entertainers before submitting them to sponsors of radio or TV shows. The United States was going through what Edward A. Shils, in a superb and unfortunately neglected book, called *The Torment of Secrecy*.[35]

The crux of the problem was the definition of "loyalty." The Federal Loyalty Program began with the sound principle that the loyalty of an individual has to be evaluated in terms of his whole life pattern. He could have belonged to twenty Communist fronts and still be loyal, or he could have belonged to none (following the "cover" procedures of intelligent espionage) and be a spy. To investigate a man's loyalty is thus to attempt a photograph of his soul. It is equivalent to the historic problem in Christian theology of determining a man's standing in the eyes of God. Like the Christian Fathers, the loyalty investigators found this task rather esoteric and began to insert into the process of subjective analysis various objective considerations—"outward and visible manifestations of inward and abiding grace" in the language of the Sacraments—which might serve as definitional shortcuts. The most important of these was the "Attorney General's List" of subversive organizations, formulated at President Truman's instruction in November, 1947, which contained the names of eighty-two groups broken down into several categories: "totalitarian," "Fascist," "Communist subversive," etc.[36]

The list was distributed (it was reissued several times with many additions and a few deletions) with a careful caveat that the United States government did not accept the principle of "guilt by association," that membership in a group or groups listed did not in itself constitute proof of disloyalty. But for the men at every level of government charged with the extremely taxing task of soul-reading, it was the answer to a prayer. At last they had something concrete upon which to base a judgment. The warning about "guilt by association" was often simply disregarded, and the individual was summoned to demonstrate that he was *not disloyal* on the basis of his membership in one or more of the proscribed groups. Again, the procedure spread rapidly. The House Committee on Un-American Activities had *its* list (which contained five times as many Communist organizations as the Attorney General's)[37] and various state, local, and private bodies set up their own card files. For a time it seemed as though stamp collectors were outnumbered by those collecting, and eagerly swapping, the names of "subversive" organizations.

Into this confused, disordered, frenetic universe strode that Prince of Nihilists, Joseph R. McCarthy, and in no time he became the idol of the Yahoos. In some ways he resembled Huey

Long—he had the same total disregard for normal ethical standards as the Kingfish; he simply transcended good and evil and seemed to get a great kick out of the solemnity with which his extravagances were greeted. Richard Rovere in his interesting appraisal of McCarthy [38] suggested that he was never really serious about anything—he just liked to turn the world upside down and chuckle at the chaos. And he got an enormous pleasure out of kicking people around. The more highly placed and revered the people, the better he liked it, but he could also settle back, lick his chops, and ruthlessly pursue the most hapless, inconspicuous victim. He was, in short, a totally destructive personality. It was fully in character that he drank himself to an early death. It is important to note, however, that McCarthy was temperamentally incapable of building an organization: he touched only to destroy.

This is no place for a history of McCarthy's fantastic safaris after "Reds." Three aspects of McCarthyism deserve comment in the perspective of this book, and the rest of his eerie career can be left for the student of political pathology. First of all, his power rested on two bases. He supplied the wandering Yahoos with a focus, and they flocked to his standard. Since, like Long, he was seemingly without racial or religious prejudices, was Catholic and had close Protestant and Jewish aides, he was able to unite in his person the ambitions of Catholic, Protestant, and Jewish extremists. In the Midwest, he rallied the bigots who had howled down Al Smith; in Boston, he addressed Communion breakfasts of the Knights of Columbus. He did this by a brilliant technique. He channeled all their variegated aggressions behind his brand of anti-Communism and let their racial and religious biases cancel each other out. He did not care what his followers thought of each other so long as they backed "Senator Joe." And he built up this wild-eyed constituency with the tacit consent of the Republican leaders who in the period 1950–52 were willing to use any technique to crush Truman and the Democrats. After McCarthy had denounced General George Marshall as a Soviet master agent, there was some rumbling in respectable G.O.P. ranks; but the position which emerged was that Marshall could remain in limbo until after November, 1952. This was confirmed when candidate Dwight Eisenhower, who worshipped Marshall and despised McCarthy, appeared in Wisconsin in a chummy pose with the Senator in the 1952 campaign. The Republicans were to rue their Machiavellian tolerance of the Wisconsin wild man when, after the great victory of 1952, it soon appeared that his psychotic drive to destroy the Establishment applied to one dominated by Republicans as well as by Democrats.

Second, despite some rumors to the contrary, a terrific counteroffensive was mounted against McCarthyism. The liberal community has always been in bad shape organizationally as far as politics in the narrow sense is concerned. Liberal Congressmen have never looked, for example, to Americans for Democratic Action for instructions, and one often suspects that Negro politicians use the NAACP more than that organization activates them. Thus it was regrettably true that in the era of the Great Fear few politicians were willing to go to war against McCarthy and his program of frenzied anti-Communism. President Truman blasted away, but his veto of the appalling Internal Security Act of 1950 was overridden in 24 hours, and in the Senate only ten of the liberals dared to vote their convictions.[39] A number of liberal Representatives and Senators explained to their friends in rueful vein that they could not "afford" to vote against it, but that their efforts had kept it from being far worse. As politicians, these liberals were exposed, highly visible targets, 1952 was looming up ominously as a good Republican year, and they felt with some justice that it was a good deal better for them to hedge a bit on this touchy issue and get reelected than go down in heroic defeat before some outright reactionary. In short, they estimated that the American public was in an ugly mood on the subject of Communism and adjusted their votes, if not their views, accordingly.[40]

Consequently it often appeared as though McCarthy was carrying everything before him on a tidal wave of extremist anti-Communism. Nobody was fighting him center stage, and the prophets of gloom were predicting the dawn of American Fascism. What the latter (and the British and European commentators were particularly apprehensive) never understood was the extent to which McCarthyism was an ideology without an organized mass base. Moreover, because they generally believe that Washington, D.C., is the United States of America—and McCarthy did have a substantial sector of Washington terrorized—these critics overlooked the vigorous containment action that was mounted elsewhere in the nation. Even in Washington, the influential *Post* lambasted the Senator day in, day out, and Herblock surely deserves a special oak-leaf cluster for his continuous and savage caricatures of McCarthy, an unshaven, apelike figure scuttling in and out of sewers and emerging from garbage pails.

Much as the Yahoos wanted to restore the Good Old Days of the Great Red Scare, they found that this time there was real resistance. Responsible national newspapers like *The New York Times*, Washington *Post*, St. Louis *Post-Dispatch*, attacked McCarthy constantly. The trade-union movement rallied to the defense of civil liberties; the National Council of the Churches of Christ called for the reform of Congressional investigative procedures; [41] and civil liberties and liberal organizations mobilized for the battle. Senator Lehman, speaking to the 39th Annual Meeting of the Anti-Defamation League in the fall of 1952, stated the real issue in stark and unmistakable terms:

these hysterical and demagogic activities . . . which are gathered under the banner of the McCarthy brand of anti-Communism are among the most vicious in America today. They are the forces responsible for the bigoted and intolerant provisions of the McCarran Immigration Act. They are the forces whose extreme elements preach and practice vigilantism. They assassinate characters by association. . . . They turn neighbor against neighbor, religion against religion, and whole bodies of our citizens against their government and the institutions of government. . . . They befoul our national heroes [an obvious reference to General Marshall] and besmirch the heroism and sacrifices of the past. All this to enhance their own prestige, in the name of anti-Communism. [42]

The American Civil Liberties Union, the Fund for the Republic, Americans for Democratic Action, the Jewish Labor Committee, the American Veterans Committee, and dozens of other groups with similar commitments went forth to war. It was rough going —one has to live through a Yahoo offensive really to believe that certain sorts of things can happen, nasty telephone threats in the middle of the night, filthy, incoherent anonymous letters in the mail (usually written in a strange childish script), hecklers at meetings who rise and with mechanical passion read from some document a long, convoluted question which is in fact an answer—but the civil liberties forces did fight back. It is a libel on the devoted men and women who bore the brunt of this assault to say, as some have, that "Everyone was afraid." The great private universities, in particular, stood like fortresses.[43]

Finally, what were the results of this period? How badly did civil liberties suffer? To what extent were the Yahoos successful in their revival? This question must be answered on different levels. On one level, disgraceful things were done to innocent people who were somehow caught in the net. No one who has read James Wechsler's *Age of Suspicion,* Arnold Forster's and Benjamin R. Epstein's *Cross-Currents,*[44] or the series of scholarly volumes issued under Robert E. Cushman's supervision dealing with various aspects of the loyalty frenzy,[45] could depreciate the harm that was done in the McCarthy era. No historical generalization can for one moment excuse or justify these abuses. History can give no absolution. However, a student of the civil liberties tradition must also put the McCarthy episode in perspective, and from this vantage point it is clear that the Yahoos failed to make a real dent. Despite all the sound and fury, the viciousness and random scurrility, McCarthyism did not fundamentally alter the power structure of American society. It was not so much a movement as a psychosis, and it never put down organizational roots.[46]

To put the matter differently, an urban society—while racked with insecurity about Communism and hardly overwhelmed by libertarianism—was no longer responsive to the slogans of the bucolic wild men. The city dweller, adapted to an impersonal existence, reacts differently to insecurity than does the rural man. He calls the police rather than getting out a length of rope or a barrel of tar. In short, he has what might be called a bureaucratic response—and in a real sense this constitutes a prerequisite of the tradition of due process of law; it is the antithesis of direct action. Against this urbanity (to indulge in a bad play on a word) the Yahoo tempest beat to no avail. It was not that their issue lacked potency—anti-Communism was a strong sentiment everywhere —but that their whole style was anachronistic; behind their surface anti-Communism, the urban citizen could sense the old racial and religious bigotry, the ancient hatred of the prurient, frustrated rustic for the temptations, corruptions, and delights of the metropolis.

Thus, freedom in our urban society, by a curious paradox, is sustained by the very impersonalization of city life and of the development of legal and political institutions which have muffled interpersonal and intergroup conflicts among people necessarily living at very close quarters with each other. Ironically, the collapse of that sense of community so highly esteemed by nostalgic sociologists seems to have created a new atmosphere of liberty and procedural due process for the nonconformist, who no longer finds himself perpetually in face-to-face relationships with his neighbors or subjugated to the coercive power of the "group"—whether it be the rural parish or the ethnic ghetto of fifty years ago. McCarthy and the militants whose perverse utopianism he represented symbolized a desperate effort to turn the clock back, to drag the United States once again to the old standards of direct action, the "direct democracy" of the lynch mob.[47] Fought by all the organizations which stood for civil liberties and equality, as well as by those who in a nonideological fashion took their stand for decency and civility, his real power rested on the willingness of conservative politicians, Republican and Democratic, to tolerate his vicious nonsense for purposes of expedience.

When after 1953 his daemon drove him to continue his destructive, nihilistic course, he was doomed. Once he had attacked the Eisenhower Administration and then desecrated the lares and penates of that exclusive club, the United States Senate, he found himself a man without an effective constituency. He had captured only the Yahoos, and the last years of his life were spent with them at a witches' sabbath, his voice getting shriller and shriller and his following smaller and smaller. The supreme irony occurred when the people of Wisconsin, after his death, amidst the wails of his bereft clansmen, replaced him in the Senate with a Harvard educated Democrat. The damage McCarthyism had done lived on, but the social and political fabric of urban America withstood the shock. Indeed, in this very period, the liberal forces in American society were organizing a great campaign for full equality and the expansion of human rights—a drive which continued unabated throughout the years of anti-Communist hysteria and internal insecurity legislation. The Yahoos had been contained.

THE STRUGGLE
FOR FULL EQUALITY

The Yahoos in the postwar period clearly banked on employing the quite understandable American insecurity about Communism and the Soviet Union as a mace to bludgeon the whole movement for civil liberty and human rights. If they could once establish in the public mind the proposition that civil rights were a component in the Communist "Plan of Conquest," they would have been in a fine strategic position. They worked diligently enough at the task, denouncing the United Nations, the United Nations Educational, Scientific and Cultural Organization (UNESCO), the National Council of the Churches of Christ, Americans for Democratic Action, the NAACP, the Anti-Defamation League, the American Civil Liberties Union, Zionist organizations, Harvard University, the State Department, and even the presence of *The Adventures of Robin Hood* (a Communist who robbed the rich and gave to the poor) in school libraries.

Here and there, from time to time, they scored. Usually it was not so much the heat as the timidity. A nice group of ladies in some small Midwestern city who were organizing the sale of United Nations Childrens Fund (UNICEF) Christmas greetings would suddenly find themselves in a fearful brawl. Letters would appear in local newspapers denouncing UNICEF as a Communist front and adducing in evidence an impressive body of pseudo-facts. (Example: these funds are spent on Red Chinese. Though one might question the morality of a person who refused to help sick children whatever the complexion of their government, in fact the only Chinese cooperating with UNICEF were on Formosa.) The nice ladies, overwhelmed by the sudden storm and totally un-equipped to cope with bogus evidence, would all too often retreat. In California the Yahoos put the great university through the wringer on the loyalty oath issue,[1] and in many communities they successfully purged the public or school libraries of "subversive" books. As late as November, 1962, in what seemed like a comic caricature, the city of Amarillo, Texas, pulled George Orwell's *1984* from the public shelves! [2] Public-school teachers, never noted for their bellicosity, displayed a similar tendency to adapt and ride out the storms which blew up when the Americanism Director of the local American Legion post discovered John Steinbeck's *Grapes of Wrath* or Howard Fast's *Freedom Road* on the library list. (The list of books was extended to include wholly nonpolitical works by authors under the anathema of the House Committee, e.g., the mysteries of Dashiell Hammett and the moldy-magnolia plays of Lillian Hellman.)

But despite their compulsive, fixated strivings, the Yahoos never established the amalgam. As was noted earlier, they were handicapped by the refusal of their heroes, Senator Joseph Mc-Carthy, Vice-President Richard Nixon, Chairman Francis Walter of the House Committee, and later Senator Barry Goldwater, ever to engage in racial or religious baiting. It was Senator James East-land who, after the Supreme Court decision barring racial segrega-tion in public schools, announced that the Court was under Com-munist influence and had attempted "to graft into the organic law of the land the teachings, preachings, and social doctrines of Karl Marx." [3] And Southern Senators and Congressmen have never be-come key figures in national extremist movements, probably be-cause their consistent internationalism and general willingness to support "Socialistic-Communistic" economic programs (agricul-tural price supports, Tennessee Valley Authority, area redevelop-ment programs, etc.) put them outside the Yahoo pale.

In particular, the extremist effort to rekindle the fires of anti-

Semitism by questioning the loyalty of American Jews fell flat on its face. In *The Trouble-Makers,* an Anti-Defamation League report on intolerance in the United States published in 1952, Arnold Forster and Benjamin Epstein reported at some length on efforts that were underway to label Zionism as a form of subversive activity. Paralleling this was the continuing drive to identify the Jewish community with Communism, a drive which picked up some steam during the prolonged trial and appeal of the Rosenberg Case. The additional fact that most of the Army employees at the Fort Monmouth Signal Corps research center who suffered infamously at the hands of Senator McCarthy's kangaroo court in 1953 were Jewish was greeted with glee by the anti-Semites and apprehension by the Jewish defense organizations. A vigorous campaign by the A.D.L. and other concerned organizations and by able defense counsel resulted in the subsequent reinstatement of twenty-eight of the thirty-six men who had been suspended—in eleven cases the Army refused even to file formal charges! [4] But, in part surely because the civil liberties groups put up such a tremendous counterattack, the old hackneyed slogan of "Jewish Communism," like the smear based on the proposition that a Zionist was an agent of a foreign power, received little public support, was explicitly repudiated by all responsible political figures, and was shunned by the leading irresponsibles.

There was in consequence little fallout from the anti-Communist frenzy on the campaign for full racial and religious equality. The same state legislature which passed a stringent loyalty bill could also establish a pioneer state fair employment practices program—indeed, precisely this occurred in New York. Moreover, a strong case can be made that public awareness of the issues underlying the confrontation between the United States and the Soviet Union stimulated the drive for full implementation of the American Dream. We will examine this proposition in more detail shortly, but it is worth noting here that a Constitution which legalized Jim Crow was something of a liability in the ideological contest with the Communists for the allegiance of the uncommitted emerging peoples of Asia, Africa, and Latin America. Certainly this was an argument which President Truman employed with full and characteristic vigor when he launched the postwar transformation in the attitude of the national government toward its Negro citizens.

It will be recalled that when the war ended, the crusade for Negro rights was still an essentially private affair. Although on March 12, 1945, New York's Governor Thomas E. Dewey approved the first state fair employment practices law in the nation,[5] the burden of the campaign was in the hands of organizations such as the National Association for the Advancement of Colored People, the A.C.L.U., the Urban League, and white civil rights organizations. These "ginger groups" were all severely limited by their lack of resources. At best their efforts were sporadic and almost by definition defensive; i.e., they rallied to fight specific grievances, lynchings, or housing problems, but could do little at the basic structural level to alter the conditions which nourished prejudice. As long as the President of the United States maintained the hands-off attitude which had prevailed since Grant left the White House, it was impossible to do more than cope in an episodic fashion with the consequences of racial flare-ups. The NAACP made a decision to concentrate its legal efforts in the area of housing (particularly with an eye to eliminating restrictive covenants) and education—an understandable priority, but one which left the right of Negroes to vote, as well as a number of other key issues, for future action when resources would permit.

It is no insult to the dedicated men and women who in season and out worked for the implementation of equality to say that their efforts alone were inadequate. However, it is clear that the decisive factor in the extension to the Negro of his American birthright was the intervention of the heavy battalions of the federal government. It had to happen someday, but without the support of the Chief Executive, the administration, and the courts, that day could have been postponed. It is hard to re-create the mood of the past because we have lived through it and conveniently forgotten our erroneous estimates of the future, but I think it is fair to say that in 1945 there were few, even among the optimists, who believed that the breakthrough could come with such speed.

It all began with Harry S. Truman, that strange combination of a small-town politician and a democratic visionary, who in January, 1947, addressed a fifteen-member group at the White House. The President declared to his freshly appointed Committee on Civil Rights: "I want our Bill of Rights implemented in fact. We have been trying to do this for 150 years. We are making progress, but we are not making progress fast enough. This country could very easily be faced with a situation similar to the one with which it was faced in 1922." [6] Of course, Truman's concern with civil rights has been blithely written off as "politics," but it is important to remember that if a President likes small children it is considered "politics"—even if he *likes* small children. Moreover, every modern President, F.D.R. included, considered civil rights to be "bad politics," a sleeping dogma that had best be tiptoed around. Finally, this committee, with an overwhelmingly liberal cast, was appointed almost two years before the election of 1948, at a time when Truman had certainly not made up his mind on where he stood in the Democratic spectrum. The President was undoubtedly influenced by a number of advisors, but the fact remains that he broke the "cake of custom" and accepted responsibility for this politically audacious commitment.

The committee's report, *To Secure These Rights,* ranks as one of the great documents in the tradition of our free society.[7] It is doubtful if any official body has ever delivered such a scorching autocritique, has ever probed so deeply into a fundamental social problem and emerged with such blunt recommendations. Indeed, there is a kind of majestic ring to the conclusion:

Mr. President:

Your Committee has reviewed the American heritage and we have found in it again the great goals of human freedom and equality under just laws. We have surveyed the flaws in the nation's record and have found them to be serious. We have considered what government's appropriate role should be in the securing of our rights, and have concluded that it must assume greater leadership.

We believe that the time for action is now. Our recommendations for bringing the United States closer to its historic goal follow.[8]

The recommendations themselves were dynamite, particularly to Southern legislators, because they effectively called for the national government to take the lead in destroying racial discrimination. The fifth recommendation, for example, was crisp and to the point: "1. In general: The elimination of segregation based on race, color, creed, or national origin, from American life; 2. For employment: The enactment of a federal Fair Employment Practice Act prohibiting all forms of discrimination in private employment, based on race, color, creed, or national origin. The enactment by the states of similar laws. The issuance by the President of a mandate against discrimination in government employment and the creation of adequate machinery to enforce this mandate; 3. For education: Enactment by the state legislatures of fair educational practice laws for public and private educational institutions, prohibiting discrimination in the admission and treatment of students based on race, color, creed, or national origin; 4. . . ." [9]

It is impossible here to summarize adequately the committee's comprehensive and wide-ranging recommendations—which were not confined to the problems of the Negro, but reached even the status of the despoiled West Coast Nisei and of the inhabitants of Guam—but it is significant to note that the President, receiving this ticking bomb, did not quail or seek to bury it. On February 2, 1948, he asked Congress to implement the *Report* by passing the necessary civil rights legislation [10] and later supported Hubert Humphrey and other liberal Democrats in their successful effort to write the *Report*'s recommendations into the platform of the Democratic Party at the nominating convention in July. This led to a walkout by the "Dixiecrats" and the formation of a fourth party to contest the Presidency in 1948, though it may simultaneously have taken some wind out of the sails of Henry Wallace's "Progressive" Party, which was already in the field.

A number of politicians have managed to maintain a concern for civil rights in the abstract with a record of singular inaction on the practical level. Mr. Truman has never been among their number. To indicate that he meant business, the President on July 26, 1948, burned his bridge to the South: he issued two precedent-breaking Executive Orders, Nos. 9980 and 9981.[11] The first instituted fair employment practices within the federal government's civilian agencies, and the second, over the signature of the Commander in Chief, ordered "equality of treatment and opportunity for all persons in the armed services without regard to race, color, religion or national origin." Liberal critics of the Man from Missouri were dumbfounded (as were his old Southern Senate friends). In one day he had done more for the cause of civil rights and racial equality than had been accomplished in almost a century. In 1941 an Army spokesman had informed a group of Negro newspapermen that "The Army did not create the [race] problem. . . . The Army is not a sociological laboratory; to be effective it must be organized and trained according to principles which will insure success." [12] Now the Armed Forces, and the civilian agencies, were at Presidential orders converted into a "sociological laboratory" in which the government of the United States would demonstrate that implementation of its ideals was the standard by which "success" must be determined. Harry S. Truman in this, as in other ways, played a decisive role in the postwar struggle for American ideals. (Young egalitarians were justifiably disturbed by his later, off-the-cuff, tasteless criticism of the Negro sit-ins, his observation that they should be kicked out of stores as trespassers. They should keep in mind the story of the two Stone Age artisans discussing a third who was reclining in luxury. "How can he get away with that?" inquired the first. "He invented the wheel," replied the second. "Yes, yes, I know," came the impatient answer, "but what has he done *lately?*")

The genie was out of the bottle: the issue of Negro rights which had been successfully depoliticized since Reconstruction was now sharply and irretrievably injected into the national conscience and onto the national, and local, political stages. With the

President leading the assault on centuries of encrusted prejudice, not just in the South, once again the nation heard the "trumpet that shall never call retreat," and the shades of the Abolitionists stirred in their graves. The battle had a new dimension: no longer was it carried principally by white liberals, but the Negroes themselves took up the burden. Most significant of all perhaps, at least for the long run, was the stirring among Southern Negroes who, living in a state of racial siege, had traditionally chosen inertia over martyrdom. Before long, the Negroes of Montgomery, Alabama, led by the Reverend Martin Luther King, Jr., would employ the principles of nonviolent resistance in a solemn testimony of defiant Christian integrity and shake the edifice of white power to its very foundations.[13]

President Truman was, of course, unsuccessful in obtaining Congressional endorsement for his views on civil rights, but the great moral and political force of the Presidency was now brought foursquare behind equality. State and local governments simultaneously began to pass laws and municipal ordinances barring various manifestations of racial discrimination. By 1962, seventeen states had statutes which to one degree or another implemented fair employment practices, and in the period 1948–60 more than forty municipalities scattered throughout the North and West outlawed employment discrimination on a city-wide basis. As New York was the pioneer in establishing F.E.P.C., so that state continued to lead the way by a 1948 law forbidding discrimination on the basis of race, color, religion, creed or national origin in higher educational institutions. Connecticut took the lead in barring discrimination in public or publicly supported housing. The legislative campaign—with the national Congress conspicuously missing—picked up increasing momentum.[14]

Yet while the National Executive and a number of state governments expressed the view that racial discrimination was contrary to public policy, the Constitution of the United States still legitimized Jim Crow. In 1896, it will be recalled, the Supreme Court had drastically perverted the meaning of the Fourteenth Amendment by holding that mandatory racial segregation, enforced by state law, did not deprive a Negro citizen of the equal protection of the laws.[16] Critics of the Supreme Court's decision outlawing segregation in 1954 seldom note that it was the Court which put Jim Crow *into* the Constitution by an incredible revision of the Fourteenth Amendment. This was still the Supreme Law of the Land in the late forties and early fifties, but a campaign was underway to get the High Court to reconsider the whole corpus of constitutional law governing race relations.

The first major victory occurred in 1948 when the Supreme Court in *Shelley* v. *Kraemer* effectively destroyed the restrictive covenant, the legal device which sustained residential segregation. The core of the decision was that a covenant—where a purchaser of realty accepted as a condition of sale a restriction on his right to convey the property to Jews, Negroes, Orientals, American Indians, Tamils, or whatever other groups happened to be the recipients of local prejudice—was not a private matter between two parties. Rather, it was founded on public power because its enforcement, usually by injunctive procedures, depended on state action. If, for example, Mr. Smith sold his home to Mr. Jones, a Negro, in violation of a covenant, the courts of the state would intervene to nullify the sale. (Curiously this restriction on an individual's sacred property rights never seemed to disturb the conservative elements in the community.)

A restrictive covenant, properly construed, the Court held, was not therefore a private arrangement, a voluntary institutionalization of personal eccentricities, but an exercise of state power in behalf of racial segregation in violation of the equal protection clause of the Fourteenth Amendment. Like any contract which violates public policy (e.g., a promise to a smuggling ring to pay $1,000 an ounce for heroin, a gambling debt, an arrangement with Murder, Inc.), a restrictive covenant was held to be unenforceable by public authority. While an individual could refuse to sell his house to a Negro, an Irish Catholic, or a member of the John Birch Society if he so elected, no state power could be invoked to limit his decision. Interestingly enough, the Department of Justice, though it was not a party to the suit, appeared before the Supreme

Court to argue the unconstitutionality of the covenants. This was apparently the first time in history that this procedure had been invoked.[16]

With the covenants successfully disposed of—at least on the legal level—the NAACP prepared for the big push. Chief Counsel (today Judge of the United States Court of Appeals, Second Circuit) Thurgood Marshall mobilized a wide coalition for the assault on the enemy fortress: *Plessy* v. *Ferguson,* the "separate but equal" decision of 1896. While some figures in the civil rights field felt that the first attack should be aimed at segregation in transportation, arguing that even militant white supremacists could hardly work themselves into a fury over the impersonal possibility that a Negro would sit in the front of a bus, the decision was made to strike to the heart of the matter: public education. Educational segregation was obviously a far more sensitive sector than transportation, but its very sensitivity was a justification for the decision. The pattern of white-Negro relationships in legally segregated areas of the nation (which included sections of southern New Jersey and many other "Northern" parts of the country) had to be shattered if real change was ever to come. What better place was there to begin the process of reeducation in democratic values than the public schools? Unlike a Court decision barring segregation in public transportation, a holding which desegregated the schools would cast a shadow over generations to come, generations which hopefully would reject the prejudices of their parents in favor of the lessons of their own experience.

The story of school desegregation, and the fearful travail which at this writing still has a contingent of military police guarding James Meredith at the University of Mississippi, has been richly chronicled elsewhere.[17] To summarize, the NAACP's first campaign against racial segregation in public institutions of higher education ended in a highly ambiguous determination. The Court in 1950 refused to overrule *Plessy* v. *Ferguson,* but chewed away at its vitality by stating that *"under these circumstances* the Fourteenth Amendment precludes differences in treatment by the state based upon race." [18] In short, the Court ducked the generic issue

—the validity of "separate but equal"—but ruled in favor of the Negro plaintiffs. The opinions were painfully obscure, but one seemed to imply that in certain professional schools (law in this instance) segregation must *inevitably* lead to unequal education, and the second that when separate facilities were provided for Negroes, they had to be equal *in an absolute sense* to those provided for whites; no corners could be cut.

Undeterred by this half-victory, the NAACP began to flood the South with lawsuits aimed at implementing and expanding the Supreme Court's holding. In state after state, a qualified Negro would apply to the graduate school of pharmacy, education, engineering, home economics, or any others that existed at the state university. The state was then confronted with a problem which almost seems comical. It had either to admit him to the white graduate school on an unsegregated basis *or* build him a separate graduate facility fully equal to that open to whites! On one day the state of Florida was confronted by seven such suits. The educational cost of white supremacy could easily be bankruptcy. To build a college of pharmacy for one Negro applicant was rather more than even Texas could bear. The economic costs of racial segregation have always been enormous (two drinking fountains, two sets of bathrooms, two waiting rooms, two Bibles in the courtrooms of some states, two churches, two ambulances, two hospitals . . .), but traditionally little was spent on Negro education, and no real effort was made to enforce the "equal" half of the "separate but equal" formula. Realizing that the whole system of segregated public education was in jeopardy, some Southern states in the late 1940's instituted crash programs to build up the Negro schools, but theirs were deathbed conversions. "Separate but equal" had been a constitutional aberration and a practical deception, and those who had sowed the wind of "separate and unequal" were now to reap the whirlwind of historic justice.

While utilizing the 1950 Court decisions to the utmost, the NAACP moved to bring the issue of the constitutionality of "separate but equal" back to the high tribunal, this time in the context of primary and secondary education. Five cases were begun, each one differing slightly from the rest: one in the District of Columbia which would challenge segregation in a federal school system, one from Kansas in which both parties stipulated that the schools for colored children were fully equal to those for whites, and three from the "Black Belt." When these cases en bloc reached the Supreme Court, a large number of organizations took the opportunity to join as *amici curiae* (friends of the court) in asking the Justices to overrule *Plessy* v. *Ferguson:* the Congress of Industrial Organizations, the A.C.L.U., the American Ethical Union, the Unitarian Fellowship, the American Federation of Teachers, the American Veterans Committee, the Anti-Defamation League, the American Jewish Committee, and the American Jewish Congress, *inter alios,* filed briefs. Although a new administration had taken office, the Solicitor General of the United States again appeared on behalf of the United States to urge an end to legalized segregation.

Even though many had hoped the Court would reverse *Plessy,* the decision in the School Segregation Cases [19] in 1954 still came as a shock. A unanimous Court, in a low-pressure, anticlimactic opinion by Chief Justice Warren, threw out "separate but equal" as a valid constitutional principle in public education, and by implication undermined the standing of mandatory segregation in all areas of national life. Perhaps because the Chief Justice had to find a common denominator which would hold all nine Justices (we have already seen Justice Frankfurter in another context objecting bitterly to the Court's attempting to become a "school board for the country"), his opinion really never came to a point. It lacked totally the moral fervor of Justice John M. Harlan's great dissent in *Plessy.* Moreover, the Court suspended any action on the ruling for a year in order to examine the problems of effective implementation.

But however disappointing the burial service, "separate but equal" was dead. The United States Constitution had become "color blind," and while the battle to eliminate segregation was only beginning, the legal rationale for the practice was destroyed. From this point on the defenders of white supremacy, no matter how strong their battlements and wily their lawyers, were put on the defensive. With their entrenched control over local governments—judges, sheriffs, juries—they could conduct rearguard actions in some places for years, but down in their hearts they knew that defeat would finally come because they had lost their claim to legitimacy. Their authority had become, in a phrase St. Augustine borrowed from Cicero, that of a "den of robbers," sustained alone by physical force and intimidation.

The Court's decision presaged a revolution in race relations. In the cities of the North, the Negroes and their neighbors in prejudice, the Puerto Ricans, began increasingly to assert their autonomy and to demand their full rights in the political community. This surge created enormous new problems in intergroup relations which cannot be solved by libertarian clichés. The objective difficulties involved, for example, in maintaining a healthy mixed neighborhood are very great indeed, and the techniques of group relations unfortunately have little impact on the crucial problem of the Negro and the Puerto Rican—his poverty which, despite his abstract "rights," imprisons him in a filthy ghetto. To say this is not for a minute to accept the notion that poverty *creates* crime—most poor children are not delinquents—but rather to argue that poverty establishes stark limits to assimilation in the broader community, it institutionalizes a cultural treadmill where no matter how much energy is expended, little forward motion occurs. Caught in this trap, the Negro and Puerto Rican communities in the big cities have often resented bitterly the power of the white political and social elite, but have been incapable of providing responsible leadership of their own. Ironically, the opening up of housing to nonwhites in better suburban residential areas, which has been taking place slowly but surely over the past decade, has made it possible for the upper-income, highly educated members of these groups, the doctors, lawyers, businessmen, teachers, who should comprise the natural leaders of the ethnic communities, to leave the ghetto for more pleasant surroundings.

Yet armed with that invaluable weapon in the process of improvement, the vote, the Negro and Puerto Rican minority groups in the North have been making substantial progress. Their difficulties, moreover, are structural rather than legal. It is the poverty, the poor educational level, the slum housing, and other environmental factors of a similar sort, not the laws of the state or the power aspirations of the white elite, which bear down upon them. For a politician in New York to be anti-Negro would, in Fouché's phrase, be worse than a crime; it would be a blunder. To put the matter differently, a number, probably a fairly large number, of citizens in the Northern states hold prejudiced views on matters of race, but their attitudes are not incorporated in public policy. On the contrary, the force of law in these states and big cities is opposed to racial discrimination. Perhaps some officials are insincere, perhaps their votes for F.E.P.C. are "politically motivated," but however motivated the outcome is the same. If in the perfect world all men would do the right thing for the right reasons, can we not settle in this contingent political universe for the right thing and leave the extended analysis of motives to spiritual and psychiatric directors?

Thus, while no one is going to proclaim enthusiastically that the Northern Negro has been well treated or warmly welcomed by the white community—he has in fact been fearfully exploited— the key consideration from the historical viewpoint is that he has obtained the instruments of self-defense, the "access rights" which give him the opportunity to push toward full equality. *De facto* residential segregation (which often results, of course, in *de facto* school segregation) has no legal foundation, and efforts to break out of the ghetto, though they may meet with great social resistance, cannot be checked by force of law or the exercise of power indirectly founded on law. Private associations, for example, which fulfill public functions—county medical associations, trade unions, bar associations, educational accrediting bodies—cannot discriminate on the basis of race, color, or creed. The Negro and the Puerto Rican certainly have a long way to go in the North before the burden can be lifted from the conscience of the white Establishment, but we can all take pride in the fact that the breakthrough has occurred and the journey has commenced. Perhaps in another generation our society will have approximated the outlook of one seven-year-old girl who was asked after her first day in a new school whether there were any Negroes in her class and replied that she didn't know, but she would look.

The awakening of the Negro to political consciousness has created great dislocations in the North, but from the outset the basic trend was discernible. The road was tortuous, and numerous barriers blocked the traveler, but the goal was in sight: Constitutional equality, equality of opportunity, the precious right to be treated as a Man on one's own merits rather than as a member of a separate and inferior category. Anxious mothers would, of course, torture themselves with the prospect of a Negro son-in-law, but this is largely a by-product of white ethnocentrism— one Negro has noted sardonically, "I find pink skin decidedly unattractive in a woman." [20] But no advocate of equality has ever tried to force Jewish wives on Catholics, or Negro husbands on Protestants, or for that matter husbands with Ph.D.'s on uneducated girls whose reading is limited to comic books. This is the dimension of private association, and, despite efforts to drag it into the argument, it is wholly irrelevant to the substantive point, namely *that individuals have the right to make these decisions for themselves.* The community neither prescribes nor proscribes but leaves social relations as a matter of free individual decision.

In the Southern states, the situation was radically different. The Supreme Court's decision was greeted with the slogan of "massive resistance" and the burgeoning of "white citizens' councils" as unofficial organs of white supremacy. In the years since Reconstruction, the white elite had successfully excluded the Negro from the political process—from any access to power—and was determined to maintain this exclusion. By 1960 it was clear that little short of physical force or a clear willingness to employ force by the federal government would dislodge segregation in the Black Belt states of Mississippi, Alabama, and South Carolina, while most of the others had established at best token desegregation, usually in the big cities. A complex dilemma confronted those who wished to break down the power of the segregationists. Where could they put their lever? In Mississippi, for example, 42 percent of the population is Negro, but in terms of effectiveness it might just as well be in Brazil—it is utterly powerless and intimidated. Whatever "nigra agitators" there were in Mississippi presumably left for Chicago or other points North, and can hardly be blamed for departing.

It is important to understand the full institutional meaning of white supremacy in a state like Mississippi. We are not dealing with abstract political theory, but with a system based on official coercion and unofficial terror. In 1890 when the Mississippi Constitution was revised to eliminate the Negroes from the electorate, it was frankly announced that "The policy of crushing out the manhood of the Negro citizens is to be carried on to success." [21] It was, in fact, a roaring success, though one unanticipated consequence was the departure of so many Negroes from the state over the next seventy years that the whites—a substantial minority in 1890 —were by 1960 the majority group. Confronted by an interlocking directorate of white officials, the Negro who wished to challenge the system was simply trapped. If he were leading a group of Negroes to try to register to vote, he could find himself dead from the "accidental discharge of a pistol" in the hands of a member of the state legislature.[22] Or, he might find his house burned down, or the mortgage foreclosed, or his job gone, or his cotton allotment decreased. Finally, he might find himself in jail for "breach of the peace"—that flexible net cast by the common law for disposing of community "troublemakers." And everywhere he looked he found the same cast of characters. The sheriff who arrested him was the chairman of the white citizens' council; the jury who assessed his guilt, members of the council and perhaps members also of the local committee of the Department of Agriculture's cotton program which cut his allotment; the state's attorney, a cousin of the businessman who fired him from his job; the judge, elected by the local machine, a state coordinator of the white citizens' councils and brother-in-law of the sheriff. The American Legion post, the National Guard, the sheriff's posse, and the white citizens' council could easily have identical members.

Southern liberals, fine people who often spent many years at considerable risk attempting to improve race relations, have often condemned "outside" efforts to alter the status quo in the South. They have argued that "agitation" inspired from the North has in fact destroyed the chances of a gradual transformation of Southern society and exacerbated Negro-white relationships. Unfortunately, if the burden of change had been left in the hands of Southern liberals, the Negroes would probably still be in slavery. No one can scorn their work, but the crucial consideration was that they never posed a real threat to the white power structure. Essentially they called upon the white community to be decent toward Negroes, but never denied that fundamental authority over the Negro lay in the hands of the whites. Once the line was drawn in terms of Negro rights rather than white *noblesse oblige*, they vanished from the scene. Thus, if change were to come, it had to be initiated from outside and fought through from without—whether by NAACP lawyers, "Freedom Riders" sponsored by the Congress of Racial Equality, the Civil Rights Division of the Department of Justice, federal judges, or federal troops. The harsh reality was that no Southern Negro, even a lionhearted Christian like Dr. Martin Luther King, Jr., could survive against the built-in power of the white elite without outside protection, financial assistance, and public support. The job could not be done from the "inside."

The elimination of white supremacy in the South is clearly going to be a long hard struggle, but the active intervention of the national government cannot be frustrated indefinitely. With the Supreme Court taking an increasingly militant posture toward Southern efforts to circumvent the impact of the desegregation ruling, and the federal district and circuit judges, willy-nilly (for most of them are graduates of the white political elite [23]), injecting themselves into the battle on behalf of Negro rights, the legal foundations of the system are doomed. For Southern Negroes the achievement of legal equality can only be the beginning of the process of fulfillment. Yet however great the hurdles that remain in their path, they know in 1963—as they have never known before—that the first great leap has been accomplished. And again without justifying the sins of the past, the historian of civil rights in the United States can feel some pride that the appalling racial pattern of centuries has in the short space of a decade been revealed as a moribund anachronism living on borrowed time. Perhaps the best augury of future development was the massive turnout of Negro voters in Georgia in 1962 which in restrained, uncommunicative fashion cast the votes that defeated a reactionary candidate for Governor, an outspoken white supremacist member of the House of Representatives, and elected a Negro to the Georgia State Senate.[24]

Any discussion of the contemporary movement for full equality must of necessity concentrate on the problems of the Negro who is just breaching the dike of prejudice. However, it is also important to examine other sectors of the front, particularly the efforts and accomplishments of the campaign to eliminate anti-Catholicism and anti-Semitism from American life. It was noted earlier that, in the decades following the shambles of 1928, while anti-Catholic stalwarts remained at their endeavors, there seemed to be little support for the movement. However, two factors have in recent years stirred the fires of anti-Popery: the church-state controversy, and the nomination of John Fitzgerald Kennedy for President of the United States. It was also pointed out that the Yahoos made vigorous efforts in the McCarthy period to refurbish the Jewish-Bolshevist-Zionist amalgam, and, even though they failed, there has been an unending campaign against other covert manifestations of anti-Semitism, manifestations which unfortunately still linger on in many sectors of American life.

The church-state imbroglio, which has come to a head in the area of federal policy toward education but has been simmering in many states with large Catholic populations for years, is peculiarly complex. A number of simplistic formulae have been provided by partisans of each position to explain exactly where a completely logical line can be drawn between the religious and the secular areas, and a great deal of research has been done to demonstrate the precise intention of the framers of the First Amendment. Alas, I find none of the formulae compelling and feel that most of the research has been based on extrasensory perception; i.e., facts have been used the way a drunk uses a lamppost: for support, not light. The best short study of the intention of the men who wrote the First Amendment, that by Dean Leonard W. Levy of Brandeis University,[25] gives us James Madison's views with precision and accuracy, but then concludes by assuming that the other framers shared Madison's convictions. This is not necessarily mistaken, but on the other hand there is little data to justify it either. And even if we knew the full intention of the framers, should we accept it as binding in 1963? Are we any more bound by their views on church and state than we are by their definition of "interstate commerce," or their view that bleeding was the most effective treatment for yellow fever?

The so-called logic which both Catholic and separationist spokesmen have elaborated hardly holds up under careful scrutiny. If one argues, for example, that Quakers confronted by military service or Orthodox Jewish storekeepers hurt by Sunday closing laws should not have to pay a penalty for their religious convictions, it is hard to escape the parallel conclusion that Catholics, who are taxed for public schools their children, on the basis of Church law, do not attend, should receive a special dispensation. And even the wildest logician of separation has never maintained that the state should not provide police and fire protection to parochial schools. On the other hand, the view that Catholics relieve the public of a burden by educating their own children and therefore merit relief could logically buttress a claim on the public for tax exemption by one who drives his car to work rather than using public transportation. Similarly, the argument that the state would by its subventions be aiding the children, not the institution, has little intrinsic merit—patently the state's funds would help the institution to educate the children. In short, history is open-ended and logic provides no easy solution; this appears to be one of those problems envisaged centuries ago by the Talmudic scholar who announced that the presence of a question was no proof of the existence of an answer. It may take a generation to evolve an answer which will meet with substantial agreement on all sides, or alter the framework of the argument.

Given this complexity, and the strong feelings on both sides, it is hardly surprising that the church-state issue has exacerbated intergroup relations. It is a problem that must be handled with great care, because legitimate differences over state aid to religious institutions can on one side feed anti-Catholic bigotry and on the other generate anti-Semitism. For understandable reasons, Jewish organizations and individuals have been in the forefront of efforts to eliminate Christian liturgical manifestations from the public schools and have as a consequence been exposed to a wave of criticism. On one level the Jesuit weekly *America* could in 1962 solemnly warn the Jews—on a "friend to friend" basis—that their concern with separation *could* lead to anti-Semitism [26] (the liberal Catholic journal *Commonweal* immediately repudiated this veiled threat [27]). On a lower level, Catholic and Protestant bigots played variations on the theme of "Jewish-atheist-Communism" and demanded a revitalization of "Christian America." On the other side of the fence, attacks on the Catholic position often have degenerated into a vicious rehashing of old libels—the ancient (1836) *Awful Disclosures of Maria Monk*, the faked memoirs of a Canadian nun which titillated the lascivious bigots of the Know-Nothing Movement in the 1840's, went into a new printing, and the bogus Knights of Columbus "Oath" once more circulated in the back country.

But the unresolved issue of the proper relations between the state and religious institutions paled in significance as a source of anti-Catholic bias as John F. Kennedy began his campaign for the Presidency. The old slogans were brought out and a widespread program was launched to "Keep the Pope out of the White House." There was, however, a tremendous difference between the anti-Smith drive in 1928 and the effort to block Kennedy; the latter was clandestine and lacked the support of any significant journals of opinion.[28] When the issue surfaced, Senator Kennedy confronted it boldly, stated his convictions on issues of church and state precisely to a group of Texas clergymen, and then gave it no further official cognizance. Vice-President Nixon vigorously disavowed any support from bigots. At the ground level of American politics, Senator Kennedy's religion was, however, a key though covert issue. Democratic workers in Boston, New York, and other centers of Catholic strength did not keep their candidate's affiliation a secret, and it took no particular political sagacity to guess that American Catholics were looking forward to breaking the religious barrier—the "unwritten law of American politics"—to the White House. The word in Boston on election day 1960 was "Vote Green!", and it is equally clear that in many areas in the West, Middle West, and South the word was "Vote Protestant!" I am convinced that Kennedy's Catholicism almost lost him the election,[29] but the long-run implication of his victory, however close (close counts only in horseshoe pitching), is the disappearance of one more traditional prejudice from American politics—at the top level, the Catholic issue is dead.

The Jewish community has yet to field its first presidential candidate, but the indications certainly point to the collapse of anti-Semitism as a vital force in American politics. It is risky to generalize from state politics to national, but the extremely good *down-state* showing of Sidney Yates, who lost narrowly to Everett Dirksen in the 1962 Senate race in Illinois, as well as the career of Abraham Ribicoff in Connecticut, a state with a tiny Jewish population (to say nothing of the phenomenal performance of Senator Jacob Javits in New York), suggest that the populations of widely separated states are prepared to accept a Jewish candidate for high office on his merits. An even more extraordinary 1962 result was the victory of Edward Brooke, a Republican Negro, over Francis Kelly for the post of Attorney General of Massachusetts. The *only* Republican to survive a Democratic sweep, Brooke observed that he had not seen one piece of hate literature during the campaign and had almost forgotten he was a Negro! [30]

With a solid backlog of accomplishment in the historically interminable fight against anti-Semitism, American Jews in the postwar era could turn their attention from the struggle for recognition and legitimacy as members of the body politic to eradicating the remaining facets of racial and religious bias. Moreover, Jewish defense organizations—no longer living in a state of siege—broadened their concerns to include vigilant campaigns against all forms of racial and religious prejudice. As was noted earlier, the American Jewish Congress gave invaluable legal assistance to the Negroes,[31] and the Anti-Defamation League worked indefatigably to counter the various efforts of the Yahoos to destroy academic freedom, to repudiate the United Nations as a Communist trick, and to convert the election of 1960 into another Religious War.[32]

An essential task of Jewish organizations has been the attainment of social equality without violating the right of private association. This is admittedly a tricky business and, because the issues are confusing, one that deserves treatment. One of the criticisms of the Anti-Defamation League, for example, has been that it tries to "force Jews" upon non-Jewish associations or institutions, e.g., college fraternities, clubs, hotels, neighborhoods, schools, etc. This tactic, it is asserted, runs head on into the right of Christians to sponsor their private institutions, barring Jews; or the right of whites to exclude Negroes; or, for that matter, the right of Jews to run closed organizations.

What has obscured this whole area is the use of irrelevant categories. The A.D.L. has, for example, never claimed that a Catholic seminary was anti-Semitic because it barred Jewish students. A closed religious institution—a parochial school, *yeshiva*, or Islamic institute—has a constituency founded on religious criteria. But when we turn to an allegedly "nonsectarian" institution, we find a different set of categories operating—and *ex hypothese* "sect" is not one of them. Thus the A.D.L. can correctly claim that a nonsectarian institution which discriminates against Jews is violating *its own proclaimed standards*. At another level, a Jewish student will hardly rejoice if he learns that a group of anti-Semitic students at his college meet once a week to exchange Yahoo gossip, but that is their affair. It becomes his problem if the college gives official recognition to this group—say as a fraternity—and treats it as an operating agency of the school. In this instance, the anti-Semitic principle has been given covert institutional endorsement. No sane Jew would want to be pledged by an anti-Semitic fraternity; the complaint is not that Jews are excluded but that the principle of Jewish exclusion receives official recognition.

In still another situation, one that has received great emphasis from the A.D.L. over the past decade,[33] a housing developer builds a community of $35,000 houses and puts them up for sale. He has established the price criterion, but then adds to it racial or religious bars. The A.D.L. has never argued that a Jew or a Negro with only $25,000 should be sold such a house as a token of intergroup esteem, but it has insisted that the *only* valid basis for exclusion is pecuniary. If a citizen appears with the requisite $35,000, his race or religion is utterly irrelevant to a business transaction: buying a house is not a religious or cultural enterprise.

Similarly, there are few commentators who would maintain that a hotel or resort is a religious institution, yet for fifty years the A.D.L. has been battering away at this confusion of roles.[34] A hotel has the right to turn away individuals who cannot pay the bill, and hopefully it will bar noisy drunks, prostitutes, typhoid carriers, and teen-agers with transistor radios despite their race, color, creed, or financial affluence. But race and religion are not relevant categories; there is no such thing as Jewish or Negro money. (Perhaps the startling hypocrisy of some resort hotels merits a parenthesis: during the season they discriminate against Jews and Negroes, but in the off-season they revert to the principles of capitalism!) It might also be noted that many so-called "private clubs," which the A.D.L. has been accused of trying to crash, have a wholly fictitious corporate existence. Any individual who demonstrates his membership in the master race can join on his way in the door, while membership is denied to "undesirable types" who are asked why they want to invade a "private" gathering. In other words, the right of private association has been used as a cloak for discriminatory activities of an essentially public character. And it has been this spurious employment of a fundamental and unquestioned principle that has aroused the opposition of the A.D.L. and other civil rights organizations.[35]

As the antidiscrimination laws of the great urban states have been tightened up, anti-Semitism has become more sophisticated, harder to identify precisely. This has called for an even greater outlay of energy, particularly in preparing elaborate statistical studies which indicate the existence of prejudice in situations where few explicit signs appear. In 1959, for instance, the A.D.L. released a careful study of the employment practices of seven great life insurance companies which indicated that Jewish executives were concentrated in sales functions outside of the home offices with little access to top managerial posts. The consistency of this pattern across the industry indicated that it was more than a statistical accident.[36]

In 1962 a nationwide survey of private clubs, bona fide clubs in this case, revealed that 67 percent of them practiced religious discrimination (of this total, one-eighth were Jewish) and raised a series of important questions about the extent to which such admittedly private discrimination militated against the effective operation of the democratic process. This is the American version of a problem which has troubled British commentators for years: the degree to which informal groupings—"old boys" clubs where the influential gather—in fact play a key role in determination of public policy.

Social discrimination and related problems will remain to absorb the interest and energies of Jewish defense organizations for years to come, but an American Jew in 1963 could look to an untrammeled future with confidence and determination. And despite the hardships, the injustices, the inner hurts and aching scars suffered by the Jewish community in the United States, it could look with real pride to a half-century of magnificent accomplishment. American Jews had not fled from their burden of prejudice nor stood immobile and paralyzed in the face of their enemies— they had accepted the challenge of freedom in a harsh but yet open society and fought back. Moreover—and perhaps this should stand as their finest tribute—they did not fight a limited war against anti-Semitism, but rather a general engagement against the whole complex of racial and religious discrimination. They were not seeking admission to the master race, but the eradication of the pernicious principle of racism wherever and against whomever it might be employed. Their record of attainment is thus both a spiritual testimony to their integrity as Jews and a vindication of their standing as Americans.

THE PAST
AND THE FUTURE

In November, 1962, President John F. Kennedy, by Executive Order, forbade the use of federal funds to subsidize segregated housing. This measure, which had long been advocated by liberal pressure groups, had formally come to the President as a recommendation of the federal Civil Rights Commission, a government body with a roving franchise created under the otherwise innocuous Civil Rights Act of 1957 which has done a superb job of investigating and publicizing the barriers confronting the Negro in his march toward full equality. If this order is fully implemented, and regrettably one can count on the development of numerous evasive tactics to forestall its impact, housing discrimination will effectively lose its economic base. This action by the President, although it brought the power of an egalitarian federal public policy to bear on a new sector of American life, was just one more episode in a long series of administrative decisions which began with President Truman in 1948. A similar policy governs employment practices in private industries under contract to the national government, and various states have already applied the principle in these and other sectors.

Perhaps this far-reaching "stroke of a pen" can serve us as a point of departure for concluding the present essay. This has in no sense been a comprehensive analysis of civil liberties in the twentieth century. It has rather been an effort to provide some perspective and depth to the remarkable transformation in American attitudes and practices that has taken place in the historically short span of half a century. An action like President Kennedy's would literally have been unthinkable in 1913. In the first place, there was no tradition of civil liberties at that time, and President Woodrow Wilson, a Southern gentleman by origins and belief, accepted racial segregation as a fact of life in the United States. In the second place, the role of the national government in American life was such that any administrative decision by the President (assuming that he felt the need for action) would have had no significant impact on the economic life of the nation. In short, there has been a radical change both in the subjective views of political leaders and in the objective role of the government in national affairs. The consequence is that today we are as a nation "civil liberties conscious," and there are at the disposal of government instruments for realizing our libertarian aspirations undreamed of fifty years ago.

It is curious how those who bemoan the present state of American freedom overlook this undeniable historical shift. They point, for example, to the many deplorable violations of civil rights in our time as proof that we are in a bad way, forgetting that the very existence of this clamor and demand for justice is a function of new social attitudes. Newspapers in 1913 seldom paid the slightest attention to a lynching, except to note that, if the victim had behaved himself, he would not have wound up dangling from a tree. Today accused Communists utilize federal courtrooms as platforms for expressing their view that the United States is on the road to Fascism; half a century ago, a Wobbly was lucky to get into a courtroom alive. In other words, *because we are now sensitive and concerned about civil rights,* deprivations are announced and denounced from the housetops. We now have statistics on police brutality; they are appalling, but at least the victim of the third degree has now achieved the right to be a statistic. Fifty years ago nobody paid the slightest attention to him—he was beaten up and ignored. If someone took the mortality statistics in 1900 and said that cancer was virtually nonexistent because it was rarely listed as a cause of death, he would be laughed out of medical circles. There was simply a diagnostic failure which led to "lung fever" or "pneumonia" being listed on an enormous number of death certificates. Similarly, the fact that we now chronicle and get exercised about civil rights problems which left our fathers and grandfathers undisturbed should never be taken as probative evidence that repression and denial of individual liberty are new and increasing phenomena.

Indeed, it is precisely this transformation in public ideals, this civil liberties consciousness, which provided the stimulus for the great Negro campaign in the summer of 1963. It is not that the Negro today suffers under a greater burden of prejudice than his father or grandfather; on the contrary, he is both objectively better off and subjectively aware of how much better off still he should be. And without in any way depreciating the initiative or the autonomy of contemporary Negro leadership, it is only fair to say that their mobilization for full freedom is occurring within an atmosphere of public concern that simply did not exist fifty, twenty-five, or even ten years ago. Does anyone doubt that the militant racists in the Deep South would not be prepared to follow the ruthless pattern of the South African whites *if they could get away with it?* The machine guns and tanks of the Alabama State Guard could, for example, maintain white supremacy in Birmingham if they could be employed for that purpose—and fifty years ago they *would* have been so utilized. In 1963 the Alabama State Guard was "nationalized" and employed to enforce national law against the Governor, the legislature, and the white elite of Alabama.

The bravery and dedication of the Negro protesters is not at issue, but—as the fate of the Hungarian Freedom Fighters demonstrated—bravery and dedication cannot alone master the repressive instruments that modern technology has devised. The fact is that the *nation* will not permit the suppression of Negro protest, will not permit the white supremacists to exercise their traditional power of life and death over Negro citizens. Thus when the American Negroes emerge victorious from what must be their final campaign for their rights, they can justly claim that they won their own place in the sun. But at the same time, and without exaggerating the role of the white man in this struggle, they should also recognize that their success was in part a consequence of the great transformation in American attitudes that we have discussed. No white American can feel anything but a sense of shame when he chronicles the travail of the Negro, but some hope for forgiveness may perhaps be found in the fact that, imperfect as it is, there is an "American conscience."

We have in this book concentrated on certain broad patterns of prejudice, and have avoided a detailed legalistic treatment which can be found elsewhere. However, it should be noted that the movement toward greater respect for individual dignity has taken place across the board. The federal courts have, for instance, in the last twenty-five years imposed upon both state and federal prosecutors an ever-tightening set of standards in the area of criminal justice. In 1961, the Supreme Court ruled in *Mapp* v. *Ohio* that the introduction of illegally procured evidence in any state prosecution violated the constitutional rights of the defendant, a decision which brought the states up to preexisting federal standards and set off a revolution in state and local police practices. Moreover, in 1963, the Court ruled that counsel must be present in all serious state prosecutions—at the pre-trial as well as at the trial proceedings. In an entirely different sector, the Court in 1962 (*Baker* v. *Carr*) drove a bulldozer through a principal bulwark of Yahoo power by holding that the equal protection clause of the Fourteenth Amendment protected a citizen from having his vote depreciated by gerrymandering. While this decision will have some long-run impact on Congress, its real punch hit those rurally dominated state legislatures where the power of the urban population has been minimized by fancy districting.

The United States, to put the matter a bit differently, has developed over the last five decades, and notably in the last three, a tradition of due process and equality which it never had before. Not equality and due process as rhetoric, but as meaningful political, social, and legal procedure. In this analysis we have concentrated perhaps too heavily on the woes of the underdog and the sins of the overdogs. The relationships have been accurately portrayed, but at the same time it must be emphasized that the attainment of a national tradition of civil liberty resulted from both the struggles of minorities for justice and equality *and* the recognition by the dominant groups in American society that these claims were legitimate. These great accomplishments, in other words, were not the outcome of a plot by the A.C.L.U., the NAACP, the A.D.L., and the A.D.A.—the Constitution was not secretly amended by libertarian conspirators.

The majority itself, in that ungainly, amorphous fashion characteristic of a huge pluralistic society, accepted the full implications of its own democratic principles and gave concrete meaning to the abstractions of the American Dream. The key to freedom in a democratic society can never be judicial decisions, Presidential orders, or even statutes. A judicial decision can focus the ideal of due process or equal protection of the laws on a question under litigation and protect individual rights against specific violation. A Presidential order can bring the moral leadership of the Chief Executive into an issue, provide a catalyst, and prod the reluctant. A statute can establish sanctions to enforce moral purposes and has enormous educational value. (It is ironic that the Southerners who loudly proclaim that morality cannot be legislated are in fact complaining that their peculiar racial legislation is being overridden! They have for centuries legislated the "morality" of white supremacy and are fighting to prevent its being "un"-legislated.) But the fundamental force that sustains liberty is the commitment of the community to those values which make individual freedom possible. To borrow a metaphor from Aristotle, if there is to be a free community, its citizens must have freedom in their souls.

In practical terms, this comes down to self-restraint on the part of whatever group or coalition of groups happens to control the instruments of authority in society—the majority, to use a shorthand word for a complex phenomenon. In essence it requires a commitment, conscious and/or unconscious, that ideals will restrain force. To use a vivid example, who has not felt murderous rage flowing into his system as he read of the brutal murder of a child? Who has not wondered what he would have done had he been the policeman who captured the murderer? Yet the bench mark of a decent society—and more than anyone realizes, democracy is the institutionalization of decency—is its reaction as a whole to such a fearful event. Does it take the guilty party and hang him to a lamp-post in an orgy of vengeance? Or does it guarantee to him decent police treatment, a fair trial, and frequently the sanctuary of a hospital for the criminally insane? A simple sort of problem, but one that separates the men from the boys in terms of political maturity. The cruel fact is that in terms of the welfare of the community the lynchers are far worse criminals than the murderer. His is an individual crime, but theirs is a betrayal of the very ideals which provide the democratic community with its *raison d'être*. He has used private power for a criminal end. They have dragged the standard of public morality with them in their return to the jungle.

I have chosen an extreme example to point up the issue, but the same proposition applies to the recognition of the rights of all minorities—criminal or law-abiding. The majority has never been reluctant to confer civil rights and equality on those it liked or respected. The bone of contention has always been that the majority could convince itself that a minority it disliked was in effect criminal or subhuman. In the 1850's all Irish were drunks and ruffians; later the Jews were thieves and subversives; and throughout, the Negro's status as *untermensch* was unchallenged. In this fashion most Americans could reconcile their democracy with their prejudices and emerge with few qualms. The Declaration of Independence set the pace by asserting the equality of all men, with the unarticulated corollary that Negro slaves were not men. The trouble was that the ideals had a logic of their own. The unarticulated corollary provoked a bloody Civil War because freedom could not survive in the same universe with slavery. And there were always those, both self-interested and altruistic, who demanded that the intrinsic potentialities of the democratic credo be realized in practice. From the time that John Adams braved the Boston mob to serve as defense counsel to the British officer accused of perpetrating the "Boston Massacre"—"Honest John" was nauseated by the local evidences of what the Communists today applaud as "People's Justice"—there have always been hard, clear voices calling Americans back to their principles.

Thus, while we have in this volume chronicled at some length the brave battles of the civil liberties groups, the fact remains that their plea to the American people to fulfill the obligations of the democratic ideal did not fall on deaf ears. When one examines, for example, the 1960 platforms of the Democratic and Republican parties, when he reads the speeches of party leaders, when he investigates the positions of the National Conference of Christians and Jews, the National Catholic Welfare Conference, the National Council of Churches of Christ, he realizes the extent to which the full achievement of human rights has become a national imperative. Not only has this become a matter of domestic importance, but in the international sphere as well the United States has taken up the standard of freedom.

Indeed, there are those who assert that the increased emphasis on civil rights in the United States is largely a result of our needs in the international arena. They argue, for example, that the expediential requirements of fighting the Cold War have led to efforts to improve the status of the American Negro. There is obviously some validity to this position, but I think it is generally a vast oversimplification which merits some discussion. As we have seen, the outrages the Nazis committed against European Jewry undoubtedly played an important role in altering American attitudes toward anti-Semitism in the 1930's and 1940's. It is assumed that because this was the reaction, it had to be the reaction, but I am not sure that history is that unilinear. It was quite possible for a people to be anti-Nazi *and* anti-Semitic; the Nazi atrocities hardly led the Poles, for example, to love their Jewish brethren; and the Stalinists, while denouncing Nazi anti-Semitism, were ruthlessly suppressing "cosmopolitanism" in the Soviet Union— and a "cosmopolitan" could best be described as a recognizable Jew. (Jews in the U.S.S.R. had the somber satisfaction of being

shot or exiled to Vorkuta as "Zionist agents of British imperialism"
or "rootless Trotskyite intellectuals" rather than as *Zhids,* to use a
favorite word of Stalin's.)

In short, the American people could have reacted—as a few
did—by adopting a pattern of nationalistic anti-Semitism: "I have
no use for Hitler, but he *has* eliminated the Jewish problem."
This did not happen, but hardly because there was no anti-Semitic
tradition for it to take root in. It did not occur because the American majority, riddled though it was with anti-Jewish prejudice,
reacted even more strongly against the indecencies of Nazism;
i.e., when the issue was put before the people in concrete terms,
they looked to their ideals for the appropriate response. This response was, of course, fortified by the reactions of their political
and spiritual leaders: President Roosevelt, Secretary of State
Cordell Hull, many leading Senators and Congressmen, and most
leading churchmen.

Similarly, the contemporary confrontation with Communist
totalitarianism has no *necessary* connection with the expansion of
freedom in the United States, particularly for the Negro. It is
quite possible to argue that the upsurge of the Negro at this time
will weaken the fabric of national unity, will provide a seedbed
for Communist propaganda; in short, that it plays into the hands
of the enemy. This in a nutshell is the position advanced by Senator James Eastland and other leading Southern racists. As far as
the need for the United States to demonstrate its libertarian convictions for the benefit of new nations emerging from colonialism,
these same spokesmen can claim that the struggle for the "minds
of the uncommitted" is essentially fictitious as a power consideration in the Cold War. The attitudes of the Burmese or the
Ghanaians, they suggest, are completely irrelevant to the balance
of nuclear terror—the best these new nations can hope for is to
escape the consequences of great power rivalry. In sum, they submit that American attitudes and practices toward our Negro minority are immaterial in the international context, that we do not
strengthen our nation by the drive for equality but weaken it, that
we should tighten up our security by clamping down on these

Communist-inspired demands for civil rights which only deflect our energy from the battle with an implacable enemy.

The fact that this sounds like a straw man which has only been set up so it may be knocked down emphasizes how far we have moved in the last generation. These are precisely the arguments (in a present-day formulation) that were employed throughout World War II to justify the maintenance of the Negro in his subordinate position in American society. Even though we were fighting a war against Nazi racism in one theater and against the Japanese—who claimed to be the champion of the colored races in the struggle against the colonialism and racism of the white man—in the other, the conservative logic proved compelling. The fact that Japanese propaganda in the Pacific harped on the sensitivities of Negro American soldiers, telling them night in, night out, of their bondage to white exploiters, led to no great change in the status of the colored troops. No one, in other words, rushed to "meet the Japanese challenge" by desegregating the aviation engineer battalions or commissioning Negro officers: the Negroes were simply forbidden under penalty of court-martial to listen to the Tokyo and Manila broadcasts.

Thus, the notion that, in a dialectical sense, the Negroes have the Communists to thank for their improvements because the Soviets have "challenged" the United States to the fulfillment of democratic precepts is a little too neat. A society can react to a challenge in more than one fashion, and, again, the crucial question which this line of argument does not answer is *why did the United States take the libertarian course?* The answer seems to me to be that the status of the Negro was by 1946 tormenting the American conscience—civil liberties and religious groups had been hammering away at this anomaly for twenty years—and the Negro himself was no longer willing to accept his traditional role as the "invisible man." The confrontation was inevitable. Given the forces that had been building up behind the civil liberties tradition, the long-run outcome could hardly be doubted; but the struggle with the pseudo-egalitarian Communists unquestionably gave the issue an urgency and a cogency that would otherwise have been absent. It is probably true that the attitude of the Ghanaians or the Burmese has today little relevance to the power equilibrium between the United States and the Soviet Union, but it should be added that those who argue this "hard-nosed" position subconsciously assume that the world will remain in this precarious balance for the rest of time. Of course, time may end with a nuclear holocaust, yet as an optimist—defined these days as one who looks to the future with *un*certainty—I suspect that there will be a long run, and that in it the American concern for the rights of all men will play an important part in the growth of a tradition of freedom throughout the world. Even if my optimism is misconceived, that ideal is worth our full support on its intrinsic merits.

One who looks at the present in the perspective of the past and finds, as I do, that there has been a vast improvement in the climate of civil liberties is always accused of joining the "celebration," of flattering the American reader's taste for a Happy Ending. Now it is my contention that in 1963 there is more respect for freedom and dedication to equality in the United States than we have ever known before, and I am prepared to argue further that every indicator points toward the future elaboration of these libertarian principles. As this book goes to press, the President of the United States and his brother, the Attorney General, are committed to a congressional battle for unprecedented civil rights legislation, measures which would throw the great power of the federal government into the struggle for Negro rights. This battle may be lost, but the war will be won. But to make this historical judgment is not to suggest for a moment that the battle is over, that the A.C.L.U., the A.D.L., the NAACP, and other defense groups should abandon their labors and leave the mopping-up operations to the state and federal governments. In the first place, it has been the pressure of private demands for the expansion of freedom, the endless agitation of private organizations, which has paced the development of public policy. This must continue; the pressure can never be let up. In the second place, there is the continuing task of community education and defense against Yahoo raids such as those instigated in the last few years by the John Birch Society.

As one who is strongly opposed to the employment of legal sanctions against extremist opinion—e.g., the Smith Act, the various subsequent internal insecurity acts, group libel laws—I feel that the liberal community must mobilize effectively for the defense of its principles on the level of community organization. Far too many liberal intellectuals, seemingly obsessed by a vision of catastrophe which in fact amounts to an acute distrust of the American people, abandon the battlefield to the Yahoos and retire to their libraries to read German history and bewail the imminence of Fascism. From this sanctuary of alienation they emerge from time to time to bleat that "all is lost," and then characteristically, when nobody listens to their funereal prophecies, denounce the lack of respect for nonconformity and the absence of freedom of opinion. In some curious fashion, they have thus confused the right to be heard with an alleged right to be taken seriously, but the constitutional right to free speech can hardly be interpreted as a legal obligation to supply an audience.

Poor old American "mass culture" takes quite a beating, but the interesting thing is that a large number of Americans seem to enjoy the critical flagellation; at least, the literature of excoriation seems to sell. At the moment, for example, there is a "Slums Were Fun" vogue which has proclaimed to the children and grandchildren of "old law" tenement dwellers that their high-rise apartments are a symbol of cultural barbarism, that in the process of getting a decent place to live they have sacrificed such irreplaceable bases of community as the organ-grinder and the block party. Modern city life is condemned by ample use of figures on juvenile delinquency, as if gang warfare was invented with lower-income public housing. Once again, I suspect, we are to a large extent victims of our statistical obsession: the startling increase in juvenile delinquency in recent decades *could* in large part be occasioned by a radical shift in police practices. When I was a youngster the New York police rarely booked a juvenile for anything less than a felony; they simply beat his ears off and sent him home to meditate on the evils of sin. He never became a statistic, but today when the juvenile offender is brought into the station house he is met by a committee: a clergyman, a social worker, a psychiatrist, and a statistician. This is, of course, a highly commendable change in social attitude, but it must lead to a skewed statistical sample. (Technology also plays a role: fifty years ago a boy was rarely arrested for hopping a ride on the back of a trolley car—the equivalent at that time of "grand theft auto.")

Despite all the anguished complaints about contemporary American life and the seemingly endless predictions of a conformist "police state," it seems clear to me that over the past half-century the American people have become committed as they never were before to the concrete achievement of their traditional values of freedom, justice, and equality. This has not occurred because of the unfolding of historical inevitability—urbanization and industrialization need not, as the German and Japanese experiences indicate, necessarily lead to the growth of freedom—but as the outcome of endless struggle in behalf of these precious ideals. Great problems have yet to be surmounted in the perpetual, many-fronted war for the defense and enlargement of the sector of freedom, and we can devote little time to self-congratulation since our commitment is to an ideal future, not a relatively better present.

Yet in the fights that lie before us we can draw some comfort and sense of comradeship from the obstacles we have overcome and from the knowledge that while the American standard may be tattered, we have in the United States achieved a level of individual freedom that hundreds of millions of human beings can only conceive of as a remote, impossible aspiration. This accomplishment stands as an eternal monument to those fearless dreamers who, despite their bruises and their scars, never lost their faith in the ultimate decency of the American people or their vision of a great, pluralistic, rambunctious community bringing to fruition on the greatest scale in human history the ideals of brotherhood and human freedom. They need no other.

NOTES

CHAPTER I

1. U. S. Bureau of the Census, *Historical Statistics of the United States, Colonial Times to 1957* (Washington, D.C., 1960), p. 25. (Henceforth *Historical Statistics.*)
2. *Ibid.*, pp. 7, 14, 712; see *Pollock* v. *Farmers' Loan and Trust Co.*, 158 U.S. 601 (1895) for the Supreme Court's position on income tax.
3. John Higham, *Strangers in the Land* (New Brunswick, Rutgers University Press, 1955), pp. 89–96.
4. See Elias Tcherikower (ed.), *The Early Jewish Labor Movement in the United States* (New York, Jewish Publications Society, 1961).
5. John P. Roche, "Pre-Statutory Denaturalization," *Cornell Law Quarterly,* Vol. 35 (1949), pp. 132–37.
6. See John P. Roche, *Courts and Rights* (New York, Random House, 1961), pp. 98, 115.
7. Hugh H. Brackenridge, *Incidents of the Insurrection* (Philadelphia, 1795), Vol. 3, pp. 136–37.
8. Cited by C. Vann Woodward, *Origins of the New South* (Baton Rouge, Louisiana State University Press, 1951), p. 218.
9. Cited by C. Vann Woodward, *Reunion and Reaction* (Boston, Little, Brown, 1951), p. 214.
10. *Ibid.*, p. 212.
11. Robert K. Carr, *Federal Protection of Civil Rights* (Ithaca, Cornell University Press, 1947), pp. 10–14, 35–47; John P. Roche, *op. cit.*, pp. 65–70, 84–90.
12. Joseph S. Ransmeier, "The Fourteenth Amendment and the Separate but Equal Doctrine," *Michigan Law Review,* Vol. 50 (1951), pp. 203–60; John P. Roche, *op. cit.*, p. 86.
13. In the family atlas which I absorbed as a child, the "Caucasian" race was represented by Benjamin Franklin and the "Negroid" by a nightmare-inspiring cannibal.
14. Cited by David Spitz, *Patterns of Anti-Democratic Thought* (New York, Macmillan, 1949), p. 140.

15. John H. Franklin, *From Slavery to Freedom* (New York, A. A. Knopf, 1947), pp. 432, 336–37, 435–36.

16. See Thomas A. Bailey, *Theodore Roosevelt and the Japanese-American Crisis* (Stanford, Stanford University Press, 1934); Eleanor Tupper and George E. McReynolds, *Japan in American Popular Opinion* (New York, Macmillan, 1937); Raymond L. Buell, "The Development of Anti-Japanese Agitation in the United States," *Political Science Quarterly*, Vol. 37 (1922), pp. 605–38.

17. John W. Burgess, *Political Science and Comparative Constitutional Law* (Boston, Ginn & Co., 1890), Vol. I, 44–45, cited by David Spitz, *op. cit.*, pp. 139–40.

18. Cited by Higham, *op. cit.*, p. 169.

19. Cited by John Higham, "Anti-Semitism in the Gilded Age: A Reinterpretation," *Mississippi Valley Historical Review*, Vol. 43 (1957), p. 573.

20. *Ibid.*, p. 577.

21. See Louis Adamic, *Dynamite* (New York, Viking Press, 1934); Robert Hunter, *Violence in the Labor Movement* (New York, Macmillan, 1914); Robert V. Bruce, *1877* (Indianapolis, Bobbs-Merrill, 1959); Leon Whipple, *The Story of Civil Liberty in the United States* (New York, Vanguard Press, 1927).

22. Vernon H. Jensen, *Heritage of Conflict* (Ithaca, Cornell University Press, 1950), esp. chaps. 4 and 5; and for the record of Harry Orchard's exploits as chief assassin see Stewart H. Holbrook, *The Rocky Mountain Revolution* (New York, Henry Holt, 1956), *passim*.

23. *Historical Statistics*, pp. 427, 428, 139, 74.

24. Howard J. Graham, "An Innocent Abroad: The Constitutional Corporate 'Person,'" *U.C.L.A. Law Review*, Vol. 2 (1955), p. 209.

25. Charles O. Gregory, *Labor and the Law* (New York, W. W. Norton, 1946); Elias Lieberman, *Unions Before the Bar* (New York, Harper & Bros., 1950), chap. 5; see *U.S.* v. *E. C. Knight Co.*, 156 U.S. 1 (1895) for the Court's position on the character of the trade of the sugar company.

26. Vernon H. Jensen has a detailed discussion of troubles in the Coeur d'Alene during the 1890's in *op. cit.*, chap. 7.

27. See *Hitchman Coal and Coke Co.* v. *Mitchell*, 245 U.S. 229 (1917).

28. Richard Hofstadter, *The Age of Reform* (New York, A. A. Knopf, 1955), p. 10.

29. Cited by Henry F. Pringle, *Theodore Roosevelt, A Biography* (New York, Harvest Reprint, 1956), p. 180.

30. Louis Filler, *Crusaders for American Liberalism* (Yellow Springs, Antioch Press, 1950), pp. 132 ff.

31. Hofstadter, *op. cit.*, pp. 77–81.

32. On the Brownsville Incident see Franklin, *op. cit.*, pp. 433–35. See generally: Gunnar Myrdal, *An American Dilemma* (New York, Harper & Bros., 1944), William Nowlin, *The Negro in American National Politics* (Boston, Stratford, 1931); Mary W. Ovington, *How the NAACP Began* (New York, n.p., 1914); Robert Jack, *History of the NAACP* (Boston, Meador, 1943); James W. Johnson, *Along This Way* (New York, Viking

Press, 1933); Charles S. Johnson, *Patterns of Negro Segregation* (New York, Harper & Bros., 1943).

33. Ira Kipnis, *The American Socialist Movement, 1877–1912* (New York, Columbia University Press, 1952), p. 131.

CHAPTER II

1. This is the view of such diverse commentators as Norman Thomas and George F. Kennan. See also Eric F. Goldman, *Rendezvous with Destiny* (New York, A. A. Knopf, 1952), and Richard C. Hofstadter, *The Age of Reform.*
2. Norman A. Graebner (ed.), *An Uncertain Tradition* (New York, McGraw-Hill, 1961), p. 9.
3. *Ibid.,* p. 12.
4. Nathan Schachner, *The Price of Liberty* (New York, American Jewish Committee, 1948), chap. 1.
5. Mark Sullivan, *Our Times* (New York, Scribner, 1936), Vol. 4, p. 44.
6. Arthur S. Link, *Woodrow Wilson and the Progressive Era* (New York, Harper & Bros., 1954), pp. 64–66.
7. See the study of Bryan's record as Secretary of State by Richard Challenger in Norman A. Graebner, *op. cit.,* p. 83.
8. Sullivan, *op. cit.,* Vol. 5, p. 38.
9. Barbara Tuchman, *The Guns of August* (New York, Macmillan, 1962), chap. 2, *passim.*
10. Cited by Sullivan, *op. cit.,* Vol. 5, p. 6.
11. Link, *op. cit.,* chap. 6, *passim.* For Bryan's "neutral money" see esp. 51 ff.
12. This was notably true of the Jewish Socialists who had close ideological ties with the powerful German Social Democratic Party. The Jewish *Daily Forward* was, for example, outspokenly pro-German.
13. Cited by John Higham, *op. cit.,* p. 197.
14. *Ibid.*
15. See United Nations, *Report of the Special Committee on Hungary* (New York, United Nations, 1954), pp. 79–80, for statements of similar sentiment.
16. Charles Seymour, *The Intimate Papers of Colonel House* (Boston, Houghton, Mifflin Co., 1928), Vol. 2, p. 361.
17. John Maynard Keynes, *Essays and Sketches in Biography* (New York, Meridian Edition, 1956), p. 267. (Quoted with permission of copyright holder, Harcourt, Brace & World, Inc.)
18. Cited by Link, *op. cit.,* p. 186.
19. Cited by John M. Blum, *Woodrow Wilson and the Politics of Morality* (Boston, Little, Brown, 1956), p. 71. This short book treats Wilson's ambivalences superbly.
20. Cited by Horace C. Peterson and Gilbert C. Fite, *Opponents of War, 1917–1918* (Madison, University of Wisconsin Press, 1957), p. 11.
21. *Ibid.,* p. 14. For a short but perceptive analysis see Harold M. Hyman, *To*

Try Men's Souls (Berkeley, University of California Press, 1959), pp. 267–315. I am indebted to Professor Hyman for providing me with a copy of Joan Maria Jensen, *The American Protective League, 1917–1919,* an unpublished doctoral dissertation prepared under his direction at the University of California, Los Angeles, 1962.

22. Cited from Emerson Hough, *The Web* (Chicago, Reilly & Lee, 1919), p. 14, by *ibid.,* p. 19.

23. Cited by Zechariah Chafee, *Free Speech in America* (Cambridge, Harvard University Press, 1946), p. 79.

24. Cited by Peterson and Fite, *op. cit.,* p. 38.

25. See *Meyer v. Nebraska,* 262 U.S. 390 (1923).

26. Chafee, *op. cit.,* pp. 40–41, 54.

27. Leonard W. Levy, *Legacy of Suppression* (Cambridge, Harvard University Press, 1960), *passim.*

28. See Justice Holmes's essay on Montesquieu in his *Collected Legal Papers* (New York, Harcourt, Brace, 1920), p. 258.

29. Chafee, *op. cit.,* pp. 108 f.

30. See Alpheus T. Mason, *Brandeis, A Free Man's Life* (New York, Viking Press, 1946), chap. 36, for a discussion of Brandeis' influence upon the older Holmes.

CHAPTER III

1. Frederick Pollock and Frederic W. Maitland, *The History of English Law* (Cambridge, Cambridge University Press, 2nd ed., 1952), Vol. I, p. 1.

2. Andrew Sinclair, *Prohibition* (Boston, Little, Brown, 1962), p. 119.

3. Cited by Daniel Bell, "Marxian Socialism in the United States," in Donald D. Egbert and Stow Persons, *Socialism and American Life* (Princeton, Princeton University Press, 1952), Vol. I, p. 283.

4. See David A. Shannon, *The Socialist Party of America* (New York, Harcourt, Brace, 1955), on "gas and water" Socialism in pp. 13–17; on Victor Berger, pp. 21–25.

5. *Ibid.,* p. 309.

6. It is interesting that Bell, Kipnis, Shannon, and Theodore Draper all have played down the impact of the war, and the St. Louis Program, on the fortunes of the party.

7. Cited by Ray Ginger, *The Bending Cross* (New Brunswick, Rutgers University Press, 1949), p. 341.

8. *Ibid.,* p. 342.

9. Shannon, *op. cit.,* pp. 5, 21.

10. Ginger, *op. cit.,* p. 343.

11. See Stewart H. Holbrook, *op. cit., passim.*

12. See Wallace Stegner, *The Preacher and the Slave* (Boston, Houghton, Mif-

flin, 1950), for a novelist's account which surpasses many of the "scholarly" analyses in its graphic and sophisticated treatment of the ambiguities of the IWW.

13. Paul F. Brissenden, *The I.W.W.* (New York, Russell & Russell, 2nd ed., 1957), p. 359.
14. *Ibid.*
15. *Ibid.*, p. 366.
16. For a discussion of the constructive Socialist position versus the nihilist Nazi one, see Peter Drucker, *The End of Economic Man* (New York, John Day, 1939); and Hermann Rauschning, *The Revolution of Nihilism* (New York, Longmans, Green, 1939).
17. For the Nazi program in the early 1930's see Carl Mayer, "On the Intellectual Origin of National Socialism," *Social Research*, Vol. 9 (1942), pp. 225–47. For a brilliant exposé of Italian fascist development in the early stages, see A. Rossi (pseud. of Angelo Tasca), *The Rise of Italian Fascism* (London, Methuen, 1938).
18. Stuart Jamieson (Bureau of Labor Statistics, Bulletin No. 836), *Labor Unionism in American Agriculture* (Washington, D.C., 1945), pp. 61–62.
19. *Ibid.*, p. 62.
20. See Ralph Chaplin, *Wobbly* (Chicago, University of Chicago Press, 1948), *passim*, esp. pp. 135 ff.
21. Brissenden, *op. cit.*, p. 263.
22. *Ibid.*, p. 266.
23. See Chaplin, *op. cit.*, pp. 149 f., for a vivid description of the Spokane "free speech fight."
24. Cited by Peterson and Fite, *op. cit.*, p. 236.
25. See Ginger, *op. cit.*, pp. 324–43, 350–59.
26. Shannon, *op. cit.*, pp. 114 ff.
27. Peterson and Fite, *op. cit.*, pp. 251 ff.
28. According to Ginger, *op. cit.*, p. 364.
29. Cited by Peterson and Fite, *op. cit.*, p. 254.
30. *Debs* v. *United States*, 249 U.S. 211, 216 (1919).
31. Cited by Ginger, *op. cit.*, p. 405.
32. Cited by Ira Kipnis, *op. cit.*, pp. 278 ff.
33. Peterson and Fite, *op. cit.*, p. 166.
34. Zechariah Chafee, Jr., *op. cit.*, p. 250.
35. *Ibid.*, p. 79.
36. *Ibid.*, pp. 304 f.
37. *Ibid.*, p. 305.
38. Peterson and Fite, *op. cit.*, pp. 238–40; Chaplin, *op. cit.*, pp. 220–24.
39. Robert K. Murray, *Red Scare* (Minneapolis, University of Minnesota Press, 1955), p. 30; also Philip Taft, "The Federal Trials of the I.W.W.," *Labor History*, Vol. 3 (1962), pp. 57–91, *passim*. Since this was written Donald Johnson's *The Challenge to American Freedoms: World War I and the Rise of the American Civil Liberties Union* (University of Kentucky

Press, 1963) has appeared with some interesting material on the early work of the A.C.L.U.

40. Cited by Peterson and Fite, *op. cit.*, p. 237.
41. *Ibid.*
42. *Ibid.*, p. 173.
43. *Ibid.*, pp. 55 f.
44. *Ibid.*, p. 60.
45. Cited by Vernon H. Jensen, *op. cit.*, p. 396.
46. *Ibid.*, p. 397.
47. *Ibid.*, pp. 394 f.
48. President's Mediation Commission, *Report on Bisbee Deportation* (Washington, D.C., 1918), *passim.*
49. Cited by Jensen, *op. cit.*, p. 406.
50. *Ibid.*
51. *Ibid.* See also Hyman's discussion of the Loyal Legion of Loggers and Lumbermen in the Pacific Northwest as a government-sponsored "union" to combat the IWW, *op. cit.*, pp. 298–315.
52. *Ibid.*, p. 404.
53. The only serious study of this era is by Murray, but he has hardly done more than chronicle the events. An analysis in depth would be valuable— these were pivotal years in the history of American radicalism.
54. Cited by Chafee, *op. cit.*, p. 110.
55. *Ibid.*, p. 128.
56. *Ibid.*
57. *Abrams* v. *United States*, 250 U.S. 616 (1919).
58. Abrams soon found himself at odds with the Bolsheviks and fled to Mexico in the 1920's where he established a Yiddish newspaper and became a vigorous democrat. For the next quarter of a century he tried to return to the United States but only when he lay at death's door in the late 1950's was he permitted a brief sojourn for medical treatment.
59. From Files of the Anti-Defamation League, Letter from Leon L. Lewis, Executive Secretary of the Anti-Defamation League, April 17, 1920.
60. Congressional Record, *Proceedings and Debates of the Second Session of the Sixty-Sixth Congress* (Washington, D.C., 1920), Vol. 59, Part I, p. 30.
61. Cited by Chafee, *op. cit.*, p. 273.
62. Cited in Sullivan, *op. cit.*, Vol. 6, p. 172.
63. Cited by Chafee, *op. cit.*, p. 280.
64. Carl Sandburg, *The People, Yes* (New York, Harcourt, Brace, 1936), p. 58.
65. See James M. Smith, *Freedom's Fetters: The Alien and Sedition Laws and American Civil Liberties* (Ithaca, 1956), *passim.*
66. See Leon E. Aylesworth, "The Passing of Alien Suffrage," *American Political Science Review*, Vol. 25 (1931), pp. 114 ff.
67. Chafee, *op. cit.*, pp. 197 f.
68. *Ibid.*, p. 179.
69. See his opinion in *Colyer* v. *Skeffington*, 265 Fed. 17 (D. Mass. 1920).
70. (Chicago, 1923).

71. Richard Drinnon, *Rebel in Paradise: A Biography of Emma Goldman* (Chicago, University of Chicago Press, 1961), pp. 117, 120.

72. *Ibid.*, p. 223.

73. See Murray, *op. cit.*, pp. 190–262, *passim*.

74. Cited by Chafee, *op. cit.*, p. 169.

75. See *ibid.*, chaps. 4 and 5 for a fuller discussion of the legal problems.

76. Murray, *op. cit.*, p. 197.

77. *Ibid.*

78. *Ibid.*, p. 192.

79. See Chafee, *op. cit.*, pp. 204–15.

80. From a conversation with the late George Roewer, Socialist and civil liberties attorney, Rockport, Mass.

81. Norman Thomas, once a newsboy for Harding in Marion, Ohio, has related the conversation he had with the President on behalf of the Debs amnesty committee. Harding then had Debs pay a call on him and was apparently quite mystified by the ferocity of the Wilson Administration toward the gaunt, kindly old agitator.

CHAPTER IV

1. Roy Basler (ed.), *The Collected Works of Abraham Lincoln* (New Brunswick, Rutgers University Press, 1953), Vol. I, pp. 108–115.

2. See Gaetano Mosca, *The Ruling Class* (New York, McGraw-Hill, 1939), pp. 120–52.

3. See *Historical Statistics*, pp. 43, 46.

4. Franklin, *op. cit.*, p. 472.

5. *Ibid.*, p. 471.

6. *Ibid.*, p. 475.

7. See *Revolutionary Radicalism* (Report of the Lusk Committee, New York, 1920), Vol. II, pp. 1476–1520, for a random collection of documents from the Negro left, including considerable material on *The Messenger* and *The Emancipator*.

8. This was originally an editorial in the *Business Chronicle* of the Pacific Northwest.

9. Cited by C. Vann Woodward, *Tom Watson* (New York, Macmillan, 1938), pp. 426–27.

10. *Congressional Record*, 62 Congress, 2 Session, p. 1020.

11. *Ibid.*, p. 797.

12. *Ibid.*, p. 1014.

13. *Ibid.*, pp. 1024, 1019.

14. See Warren D. St. James, *The National Association for the Advancement of Colored People* (New York, Exposition Press, 1958), pp. 38–43, 166–71.

15. *Ibid.*, p. 54.

16. For general background see C. P. Connolly, *The Truth about the Frank*

Case (New York, American News, 1915); Charles and Louise Samuels, *Night Fell on Georgia* (New York, Pocket Books, 1956).

17. Cited by Connolly, *op. cit.*, pp. 11, 42, 44.
18. Watson attacked Hearst as a tool of the Jews and advanced this movie as evidence. See *Watson's Magazine*, Vol. XXI, No. 4, August, 1915.
19. See *Frank v. Mangum*, 237 U.S. 309 (1915).
20. Cited by Woodward, *Tom Watson*, p. 439.
21. Cited by Samuels, *op. cit.*, p. 209.
22. *Watson's Magazine*, Vol. XXI, No. 4, August, 1915, p. 234.
23. Cited by Samuels, *op. cit.*, p. 219.
24. Cited by Woodward, *Tom Watson*, p. 486.
25. Two Georgians associated with the trial have argued that Conley confessed his guilt to his attorney, William Smith, who could not reveal the fact without violating the lawyer-client relationship. Apparently Smith did tell the presiding Judge L. S. Roan and Judge Arthur G. Powell, who in turn informed Governor Slaton. See Arthur G. Powell, *I Can Go Home Again* (Chapel Hill, University of North Carolina Press, 1943); Allen L. Henson, *Confessions of a Criminal Lawyer* (New York, Vantage, 1959). The files of the Anti-Defamation League have a summary of an interview with John Slaton by Samuel A. Boorstin, formerly of Atlanta, on Oct. 12, 1953, in which Slaton reported that Watson had written offering to make him Senator if he would "let Frank hang."
26. The documentation for the following items is all on file at the A.D.L.
27. Nathan Schachner, *op. cit.*, pp. 72–73.
28. See the annual reports of the A.C.L.U. and the files of this organization in the New York Public Library. Curley's reprimand is reported in *Free Speech*, 1923, p. 19.
29. Reported to me by the late George Roewer of Rockport, Mass., then a close associate of Hillquit's in the Socialist Party.

CHAPTER V

1. See, for example, Daniel Boorstin, *The Genius of American Politics* (Chicago, University of Chicago Press, 1953), Louis Hartz, *The Liberal Tradition in America* (New York, Harcourt, Brace, 1955), Hans Kohn, *American Nationalism* (New York, Macmillan, 1958), Clinton L. Rossiter, *Marxism: The View from America* (New York, Harcourt, Brace, 1960).
2. Letter of Feb. 3, 1825, to Joseph Cabell, in *The Early History of the University of Virginia as Contained in the Letters of Thomas Jefferson and Joseph C. Cabell* (Richmond, 1856), p. 339. See also my "American Liberty: An Examination of the 'Tradition' of Freedom," in Milton Konvitz and Clinton L. Rossiter (eds.), *Aspects of Liberty* (Ithaca, Cornell University Press, 1958).
3. See Edmund A. Moore, *A Catholic Runs for President: The Campaign of*

1928 (New York, Ronald Press, 1956), pp. 101–2. (Quoted with permission of Ronald Press).

4. *Ibid.*, p. 114.

5. *Ibid.*, p. 131.

6. Irving Bernstein, *The Lean Years* (Boston, Houghton, Mifflin, 1960).

7. The story of Foster's pilgrimage to Moscow and development into an *apparatchik* is told in Theodore Draper's superb volume, *American Communism and Soviet Russia* (New York, Viking Press, 1960).

8. Samuel Lubell, *The Future of American Politics* (2d ed., Garden City, Doubleday, 1956).

9. See Edgar Eugene Robinson, *The Presidential Vote, 1896–1932* (Palo Alto, Stanford University Press, 1934), and *Historical Statistics*, pp. 686–87.

10. See Ray Ginger's vivid description of the Scopes Trial, *Six Days or Forever?* (Boston, Beacon Press, 1958).

11. According to Surgeon General Thomas Parran, there were in 1936 six million cases of syphilis in the United States, Sinclair, *op. cit.*, p. 406.

12. *The New York Times*, July 9, 1962, p. 18.

13. Sinclair, *op. cit.*, pp. 336–37.

14. Richard C. Hofstadter, *The Age of Reform*, pp. 289–300, is very perceptive on the tension of this era and the reactions of the intellectuals. See also Malcolm Cowley, *Exile's Return* (New York, Viking Press, 1951), and Alfred Kazin, *On Native Grounds* (New York, Anchor ed., 1956), pp. 147–238.

15. *Free Speech, 1925* (New York, A.C.L.U., 1926), p. 10.

16. See Edmund D. Cronon, *Black Moses* (Madison, University of Wisconsin Press, 1955). Garvey, a "black supremacist," responded to W.E.B. DuBois' criticism of his movement by saying, "Well, what could you expect of that quadroon." I am indebted to my friend Professor Ira de A. Reid of Haverford College for this piece of information.

17. Franklin, *op. cit.*, pp. 489–511.

18. Discussed by Gustavus Myers in his extremely useful *History of Bigotry in the United States* (New York, Random House, 1943), pp. 294–95.

19. Moore, *op. cit.*, pp. 186–87.

20. *Ibid.*, p. 150.

21. Walsh's dilemma is discussed *ibid.*, pp. 92–99. The phrase "almost a Protestant" was my father's designation of Walsh which he recalled as a common wisecrack among New York Smith militants.

22. *Ibid.*, p. 182.

23. See *infra*, pp. 253–54.

24. See Thomas T. McAvoy, *The Great Crisis in American Catholic History, 1895–1900* (Chicago, Regnery, 1957), for a fascinating examination of the "phantom heresy" of "Americanism."

25. See John Courtney Murray, S.J., "The Church and Totalitarian Democracy," *Theological Studies*, Vol. XII, No. 4 (Dec., 1952), p. 552. Father Murray has explored at length the meaning and impact of LeoXIII's views; see his "Leo XIII: Separation of Church and State," "Leo XIII: Two Concepts of Government," and "Leo XIII on Church and State: The General

Structure of the Controversy," in *ibid.*, Vol. XIV, No. 2 (June, 1953), Vol. XIV, No. 4 (Dec., 1953), Vol. XV, No. 1 (March, 1954), and Vol. XIV, No. 1 (March, 1953). See also his "Problem of Pluralism in America," *Thought*, Vol. XXIX, No. 113 (Summer, 1954).

26. Moore, *op. cit.*, pp. 179–93. See generally Oscar Handlin, *Al Smith and His America* (Boston, Little, Brown, 1958).

27. Myers, *op. cit.*, p. 310.

28. See Virginius Dabney, *Dry Messiah, The Life of Bishop Cannon* (New York, A. A. Knopf, 1949).

29. Moore, *op. cit.*, pp. 48–49.

30. *Ibid.*, pp. 164, 48.

31. *Ibid.*, p. 173.

32. *Ibid.*, p. 145.

33. Keith Sward, *The Legend of Henry Ford* (New York, Rinehart, 1948), pp. 146–49. There was a sort of disembodied cast to Ford's anti-Semitism: his neighbor and friend Rabbi Leo M. Franklin, a leader of B'nai B'rith and a founder of the A.D.L., was appalled by Ford's attack and protested personally. Ford seemed startled by Franklin's dismay; he had expected "good Jews" to support him! *Ibid.*, p. 147 and files of the A.D.L.

34. *Ibid.*, p. 144.

35. Sward, *op. cit.*, p. 159.

36. *Ibid.*, p. 158.

37. Lucien Wolf, "The Nonsense of Nilus," cited by Sigmund Livingston, *Must Men Hate?* (Cleveland, n.p., 1944), pp. 42–43.

38. *Ibid.*, p. 44.

39. This was probably an overestimate at that time, but careful investigation suggests that by 1924—its peak year—the Klan had roughly four million members *largely outside of the old South:* about half a million in Indiana and Ohio, 415,000 in Texas, 200,000 in California, New York, Oklahoma, and Oregon, and between 50,000 and 200,000 in Alabama, Arkansas, Florida, Georgia, Illinois, Kansas, Kentucky, Louisiana, Maryland, Michigan, Mississippi, Missouri, New Jersey, Tennessee, Washington, and West Virginia. See Arnold S. Rice, *The Ku Klux Klan in American Politics* (Washington, Public Affairs Press, 1962), p. 13. See also Myers, *op. cit.*, pp. 267–312. A fascinating footnote to the Klan's invasion of the North was the counterattack by the city of Chicago, where the City Council barred Klansmen from the public payroll (Chicago *Tribune*, Jan. 18, 1923), Chief Justice Michael L. MacKinley of the Criminal Court prohibited them from serving on the grand jury (*New York Times*, Dec. 5, 1922), and Superior Court Judge Joseph B. David excluded them from petty juries (*New York Times*, Nov. 12, 1922). On Jan. 17, 1923, a Chicago Democrat named O'Grady introduced into the state Legislature a bill calling for an investigation—and purge—of Klansmen among state employees (Chicago *Tribune*, Jan. 18, 1923). It would be interesting to discover whether other Northern cities set up similar "security programs." I want to thank my friend Professor Richard C. Wade of the University of Chicago for bringing this material to my attention.

40. Myers, *op. cit.*, p. 346; Sward, *op. cit.*, p. 150.
41. Schachner, pp. 90–91. The organizations which sponsored the Jewish counter-attack were the American Jewish Committee, B'nai B'rith, the A.D.L., the Zionist Organization of America, Union of American Hebrew Congregations, Union of Orthodox Jewish Congregations, United Synagogue of America, Provisional Organization for American Jewish Congress, Central Conference of American Rabbis, Rabbinical Assembly of Jewish Theological Seminary, and the Union of Orthodox Rabbis of United States and Canada.
42. Myers, *op. cit.*, p. 357.
43. Sward, *op. cit.*, p. 157.
44. Ford disavowed anti-Semitism so suddenly that even Cameron was apparently caught unawares. Sward, *op. cit.*, pp. 158–59.
45. See Charles Reznikoff (ed.), *Louis Marshall: Champion of Liberty* (Selected papers and addresses) (Philadelphia, Jewish Publication Society, 1957), p. 380, letter to Cyrus Adler.
46. Myers, *op. cit.* (paperback edition of 1960), p. 311, quotes the letter to Livingston in full.
47. Myers, *op. cit.*, p. 310.
48. Sward, *op. cit.*, p. 158.
49. Milton Konvitz, *The Constitution and Civil Rights* (Ithaca, Cornell University Press, 1947), pp. 109–20.
50. *Ibid.*, p. 123.
51. *Ibid.*, p. 76.
52. *Meyer* v. *Nebraska*, 262 U.S. 390 (1923).
53. *Pierce* v. *Society of Sisters*, 268 U.S. 510 (1925).
54. Chafee, *op. cit.*, p. 319.
55. *Gitlow* v. *New York*, 268 U.S. 652 (1925).
56. See Roche, *Courts and Rights*, pp. 58–71, for a brief discussion of the historical background.

CHAPTER VI

1. See John D. Black, *Agricultural Reform in the United States* (New York, McGraw-Hill, 1929).
2. Coolidge may never have used this exact phrase, but it was his wife who observed that *if* he had made a comment, this would have been it. Karl Schriftgiesser, *This Was Normalcy* (Boston, Little, Brown, 1948), p. 169.
3. Ross M. Robertson, *History of the American Economy* (New York, Harcourt, Brace, 1955), p. 377.
4. Louis Morton, "Germany First," in *Command Decisions* (New York, Harcourt, Brace, 1959), p. 7.
5. *Historical Statistics*, pp. 139, 73. (The figure on unemployment does not include those employed part-time.)
6. (New York, Harcourt, Brace, 1956). I owe James M. Burns an incalculable

debt. Many of the ideas advanced here first saw the light of day in discussions with him held over the last decade.

7. See Raymond Moley, *After Seven Years* (New York, Harper & Bros., 1939).
8. Burns, *op. cit.*, pp. 156–57.
9. Moley, *op. cit.*, p. 48.
10. *Ibid.*, p. 160.
11. See, for example, a collection of articles from the magazine *Common Sense*: Alfred M. Bingham and Selden Rodman (eds.), *Challenge to the New Deal* (New York, McGraw-Hill, 1934). The Communist view was elaborated in *The Communist*, Vol. 13 (May, 1934), "The Present Situation and the Tasks of the C.P.U.S.A., Resolutions of the 8th National Convention," pp. 427–506.
12. *The Secret Diary of Harold L. Ickes* (3 vols.; New York, Simon & Schuster, 1953–54).
13. F.D.R.'s use of Moley (who believed that the New Deal should have an essentially autarchic foreign economic policy) as a counter to Hull (who believed in free trade) at the London Economic Conference of 1933 was a notable piece of finagling. With two teams in the field, Roosevelt could feel his way along in terms of the domestic economic situation, and then either back Hull, or make Moley the scapegoat for repudiating Hull's views. He took the latter course, and Moley never knew what hit him. See *After Seven Years*, pp. 270–77.
14. Roy P. Basler (ed.), *op. cit.*, Vol. IV, pp. 317–18.
15. *Historical Statistics*, p. 725.
16. I assume that there was *not* a radical shift in the actual membership of this 5 percent over the four-year period. *Historical Statistics*, p. 167.
17. Cited in Moley, *op. cit.*, p. 291.
18. Hofstadter, *op. cit.*, p. 323.
19. Moley, *op. cit.*, pp. 177–78.
20. In his perceptive *Rendezvous with Destiny*.
21. *Stromberg* v. *California*, 283 U.S. 359 (1931).
22. *Near* v. *Minnesota*, 283 U.S. 697 (1931).
23. *Grosjean* v. *American Press Co.*, 297 U.S. 233 (1936).
24. *Lovell* v. *Griffin*, 303 U.S. 444 (1938).
25. This was the so-called "Third Period" of Comintern development which began with the Sixth Congress in 1928. See Draper, *op. cit.*, pp. 300–14.
26. *Ibid.*, pp. 315–56. The map may be found in the pamphlet by James S. Allen, *Negro Liberation* (New York, International Publishers, 2nd ed., 1933).
27. *Herndon* v. *Lowry*, 301 U.S. 242 (1937).
28. See Allan Knight Chalmers, *They Shall Be Free* (Garden City, Doubleday, 1951) for a thoughtful survey of the trial and its tribulations by one of the key figures in the defense movement.
29. *Powell* v. *Alabama*, 287 U.S. 45 (1932).
30. *Norris* v. *Alabama*, 294 U.S. 587 (1935).
31. See Burns, *op. cit.*, pp. 291–315.
32. See Irving Howe and Lewis Coser, *The American Communist Party* (Boston, Beacon Press, 1957), pp. 236–72.

33. Irving Bernstein, *op. cit.*, pp. 506–7.
34. See Philip Taft and John A. Sessions (eds.), *Seventy Years of Life and Labor: An Autobiography by Samuel Gompers* (New York, Henry Holt, 1957), pp. 251–52.
35. Bernstein, *op. cit.*, p. 495.
36. See Charles O. Gregory, *Labor and the Law* (New York, W. W. Norton, 1946), pp. 191–94.
37. Bernstein, *op. cit.*, p. 476.
38. Sward, *op. cit.*, p. 223.
39. See Walter Galenson, *The C. I. O. Challenge to the A. F. of L.* (Cambridge, Harvard University Press, 1960).
40. See Irving Bernstein, *The New Deal Collective Bargaining Policy* (Berkeley, University of California Press, 1950).

CHAPTER VII

1. See Ruth Fischer, *Stalin and German Communism* (Cambridge, Harvard University Press, 1948). A less pejorative account, which is perhaps even more damning in its objectivity, is Alan Bullock, "The German Communists and the Rise of Hitler," in *The Third Reich* (London, Weidenfeld & Nicolson, 1955). See also the remarkable details by "Ex-Insider," "Moscow-Berlin, 1933," in *Survey*, Oct., 1962, pp. 153–64.
2. For a general account of the alliances the French Communists formed, see Henry W. Ehrmann, *French Labor from Popular Front to Liberation* (New York, Oxford University Press, 1947).
3. Cited by Rexford G. Tugwell, *The Democratic Roosevelt* (Garden City, Doubleday, 1957), pp. 268–69.
4. *Historical Statistics*, p. 14.
5. See Alfred M. Bingham and Selden Rodman, *op. cit.*, esp. pp. 142–46.
6. See Carey McWilliams, "Upton Sinclair and his E.P.I.C.," 80 *New Republic*, August 22, 1934, p. 41.
7. Cited by Allan P. Sindler, *Huey Long's Louisiana* (Baltimore, Johns Hopkins Press, 1956), p. 98.
8. See Harnett T. Kane, *Louisiana Hayride* (New York, Morrow, 1941), p. 118.
9. *Ibid.*, p. 38.
10. See Carlton Beals, *The Story of Huey P. Long* (Philadelphia, Lippincott, 1935), p. 384.
11. Kane, *op. cit.*, p. 101.
12. Sindler, *op. cit.*, pp. 86, 126–27.
13. *Forerunners of American Fascism* (New York, Julian Messner, 1935), pp. 74–75.
14. *Op. cit.*, p. 410. (Quoted with permission of J. B. Lippincott Co.)
15. *Op. cit.*, pp. 100–101.
16. Cited by Kane, *op. cit.*, p. 126.
17. Cited by Beals, *op. cit.*, pp. 300–303.
18. *Ibid.*, pp. 308–9.

19. *Op. cit.*, p. 349.
20. Swing, *op. cit.*, p. 58–61. A very interesting brief analysis of American "Fascism" in the 1930's is Morris Janowitz, "Black Legions on the March," in Daniel Aaron (ed.), *America in Crisis* (New York, A. A. Knopf, 1951).
21. Father Charles E. Coughlin, *Eight Lectures on Labor, Capital and Justice* (Royal Oak, Radio League of the Little Flower, 1934), pp. 79–81.
22. *Ibid.*, p. 83.
23. *Ibid.*, p. 100.
24. Swing, *op. cit.*, pp. 34–46.
25. Coughlin, *A Series of Lectures on Social Justice* (Royal Oak, Radio League of the Little Flower, 1936), p. 41.
26. Swing, *op. cit.*, p. 57.
27. See Gustavus Myers, *op. cit.*, p. 432.
28. *Historical Statistics*, p. 73.
29. See Berthold Hoselitz, *The Progress of Underdeveloped Areas* (Chicago, University of Chicago Press, 1952).
30. See Raymond Moley, *op. cit.*, *passim*.
31. *Historical Statistics*, p. 682.
32. Cited by Myers, *op. cit.*, p. 442.
33. (New York, Jewish Labor Committee, 1939).
34. See Hadley Cantril (ed.), *Public Opinion* (Princeton, Princeton University Press, 1951), pp. 1075, 1136.
35. *An Answer to Father Coughlin's Critics* (Royal Oak, Radio League of the Little Flower, 1940).
36. See *Report No. 153*, House of Representatives, 74th Congress, 1st Session, Feb. 15, 1935.
37. See Robert A. Divine, *The Illusion of Neutrality* (Chicago, University of Chicago Press, 1962).
38. See Wayne S. Cole, *America First* (Madison, University of Wisconsin Press, 1953).
39. See Cantril, *op. cit.*, pp. 1136–37, 1162, and *esp.* p. 1185.
40. Cited by Myers, *op. cit.*, pp. 425, 469.
41. *Ibid.*, p. 464. See the anti-Coughlin radio addresses of the Reverend William C. Kernan, an Episcopal minister in Newark, *The Ghost of Royal Oak* (New York, Free Speech Forum, 1940).
42. *Ibid.*, pp. 420–29.
43. (Harrisburg, Telegraph Press, 1935), p. 6.
44. A poll taken by Elmo Roper in the spring of 1948 is the evidence for this. It can be treated with some reserve as 1948 was not a good year for the pollsters. See New York *Herald Tribune*, May 27, 1948.
45. See Tugwell, *op. cit.*; Frances Perkins, *The Roosevelt I Knew* (New York, Viking Press, 1946); and James M. Burns, *op. cit.*
46. Cantril, *op. cit.*, p. 1148.
47. See Eugene Gressman, "The Controversial Image of Mr. Justice Murphy," 47 *The Georgetown Law Journal* (1959), pp. 631–54; J. Woodford Howard, Jr., "Frank Murphy and the Sit-down Strikes of 1937," 1 *Labor History* (1960), pp. 103–40; and John P. Roche, "The Utopian Pil-

grimage of Mr. Justice Murphy," 10 *Vanderbilt Law Review* (1957), pp. 369–94.

CHAPTER VIII

1. See John P. Roche, *Justice and Ancestry* (unpublished Master's thesis, Cornell University, Ithaca, 1947), pp. 42, 57–58.
2. Private communication, Francis Biddle to author, Feb. 6, 1956. See also Hyman, *op. cit.*, pp. 327–28.
3. Cited by John P. Roche, *supra*, n. 1, pp. 101–2, 107–8.
4. See Ernst Haas and Allen S. Whiting, *The Dynamics of International Relations* (New York, McGraw-Hill, 1957) for a good discussion of this point.
5. See Paul Willen, "Who 'Collaborated' with Russia?" *The Antioch Review*, Vol. 14 (1954), pp. 259–83, *passim*.
6. *Harper's*, Vol. 191 (1945), pp. 193–201; "The Japanese-American Cases," *Yale Law Journal*, Vol. 54 (1945), pp. 489–533.
7. *Historical Statistics*, p. 66. These figures only refer to those born on foreign shores and therefore do not include their children born in America.
8. 160 U.S. 649.
9. See Morton Grodzins, *Americans Betrayed* (Chicago, University of Chicago Press, 1949), pp. 3, 4–15 *passim*.
10. *Terrace* v. *Thompson*, 263 U.S. 197 (1923).
11. *Oyama* v. *California*, 332 U.S. 633 (1948).
12. See Jacobus ten Broek, Edward N. Barnhart, and Floyd W. Matson, *Prejudice, War, and the Constitution* (Berkeley, University of California Press, 1954), p. 304.
13. See M. Grodzins, *op. cit.*, Part 1.
14. See Ten Broek, *op. cit.*, pp. 70–72.
15. *Ibid.*, p. 85.
16. *Ibid.*
17. *Ibid.*
18. Roche, *Justice and Ancestry*, pp. 65–66.
19. *Ibid.*, pp. 48–49.
20. *Ibid.*
21. *Ibid.*, p. 65.
22. *Ibid.*, p. 164.
23. Cited by J. ten Broek, *op. cit.*, pp. 357–58.
24. *Ibid.*
25. 7 *Fed. Reg.*, 1407.
26. 56 *Stat. at L.* 173 (1942).
27. Israel Ampter, writing in *The Communist*, labeled Norman Thomas, "A Spearhead of Fascism," in Vol. 21 (1942), pp. 450–57. The Communist view of evacuation can be found in their West Coast paper, *People's World*.

See, e.g., Jan. 31, 1942, p. 1, where Foreign Editor John Pittman endorsed it as "prudent and basically humane."

28. See Dorothy S. Thomas and Richard Hishimoto, *The Spoilage* (Berkeley, University of California Press, 1957).
29. *Korematsu* v. *United States*, 323 U.S. 214 at 219–20, 223–24.
30. *Ibid.*, at 225.
31. *Ibid.*, at 242, esp. 249–50.
32. *Ibid.*, at 233, 236.
33. 323 U.S. 283, at 302–04 (1944).
34. See Ten Broek, *op. cit.*, p. 153.
35. *Ibid.*, p. 163.
36. *Ibid.*, pp. 168–70.
37. See David Manwaring, *Render unto Caesar* (Chicago, University of Chicago Press, 1962), pp. 82–84.
38. *Cantwell* v. *Connecticut*, 310 U.S. 296 (1940).
39. *Minersville School District* v. *Gobitis*, 310 U.S. 586, 598 (1940).
40. *Ibid.*, at 601.
41. *Op. cit.*, p. 143.
42. Cited in Alpheus T. Mason, *Harlan Fiske Stone* (New York, Viking Press, 1956), p. 528.
43. See Manwaring, *op. cit.*, p. 173.
44. *The New York Times*, September 26, 1962, p. 1.
45. *Jones* v. *Opelika*, 316 U.S. 584, 623–24 (1942).
46. *Barnette* v. *West Virginia State Board of Education*, 47 F. Supp. 251 (1942), 319 U.S. 624 (1943); for a statement of Justice Rutledge's views, see D. Manwaring, *op. cit.*, pp. 202–03.
47. 319 U.S. 624, 634–5 (1943).
48. *Ibid.*, at 642.
49. See *Daily Worker*, Dec. 19, 1942, p. 5, for an account of how the conviction of the Minneapolis Trotskyites had "drawn the fangs" of a vicious group of traitors to the working class. For more on the Trotskyites see *Daily Worker*, Sept. 13, 1944, p. 5. The *Worker* consistently suggested that Father Coughlin, Charles A. Lindbergh, Norman Thomas, John Haynes Holmes, and all whose views on the war it opposed, be handled as "traitors"; see, e.g., Feb. 2, 1942, p. 6, Dec. 25, 1941, p. 5, Jan. 11, 1942, p. 4. *Worker* reporter Art Shields cheered on the trial of the "Nazi plotters" in the summer of 1944; see *Daily Worker*, Aug. 8, Sept. 6, 7, 8, 9, 12, 13, 14, 17, 24, 1944. Browder called for the arrest of Col. Robert McCormick, *ibid.*, Sept. 26, 1944, p. 2.
50. See Maximilian J. St. George, *A Trial on Trial* (National Civil Rights Committee, 1946) for an evaluation by one of the defendants.
51. *Hartzel* v. *United States*, 322 U.S. 680 (1944).
52. *Schneiderman* v. *United States*, 320 U.S. 118 (1943); *Baumgartner* v. *United States*, 322 U.S. 665 (1944).
53. *United States* v. *Wursterbarth*, 249 Fed. 908 (D. N. J. 1919).
54. John P. Roche, "Memoirs of a Subversive," *New Republic*, Vol. 132 (1955), pp. 22–24.

55. A. Philip Randolph reportedly made this comment to an official of the War Production Board.
56. S/Sgt John P. Roche, 32895640. For a first-hand account see the recent semi-autobiographical novel by the Negro author John Oliver Killens, *And Then We Heard the Thunder* (New York, A. A. Knopf, 1963).
57. See Louis Ruchames, *Race, Jobs, and Politics* (New York, Columbia University Press, 1953), esp. chap. 2.
58. See John H. Franklin, *op. cit.*, p. 567.
59. *Ibid.*, p. 571.
60. *Ibid.*

CHAPTER IX

1. See Irving Howe and Lewis Coser, *op. cit.*; Melech Epstein, *The Jew and Communism* (New York, Trade Union Sponsoring Committee, 1959).
2. See Theodore Draper, *The Roots of American Communism, op. cit.*
3. *Ibid.*; and the second volume of this study, *American Communism and Soviet Russia* (New York, Viking Press, 1960).
4. See Hugh Seton-Watson, *From Lenin to Khrushchev* (New York, Praeger, 1960), p. 200.
5. Cited by I. Howe and L. Coser, *op. cit.*, pp. 329–30.
6. *Ibid.*, pp. 348, 366–67; Nathan Glazer, *The Social Basis of American Communism* (New York, Harcourt, Brace, 1961), p. 154.
7. See William Goldsmith's study, "The Communists and the I.W.O.," in the forthcoming volume, John P. Roche (ed.), *Studies in Infiltration* (Ithaca, Cornell University Press, 1964).
8. See I. Howe and L. Coser, *op. cit.*, p. 351.
9. See Daniel Aaron, *Writers on the Left* (New York, Harcourt, Brace, 1961).
10. See the literature of disillusionment: Granville Hicks, *Where We Came Out* (New York, Viking Press, 1954); Joseph Freeman, *An American Testament* (New York, Farrar, 1936); and Richard H. S. Crossman (ed.), *The God That Failed* (New York, Harper & Bros., 1950).
11. See Whittaker Chambers, *Witness* (New York, Random House, 1952), pp. 282–83; Elizabeth Bentley, *Out of Bondage* (New York, Devin-Adair, 1951).
12. See I. Howe and L. Coser, *op. cit.*, chap. 9; Paul Willen, "Who 'Collaborated' with Russia?" *The Antioch Review*, Vol. 14 (1954), pp. 259–83.
13. Cited by I. Howe and L. Coser, *op. cit.*, p. 433.
14. *Ibid.*, p. 432.
15. *Ibid.*, p. 433.
16. *Ibid.*, p. 427.
17. *Ibid.*, pp. 442–48.
18. *Ibid.*, p. 442.
19. See Chester Wilmot, *The Struggle for Europe* (New York, Harper & Bros., 1952); for another version which argues a different viewpoint—badly—

see Forrest C. Pogue, "The Decision to Stop at the Elbe," in *Command Decisions, op. cit.,* p. 374.

20. See Louis Morton, "Soviet Intervention in the War with Japan," *Foreign Affairs,* July, 1962, pp. 653–62.

21. See Wilmot, *op. cit.,* and Samuel P. Huntington, *The Soldier and the State* (Cambridge, Harvard University Press, 1958).

22. *Historical Statistics,* p. 718.

23. See Benjamin I. Schwartz, *Chinese Communism and the Rise of Mao* (Cambridge, Harvard University Press, 1951); Robert C. North, *Moscow and Chinese Communists* (Stanford, Stanford University Press, 1953).

24. See Richard H. Rovere, *The Eisenhower Years* (New York, Farrar & Strauss, 1956).

25. See Clifton Brock, *Americans for Democratic Action* (Washington, Public Affairs Press, 1962).

26. See Eleanor Bontecou, *The Federal Loyalty-Security Program* (Ithaca, Cornell University Press, 1953), pp. 172–73.

27. See Robert K. Carr, *The House Committee on Un-American Activities* (Ithaca, Cornell University Press, 1952), chaps. 1 and 2.

28. *Ibid.,* pp. 55–78.

29. (New York, Viking Press, 1953).

30. *Public Opinion* (New York, Harcourt, Brace, 1922).

31. For examinations of the Hiss Trial see Alistair Cooke, *A Generation on Trial* (New York, A. A. Knopf, 1950); William Jowitt, *The Strange Case of Alger Hiss* (London, Hodder & Stoughton, 1953).

32. There is no authoritative statement on this episode; but see R. Carr, *op. cit.,* pp. 114–17. (And see as well W. Chambers, *op. cit.*)

33. See R. Carr, *supra,* pp. 290–93.

34. See Lawrence H. Chamberlain, *Loyalty and Legislative Action* (Ithaca, Cornell University Press, 1951); Edward L. Barrett, Jr., *The Tenney Committee* (Ithaca, Cornell University Press, 1951); and Vern Countryman, *Un-American Activities in the State of Washington* (Ithaca, Cornell University Press, 1951).

35. (Glencoe, Free Press, 1956). Sandor Voros, long a top Communist in the Middle West, makes the point in his *American Commissar* (Philadelphia, Chilton, 1961) that even key cadres such as he were unaware of the espionage *apparats.* There is a solid integrity about his presentation which leads me to believe him.

36. Cited by E. Bontecou, *op. cit.,* pp. 170–71.

37. *Ibid.*

38. *Senator Joe McCarthy* (New York, Harcourt, Brace, 1959).

39. Senators Douglas, Humphrey, Murray, Chavez, Lehman, Graham, Greene, Leahy, Kefauver, Kilgore. See *C.Q. Almanac,* Vol. 6 (Washington, Congressional Quarterly, 1950), pp. 390–98, 543.

40. See Samuel A. Stouffer, *Communism, Conformity, and Civil Liberties* (Garden City, Doubleday, 1955), chap. 2.

41. A policy statement adopted by the General Board (March 17, 1954).

42. Cited by *ADL* (Anti-Defamation League) *Bulletin,* Vol. 9 (1952), p. 8.

43. See Richard Hofstadter and Walter P. Metzger, *The Development of Academic Freedom in the United States* (New York, Columbia University Press, 1955), for an account of how inadequately academic freedom was defined and maintained in World War I.
44. (Garden City, Doubleday, 1956).
45. The series includes the volumes cited in n. 34, *supra*, and the studies of E. Bontecou, R. Carr, *op. cit.*, and Walter Gellhorn, *Security, Loyalty, and Science* (Ithaca, Cornell University Press, 1950).
46. See the author's analyses: "The McCarthy Issue," *Current History*, Vol. 27 (1954), pp. 241–48; "We've Never Had More Freedom," *New Republic*, Vol. 134 (1956), January 23, pp. 12–15, January 30, pp. 13–16, and February 6, pp. 13–15.
47. See John P. Roche, "American Liberty: An Examination of the 'Tradition' of Freedom," *op. cit.*, pp. 129–62.

CHAPTER X

1. See George R. Stewart, *The Year of the Oath* (Garden City, Doubleday, 1950).
2. *The New York Times*, Nov. 1, 1962, p. 14.
3. Cited in John P. Roche, *Courts and Rights, op. cit.*, p. 115.
4. See Arnold Forster and Benjamin R. Epstein, *Cross-Currents* (Garden City, Doubleday, 1956), pp. 119–21.
5. See Milton R. Konvitz and Theodore Leskes, *A Century of Civil Rights* (New York, Columbia University Press, 1961), pp. 198–201.
6. See Harry S. Truman, *Years of Trial and Hope* (Garden City, Doubleday, 1956), p. 181.
7. President's Committee on Civil Rights (Washington, D.C., 1947).
8. *Ibid.*, p. 149.
9. *Ibid.*, pp. 166–68.
10. See H. Truman, *op. cit.*, p. 181.
11. 13 *Fed. Reg.* 4311–3.
12. Cited in *The Annals*, "Racial Desegregation and Integration," Vol. 304 (1956), p. 78.
13. See Martin Luther King, Jr., *Stride Toward Freedom* (New York, Harper & Bros., 1958).
14. See M. Konvitz and T. Leskes, *op. cit.*, chaps. 7–9, passim.
15. *Plessy* v. *Ferguson*, 163 U.S. 537 (1896).
16. *Shelley* v. *Kraemer*, 334 U.S. 1 (1948); see Clement E. Vose, *Caucasians Only* (Berkeley, University of California Press, 1959).
17. See the journal presenting current litigation, legislation, and administrative activities in the field of civil rights, *Race Relations Law Reporter*, and the *Report on Education, 1961*, of the U.S. Commission on Civil Rights (Washington, D.C., 1962).
18. *McLaurin* v. *Regents*, 339 U.S. 634 at 641; and *Sweatt* v. *Painter*, 339

U.S. 629 (1950). See John P. Roche, "Education, Segregation, and the Supreme Court—A Political Analysis," *University of Pennsylvania Law Review*, Vol. 99 (1951), pp. 949–59.

19. *Brown* v. *Board of Education*, 347 U.S. 483 (1954).
20. Sociological research suggests that intermarriage frightens whites the most, and interests Negroes the least, of all aspects of racial equality. See W. S. M. Banks, II, "The Rank Order of Sensitivity to Discriminations of Negroes in Columbus, Ohio," *American Sociological Review*, Vol. 15 (1950), pp. 529–34.
21. Cited by Kenneth D. Kemper, "Restrictions on Negro Voting in Mississippi History" (Author's files), p. 31, from the Jackson, Miss., *Clarion-Ledger*, July 4, 1890.
22. *The New York Times*, Oct. 24, 1961. "I must have pulled the trigger unconsciously," Representative E. H. Hurst told the sympathetic, white coroner's jury. They agreed.
23. See Jack W. Peltason, *58 Lonely Men* (New York, Harcourt, Brace, 1961).
24. See *Congressional Quarterly Weekly Report*, Vol. 20 (1962), pp. 1545, 1721, and 2151.
25. "School Prayers and the Founding Fathers," *Commentary*, Vol. 34 (1962), pp. 225–30.
26. *America*, Sept. 1, 1962.
27. *The Commonweal*, Sept. 7, 1962.
28. See the A.D.L. analysis, "The 1960 Election Campaign," *Facts*, March, 1961.
29. See Philip E. Converse, *et al.*, "Stability and Change in 1960: A Reinstating Election," *American Political Science Review*, Vol. 55 (1961), pp. 269–80.
30. Even more to the point, one has to consider that fact that the Negro population in Massachusetts comprises slightly less than 2 percent of the total.
31. See "Private Attorneys-General: Group Action in the Fight for Civil Liberties," *Yale Law Journal*, Vol. 58 (1949), p. 590.
32. See A. Forster and B. Epstein, *op. cit.*, and their earlier study, *The Trouble-Makers* (Garden City, Doubleday, 1952), and the pamphlets published by the Anti-Defamation League.
33. See the Anti-Defamation League's periodic reports on discrimination in housing, employment, and public corporations. On housing, see the bulletin *Rights*, Vol. 2, No. 5 (1958); Vol. 2, No. 6 (1959), and earlier, Vol. 1, No. 8 (1957); and Vol. 2, No. 2 (1958).
34. On discrimination in resorts and supposedly private clubs, see *Rights*, Vol. 1, No. 3 (1956); Vol. 1, No. 7 (1957); Vol. 2, No. 7 (1959); and Vol. 4, No. 3 (1962).
35. See Arnold Forster and Benjamin R. Epstein, *Some of My Best Friends* (New York, Farrar, Straus & Cudahy, 1962). Also N. C. Belth (ed.), *Barriers, Patterns of Discrimination Against Jews* (New York, Friendly House, 1958.)
36. See *Rights*, Vol. 2, No. 8 (1959). See also *The New York Times* (Oct. 9, 1962) reporting agreement between seven insurance companies and New York State Attorney General Louis J. Lefkowitz on eliminating discriminatory practices as a result of A.D.L.'s survey.

INDEX

Abrams, Jacob, arrested for sedition, 69–70

Adams, Henry, anti-Semitism of, 14

Adams, John, 263–264

Addams, Jane, 86

Advise and Consent, 97

African Methodist Episcopal Church, 24

Age of Reform (Hofstadter), 21

Age of Roosevelt, minority groups in, 151

Age of Suspicion (Wechsler), 231

Age of Suspicion, Wechsler on, 224

Agrarianism, transition from, to urban industrialism, 26–27

Agricultural Adjustment Acts, 156

Alabama, segregation in, 248

Algeria, European Secret Army in, 55

All the King's Men (Warren), 163

Amarillo, Tex., and Orwell's *1984*, 235

America, on anti-Semitism, 253

America First Committee, 175, 176, 177

American Civil Liberties Union, 63, 96, 197, 237, 245, 262, 267; birth of, 101; fight for civil liberties, 230; and Gobitis Case, 201; 1926 *Annual Report* of, 104; Yahoos attack, 234

American Communist Party, 147, 210–223 *passim*; as dependent of Moscow, 218; and Smith Act, 226; and Trade Union Unity League, 152; and Whittaker Chambers, 216. *See also* Communism; Communist Labor Party; Communists

American-English, 1

American Fascists, 209

American Federation of Labor, 56, 108; and Bisbee strike, 65; and Communists, 152; Executive Council, 155; in 1930's, 151–153; as radical, 68; Socialists in, 53; and Socialists, 152; and World War I, 53

American Institute of Public Opinion, 182

American Jewish Committee, 23, 102, 121, 124; and Coughlin, 163; formed, 87, 88; and Henry Ford, 123

American Jewish Congress, Council on Law and Social Action of, 254

American League Against War and Fascism, 213

American League to Combat Anti-Semitism, 177, 178

American League for Peace and Democracy, 213, 214

American Legion, and Jehovah's Witnesses, 202; and minority groups, 191; and nativism, 191

"American Nationalist Confederation," 175

American Peace Mobilization, 217

American Plan (the "open shop"), 68; and trade-union movement, 104

American Protective League, and IWW, 64; as vigilante group, 43

American Socialist Party, 8; formation of, 51

American Sugar Refining Company, 20

American Union Against Militarism, 101

American Veterans Committee, 245; and fight for civil liberties, 231

American Way, 68

American worker, status in 1933, 153–154

American Writers Congress, 215

Americanism, hyphenated, 42–43; perverted, 82; positive, during World War I, 45

Americanization, 30, 42

Americans for Democratic Action, 221, 229, 262; and fight for civil liberties, 230; Yahoos attack, 234

Amidon, C. F., 47

Ancient Order of Hibernians, 184

Anderson, Judge George, on fair hearing for aliens, 73

Anticapitalism, 158

Anti-Catholicism, 104, 178, 251; bigotry of, 253; in 1928 presidential campaign, 115–120. *See also* Catholics; Minority groups

Anti-Defamation League of B'nai B'rith, 23, 70, 102, 230, 236, 262, 267; and anti-Semitism, 98; as pioneer civil rights group, 24; protests *The Merchant of Venice*, 94–95,

Immigration and Naturalization Service, 180

Income Tax Amendment, passage of, 32

Independent, 129

Industrial production, transportation revolution and spectacular growth in, 16

Industrial Workers of the World, appraisal of, 53–54; and Bisbee deportation, 65–66; contribution to civil liberty, 57–58; exploitations, reason for, 55–57; Kansas City trial of, 69; legal proceedings against, 59; mass trial of, in Chicago, 62; membership of, 54; nihilism of, 54–55; as radical, 68; resemblance to syndicalist-Fascist movements, 53, 54–55; suppression of, 55, 58–59, 63–66; turnover in, 54; and Wheatland Riot, 56

Industrialism, transition from agrarianism to, 26–27

Industrialization, effects of, 105; growth of massive, 16–20

Institute for Propaganda Analysis, 173

Internal Security Act, and J. P. Roche, 212; Truman vetoes, 229

Intergroup relations, in U.S.A., 251–253; violence and, 76–77

The International Jew: The World's Problem, 99, 121–122; foreign translation of, 125

International Labor Defense, 149, 214

International Ladies Garment Workers Union, 152, 188

International Workers Order, 214

Interstate Commerce Act, 21

Irish, effect of World War I on, 35–36; political talents of, 6; support for Old Country movements, 29. *See also* Minority groups

Isolationism, of U.S.A., 27–33; and Woodrow Wilson, 27; and World War II, 175–177

Italy, declares war on U.S.A., 187

Jackson, Robert, 186; and Gobitis Case, 203–204; on West Coast Japanese in World War II, 198

Japan, and United States, at war, 182

Japanese, as minority group, 190–193

Japanese-Americans, plight in World War II, 185, 190, 193–200. *See also* Nisei; Sansei

Javits, Jacob, 254

Jefferson, Thomas, 27; and fears of urbanization, 5; on Federalist principles, 107

The Jeffersonian, 84; quoted, 89

Jehovah's Witnesses, 147; and American Legion, 202; and flag salute, 200–202; as minority group, 200–202

Jenner, and McCarthy committees, 222

Jewish Activities in United States (1921), 122

"Jewish Bolshevism," 209

Jewish Community, task of, 254–257. *See also* Jews

Jewish Influences in American Life (1921), 122

Jewish Labor Committee, and Coughlin, 173; and fight for civil liberties, 231

Jewish Peoples Fraternal Order, 214

Jews, attacks on, 51; and Catholics, 112; effect of World War I on, in U.S.A., 35–36; "dual allegiance" of, 118; and Henry Ford, 114; immigrants, as anarchists, 5–6; and intolerance, 78; support for Old Country movements, 29. *See also* anti-Semitism; Minority groups

Jim Crow, 236; and Constitution, 241–242; in federal administration in 1913; legislation, 11–12. *See also* Minority groups; Negroes

Joel, Moses, 122

John Birch Society, 242, 267

Johnson, Hugh, 162; and Huey Long, 163–167

Johnson, James Weldon, and "Red Summer," 82

Joly, Maurice, 122

The Jungle (Sinclair), 21

Jurisdictions, conflict of, 8–9

Kafka, Franz, 121, 194

Kansas, and segration in federal school system, 245

Keep America Out of War Congress, 175

Kelly, Francis, and E. Brooke, 254

Kennedy, J. F., campaign for Presi-

dency, 253; and Catholicism, 253–
254; character of, 158; and Execu-
tive Order on use of federal funds
and segregated housing, 257; nomi-
nation of, 251
Kersner, Jacob, denaturalized, 74
Keynes, John Maynard, 137; on Wil-
son, 40–41
Khrushchev, Nikita, 117
King, Martin Luther, Jr., 250; and
nonviolent resistance, 241
Knights of Columbus "Oath," 253
Know-Nothing Movement, 253
Knoxville, race riots in, 83
Korea, U.S.A. and, 210
Korean War, and Truman Adminis-
tration, 221
Korematsu v. *United States*, 198
Kossuth, Louis, 30
Ku Klux Klan, 102, 118, 129; bigotry
of, 112; membership in 1920, 122;
revival of, 82
Kun, Béla, 174

Labor, restrictions on minorities, 22;
rights of, 126; and Supreme Court
of United States, 19; and U.S. Gov-
ernment in 1930's, 151–157; and
violence in U.S.A. before World War
I, 15–16, 19
La Follette Committee, 155
La Guardia, Fiorello, 51; and anti-
Semitism, 202
Lake Geneva Herald, 177
Landis, Kenesaw M., 71; and Berger,
61–62; and trial of IWW's, 63
Landon, Alfred M., in 1936 election,
172
Lansing, Secretary of State Robert, 40;
protests British blockade, 35
Lawrence, Mass., textile strike, 57
Lawson, John Howard, and motion
picture *Blockade*, 223
League of Nations, 67; Communists
and, 214
The League for Peace and Democracy,
216–217
League for Peace and Freedom, 22
The Lean Years (Bernstein), 103
Lee, Robert E., loyalty to state in Civil
War, 39
*Left-Wing Communism: An Infantile
Disorder*, 211

"Left Wing Manifesto," Z. Chafee on,
127
The Legend of Henry Ford (Sward),
120, 121
Lehman, Herbert, on McCarthyism,
230–231
Lemke, William, 169, 170, 172
Lenin, Vladimir I., 28, 139, 145, 211,
219; on German revolutionaries, 51;
as Jew, 88; on the state, 105
Leo XII, Pope, 117
Leo XIII, Pope, encyclicals of, 161
Leo Frank Case. *See* Frank, Leo
Levine, Isaac Don, on opposition of
Russian Jews to Bolshevism, 70
Levy, Leonard W., on James Madison,
252; and study of intention of men
who wrote First Amendment, 252
Liberals, under Truman Administra-
tion, 208
Liberty League, and F.D.R., 135, 171
Liebold, Ernest, 120, 121, 124
Life, on NKVD, 217
Lincoln, Abraham, 219; and David
Davis, 45; on disregard for law in
U.S.A., 77–78; on "half-slave and
half-free," 39; and Seward, 139;
and Woodrow Wilson, 42
Lindbergh, Charles, and quasi-anti-
Semitism, 175–176
Lippmann, Walter, on F.D.R., 160;
on Japanese in California, 194; on
stereotypes, 224
Literary Digest, 171
Little, Frank, hanging of, 64
Livingston, Sigmund, 125
Locke, John, 8
London *Times*, 122, 123
Long, Huey, 147, 178, 227–228; as-
sassination of, 166–167; and F.D.R.,
163, 171; and Jim Farley, 164; and
Mussolini, 163; and Nazism, 163; as
Yahoo, 161–167
Longinqua oceani (Leo XIII), 117
Los Angeles, racial violence in, 205
Louisiana, Socialists in, 24; Bureau of
Investigation, 165
Lovejoy, Elijah, murder of, 77
Lubell, Samuel, on new alignment of
presidential politics, 109
Luce, Henry, 188
"Lumpenproletariat," Marx on, 54
Lusitania, 39, 40
Lynching, 84–85, 86

My First Days in the White House
(Long), 178

NKVD, *Life* on, 217
Nation, on Negro in 1877, 10–11
National Association for Advancement
of Colored People, 102, 113–114,
149, 229, 250, 262, 267; campaign
against segregation, 243–251 *pas-
sim;* as champion of Negro rights,
86; foundation of, 24; and housing,
237; and Negroes' fight for equal
status, 236–251 *passim;* Yahoos at-
tack, 234
National Association of Manufacturers,
140
National Brotherhood Workers of
America, 83
National Catholic Welfare Conference,
120, 264
National Civil Liberties Bureau, 101;
and legal lawlessness, 59
National Conference of Christians and
Jews, 120
National Council of Christians and
Jews, 264
National Council of the Churches of
Christ, 264; fight for civil liberties,
230; Yahoos attack, 234
National Fair Employment Practices
Commission, 206
National Gentile League, 175
National Industrial Recovery Act, 137,
155
National Intelligencer, on Southern race
relations, 11
National Labor Relations Act, 154,
171, 209
National Labor Relations Board, staff
of, 155, 182; work of, 181
National Socialist Party, 54
National Union for Social Justice, 167
Nationality, laws of, codified, 6
Native Sons of the Golden West, and
minority groups, 191
Nativism, and antiradicalism, 67
Nazism, 1; Communists and, 215; and
Russia, 216; and Stalin, 212
Near v. Minnesota, 145, 146–147
Negro plasma, and Red Cross, 206
Negro Zionism, of Marcus Garvey, 114
Negroes, and Bolsheviks, 83–84; and
Communism, 147–148; contempo-
rary status of, 265–266; depression

of, in South, 22; and Eleanor Roosevelt, 182; intolerance and, 78; migration of, to North, and racial conflict, 50, 68, 80–81; as minority,
79–87; and nonviolent resistance,
241; in North, 246–247; optimism
of, 9; place of, after Civil War,
10–12; plight of, in Army in World
War II, 205–206; plight of, in
North, 81–83; population distribution of, 79, 80, 81; Reform movement, 24; restrictions by labor on,
22; status of, 113–114; status of,
and Civil War, 106; status of, in
1920's, 129, 132; status of, in 1940's
and 1950's, 134, 183, 236–251;
status of, in World War II, 185,
205–297 *passim;* and white "supremacy," 11–12, 79, 111–112
"New America" movement, 161
New Deal, 103; and civil liberty, 130–
157 *passim;* effect of, on U.S.A.,
158–183 *passim;* and Republican
Party, 143, 172
New Dealers, 143
New York *Call,* as newspaper of Socialist Party, 62
New York City, as center of world
Jewry, 5
New York State, Assembly expels Socialist members, 71–72; Assembly
and repressive acts against "revolu-
tionary radicals," 72; Civil Rights
Act, amendments to, 126; and fair
employment practices, 241
New York Times, and Alfred E. Smith
campaign for President, 119; attacks McCarthy, 230; on deportation of "subversives," 74; on Ger-
man-American Alliance, 37; on
Henry Ford and Hitler, 121; on
IWW's, 64; pro-British policies of,
during World War I, 36; reprints
Grave's analysis of *Protocols,* 123
New York World, 42
New York *World-Telegram,* publishes
Duclos article on Browder, 218
Niagara Conference, 24, 86
Nilus, Serge, 121, 122
1984 (Orwell), 2, 3, 235
1919 (Dos Passos), 67
1920 census, 107
1920's as decade of transition, 107–
113; in U.S.A., 1, 103–129

United States (*continued*)
reform movements in, and civil liberty, 21–25
restrictions on aliens, 73–75
revenues in 1900, 4
as rural in 1900, 4
and Russia in World War II, 188
Special Committee of House of Representatives, investigates German propaganda activities, 174
Supreme Court, 190, 198
and Abrams Case, 70
on alien land laws, 192
attempts to define pornography, 96
and *Baker* v. *Carr*, 261
decision outlawing segregation, 242–251 *passim*
decisions of, in 1930's, 145–151 *passim*
decisions under Espionage Act, 204–205
and due process, 150, 200
and *Ex parte Milligan*, 46
expands protection of Constitution, 144
and First Amendment, 46–47, 49, 101
on foreign-language cases, 126–127
and Fourteenth Amendment, 11, 127, 241–242
and Gitlow Case, 127–128
and Gobitis Case, 201–202, 203
and K. M. Landis, 62
and labor, 18–20
and *Mapp* v. *Ohio*, 261
and *Near* v. *Minnesota*, 145
in 1918 and 1919, 49
and *Norris* v. *Powell*, 150
on Oregon school law, 127
and *Plessy* v. *Ferguson*, 11–13, 100, 243, 245
protects corporate interests versus labor, 18–20
Reporter, Justice Murphy in, 198
and restrictive covenants, 242–243
and scope and content of civil rights, 126
and *Shelley* v. *Kraemer*, 242
and states' rights, 46–47
and *Stromberg* v. *California*, 145
suppresses Mormonism, 8
urban-rural schism in, 5, 7

violence in, before World War I, 15–16, 19
War Relocation Authority, 199
Works Project Administration, 171
and World Court, 168
and World War I, 1, 25, 26–49 *passim*, 50, 52–53, 107, 184
and World War II, 1, 175, 184–207 *passim*, 190, 220
in years before World War I, 1–25 *passim*
United States Steel Corp., 18, 153; growth of, 16
United States v. *Wong Kim Ark*, 190
Universal Negro Improvement Association, 114
Urban League, 237
Urban reform, 22–23
"Urbanity," and due process, 232
Urbanization, adaptation to, 116; American fear of, 5; effects of, 105

de Valera, Eamon, and Gallagher, 169
van Dyke, Henry, and Alfred E. Smith's campaign for Presidency, 119
Veblen, Thorstein, 63
Villard, Oswald Garrison, 86; on American conservative, 68
Volstead Act, 111
Voluntarism, 153, 155

Wagner Act, 172, 181
Wald, Lillian, 86
Walker, Dr. Hugh K., and Alfred E. Smith's campaign for Presidency, 119
Wallace, Henry A., 162; and Progressive Party, 239
Walter, Francis, 235
War Amendments (Thirteenth, Fourteenth, and Fifteenth), to Constitution, 10
Warren, Earl, and Nisei, 195; and "separate but equal" as principle, 245
Warren, Robert Penn, 163
Washington, Booker T., 84; against immigration, 14
Washington, George, 27, 219
Washington, D.C., racial strife in, 83
Washington *Post*, on McCarthy, 230
Watnick, Morris, on Communist leadership, 171

QUADRANGLE PAPERBACKS

American History

Frederick Lewis Allen. *The Lords of Creation.* (QP35)
Lewis Atherton. *Main Street on the Middle Border.* (QP36)
Thomas A. Bailey. *Woodrow Wilson and the Lost Peace.* (QP1)
Thomas A. Bailey. *Woodrow Wilson and the Great Betrayal.* (QP2)
Charles A. Beard. *The Idea of National Interest.* (QP27)
Carl L. Becker. *Everyman His Own Historian.* (QP33)
Ray A. Billington. *The Protestant Crusade.* (QP12)
Allan G. Bogue. *From Prairie to Corn Belt.* (QP50)
Kenneth E. Boulding. *The Organizational Revolution.* (QP43)
David M. Chalmers. *Hooded Americanism.* (QP51)
John Chamberlain. *Farewell to Reform.* (QP19)
Alice Hamilton Cromie. *A Tour Guide to the Civil War.*
Robert D. Cross. *The Emergence of Liberal Catholicism in America.* (QP44)
Richard M. Dalfiume. *American Politics Since 1945.* (NYTimes Book. QP57)
Chester McArthur Destler. *American Radicalism, 1865-1901.* (QP30)
Robert A. Divine. *American Foreign Policy Since 1945.* (NYTimes Book, QP58)
Robert A. Divine. *The Illusion of Neutrality.* (QP45)
Elisha P. Douglass. *Rebels and Democrats.* (QP26)
Herman Finer. *Road to Reaction.* (QP5)
Felix Frankfurter. *The Commerce Clause.* (QP16)
Lloyd C. Gardner. *A Different Frontier.* (QP32)
Edwin Scott Gaustad. *The Great Awakening in New England.* (QP46)
Ray Ginger. *Altgeld's America.* (QP21)
Gerald N. Grob. *Workers and Utopia.* (QP61)
Louis Hartz. *Economic Policy and Democratic Thought.* (QP52)
William B. Hesseltine. *Lincoln's Plan of Reconstruction.* (QP41)
Granville Hicks. *The Great Tradition.* (QP62)
Dwight W. Hoover. *Understanding Negro History.* (QP49)
Stanley P. Hirshson. *Farewell to the Bloody Shirt.* (QP53)
Frederic C. Howe. *The Confessions of a Reformer.* (QP39)
Louis Joughin and Edmund M. Morgan. *The Legacy of Sacco and Vanzetti.* (QP7)
William Loren Katz. *Teachers' Guide to American Negro History.* (QP210)
Edward Chase Kirkland. *Dream and Thought in the Business Community, 1860-1900.* (QP11)
Edward Chase Kirkland. *Industry Comes of Age.* (QP42)
Adrienne Koch. *The Philosophy of Thomas Jefferson.* (QP17)
Gabriel Kolko. *The Triumph of Conservatism.* (QP40)
Walter LaFeber. *John Quincy Adams and American Continental Empire.* (QP23)
David E. Lilienthal. *TVA: Democracy on the March.* (QP28)
Arthur S. Link. *Wilson the Diplomatist.* (QP18)
Huey P. Long. *Every Man a King.* (QP8)
Gene M. Lyons. *America: Purpose and Power.* (QP24)
Jackson Turner Main. *The Antifederalists.* (QP14)
Ernest R. May. *The World War and American Isolation, 1914-1917.* (QP29)
Henry F. May. *The End of American Innocence.* (QP9)
George E. Mowry. *The California Progressives.* (QP6)
William L. O'Neill. *American Society Since 1945.* (NYTimes Book, QP59)
Frank L. Owsley. *Plain Folk of the Old South.* (QP22)
David Graham Phillips. *The Treason of the Senate.* (QP20)
Julius W. Pratt. *Expansionists of 1898.* (QP15)
Moses Rischin. *The American Gospel of Success.* (QP54)
John P. Roche. *The Quest for the Dream.* (QP47)
David A. Shannon. *The Socialist Party of America.* (QP38)
Andrew Sinclair. *The Available Man.* (QP60)
John Spargo. *The Bitter Cry of the Children.* (QP55)
Richard W. Van Alstyne. *The Rising American Empire.* (QP25)
Willard M. Wallace. *Appeal to Arms.* (QP10)
Norman Ware. *The Industrial Worker, 1840-1860.* (QP13)
Albert K. Weinberg. *Manifest Destiny.* (QP3)
Bernard A. Weisberger. *They Gathered at the River.* (QP37)
Robert H. Wiebe. *Businessmen and Reform.* (QP56)
Bell I. Wiley. *The Plain People of the Confederacy.* (QP4)
William Appleman Williams. *The Contours of American History.* (QP34)
William Appleman Williams. *The Great Evasion.* (QP48)
Esmond Wright. *Causes and Consequences of the American Revolution.* (QP31)

European History

William Sheridan Allen. *The Nazi Seizure of Power.* (QP302)
W. O. Henderson. *The Industrial Revolution in Europe.* (QP303)
Raul Hilberg. *The Destruction of the European Jews.* (QP301)
Telford Taylor. *Sword and Swastika.* (QP304)

Philosophy

F. H. Bradley. *The Presuppositions of Critical History.* (QP108)
William Earle. *Objectivity.* (QP109)
James M. Edie, James P. Scanlan, Mary-Barbara Zeldin, George L. Kline. *Russian Philosophy.*
  (3 vols, QP111, 112, 113)
James M. Edie. *An Invitation to Phenomenology.* (QP103)
James M. Edie. *Phenomenology in America.* (QP105)
Manfred S. Frings. *Heidegger and the Quest for Truth.* (QP107)
Moltke S. Gram. *Kant: Disputed Questions.* (QP104)
Lionel Rubinoff. *Faith and Reason.* (QP106)
Paul Tibbetts. *Perception.* (QP110)
Pierre Thévenaz. *What Is Phenomenology?* (QP101)

Social Science

George and Eunice Grier. *Equality and Beyond.* (QP204)
Charles O. Lerche, Jr. *Last Chance in Europe.* (QP207)
David Mitrany. *A Working Peace System.* (QP205)
Martin Oppenheimer and George Lakey. *A Manual for Direct Action.* (QP202)
Fred Powledge. *To Change a Child.* (QP209)
Lee Rainwater. *And the Poor Get Children.* (QP208)
Clarence Senior. *The Puerto Ricans.* (QP201)
Arthur L. Stinchcombe. *Rebellion in a High School.* (QP211)